POLEMICAL JUDO

MEMES FOR OUR POLITICAL KNIFE-FIGHT

ABOUT BOOKS BY DAVID BRIN

Temple Grandin, author of *Thinking in Pictures* - "David Brin's *Existence* is a book that makes you think deeply about both the future and life's most important issues. I found it fascinating and I could not put it down."

Stewart Brand, The Long Now Foundation - "New tech is handing society tough decisions to make anew about old issues of privacy and accountability. In opting for omni-directional openness, David Brin takes an unorthodox position, arguing knowledgeably and with exceptionally balanced perspective."

George B. Dyson, author of *Darwin Among the Machines* - "As David Brin details the inevitability of ubiquitous surveillance, your instinct, as an individual facing this one-way mirror, is to hope that he is wrong about the facts. As you follow his argument (in *The Transparent Society*), you realize your only hope is that he is right."

Howard Rheingold, author of *The Virtual Community* - "David Brin is one of the few people thinking and writing about the social problems we are going to face in the near future as the result of new electronic media. *The Transparent Society* raises the questions we need to ask now, before the universal surveillance infrastructure is in place. Be prepared to have your assumptions challenged."

Vernor Vinge, author of *Rainbow's End* - "More than any writer I know, David Brin can take scary, important problems and turn them sideways, revealing wonderful opportunities."

Publisher's Weekly - "The Postman successfully and dramatically deepens Brin's theme of responsibility in surprising and provocative ways."

Thomas M. Disch - "Brin is a physicist of note who knows how to turn abstractions into high adventure.... He excels at the essential craft of the page-turner. Earth resembles Herman Wouk's *The Winds of War*, except that the history Brin is dramatizing, though also on a similar global scale, explores a possible future."

Poul Anderson - "*Startide Rising* is an extraordinary achievement, a book so full of fascinating ideas that they would not have crowded each other at twice its considerable length."

David Brin's science fiction novels have been New York Times Bestsellers, winning multiple Hugo, Nebula and other awards. At least a dozen have been translated into more than twenty languages. As an astrophysicist, Brin serves on advisory boards for NASA, but also consults for corporations and intelligence agencies. His nonfiction book about the information age - *The Transparent Society* - won the Freedom of Speech Award of the American Library Association.

(http://www.davidbrin.com)

POLEMICAL JUDO

MEMES FOR OUR POLITICAL KNIFE-FIGHT

David Brin

A Brazen Guide for Sane Americans To Bypass Trench Warfare And Win Our Life or Death Struggle for Civilization

Dedicated to George Marshall and
The best (Eleanor) Roosevelt…
To MLK and Sequoia and Lincoln and
Those flawed Americans who pushed the needle forward…
And to Ike and Barry…for showing how you can
Stand on that side with humanity and nobility of spirit.
And to fighters for our Enlightenment Experiment.

*

Polemical Judo: ISBN: 9781704368030

E-book formatting by Cheryl Brigham

Print formatting and cover design
by Larry Yudelson

Contents

Every great movement must experience three stages: ridicule, discussion, adoption.
– John Stuart Mill

Chapter 1

Introduction – The Need for Judo Polemic

It was a brilliant political maneuver – and no Democrat seemed willing to learn from it. In 1994, Newt Gingrich's innovative "Contract With America" made the Republican Party appear serious, pragmatic, reformist. No matter that every decent promise in the Contract later wound up neutered or betrayed. The electoral triumph that Gingrich wrought with this bait-and-switch was a historic phase change, demolishing what remained of the Roosevelt-era social and political compact.

The aftermath was even more tectonic. Even under Ronald Reagan, legislators assumed that their mission was to stake bargaining positions, then negotiate and ultimately legislate, adjusting our laws for changing times and needs. Gingrich retained that tradition for one more year – the *anno mirabilis* 1995 – making deals with Bill Clinton to get budget surpluses and welfare reform. Foreign policy was a collaborative neutral zone.

Revolutions often eat their own. Soon Newt was toppled by Dennis Hastert, whose eponymous "Rule" threatened political extinction for any Republican who dared to discuss tradeoffs or common ground with any Democrat, ever. Across America, "Tea Party" movements enforced the Hastert Rule on representatives with fervent passion. As a result, every following congress – except for the brief, Pelosi-led 111th (2009-2011) – would be among the most rigidly partisan in U.S. history. Also the *laziest,* holding among the fewest days in session, or bills passed, or hearings (except those spent fruitlessly pursuing Clintons), but setting all-time records at fund-raising.

Oh, about the central architect of this era that bears his name – Dennis Hastert, chosen by his party to be Speaker of the House and top Republican in the nation? Hastert later served time in federal prison for lying about decades of grotesque, serial child predation.

Why do I begin with all of that, in a book about "Judo Politics"?

Because the key feature from that entire era was *not* Republican canniness, or laziness or turpitude; it was Democrats' obstinate inability to learn and adapt.[1] What Newt Gingrich's "Contract" and the "Hastert Rule" illuminate is how liberals, moderates and Democratic politicians keep getting outmaneuvered, time and again, refusing ever to understand their mistakes – like Barack Obama attempting for eight years to *negotiate across party lines* with opponents who had literally and explicitly banished that phrase from their caucus. Yes, it was wise and mature to keep trying. And yet there are reasons why Obama failed.

Consider the Democrats' two lonely triumphs, across the last 30 years. In both 1992 and 2008, frustration with Republican misrule boiled over. Massive outpourings of activism led to registration and get-out-the-vote campaigns, bringing millions to the polls who formerly sat out elections. In each case, the Democratic-controlled legislative and executive branches got busy, trying to steer the ship of state… only to lose control of Congress just two years later, in 1994 and 2010, when those new voters stayed home. Is history repeating, yet again? Are the chess-masters already planning for 2022?

Repeatedly, Democrats and their allies are lured onto battlegrounds of the enemy's choosing, as Donald Trump tweet-controls every news cycle. Sure, talk show hosts mine each day's outrage for humor, indignation and ratings. But it's rare to find even a single pundit (other than cognitive linguist George Lakoff) asking: "Hey, what actually happened, just now?"

---

[1] "Should Democrats Issue Their Own 'Contract with America'?" http://www.davidbrin.com/nonfiction/contract.html An aside: A few dems thought they were clever, calling Gingrich's ploy a "Contract ON America." Heh. A pathetically useless snark, it was diametrically opposite to 'judo.'

What's happened? We've entered a crucial phase – so far, not hot – of America's 250-year-old civil war, a battle for survival of the Enlightenment Experiment. Moreover, we've been tricked into fighting chest-to-chest, grunting and shoving, in the polemical equivalent of trench warfare. Or else Sumo wrestling.

David Axelrod put it well, citing how we respond to every Trumpian or Fox News provocation with righteous indignation:[2]

"My advice to the Democratic nominee next year is: Don't play. … Wrestling is Mr. Trump's preferred form of combat. But beating him will require *jiu-jitsu,* a different style of battle typically defined as the art of manipulating an opponent's force against himself…."

Absolutely. Moreover, it must begin with *un-learning* our most comforting – and futile – reflexes.

TICKING CLOCKS AND URGENCY[3]

It may surprise you that the author of *Earth* and *Startide Rising*, a lifetime member of environmental NGOs and a caring father who lives by pondering the near and far future, will write so little in this book about some of the critical crises facing our nations, citizens, and biosphere – like global heating, deforestation, water scarcity, mass species extinction, and the spread of populist fascism. I *will* get to them all! But they aren't our main focus here.

That's because I am both hyper-optimistic and super-pessimistic, at the same time.

Just in my own lifetime, I've witnessed so many examples of humanity's genius at innovating spectacular solutions to daunting problems. I know how far that record goes back in time and where it might take us, if truly fed and empowered. For reasons that I won't go into, here, I think it's likely that humans are rare across the cosmos – unusually creative, for a naturally evolved intelligent species. But that creativity only burgeoned

---

[2] New York Times op-ed by David Axelrod, who was senior strategist for Barack Obama's 2008 campaign: "Let Trump Destroy Trump: The Democratic nominee, whoever it turns out to be, should use the president's contortions and carrying-on against him." https://www.nytimes.com/2019/09/11/opinion/trump-2020.html

[3] Speaking of *urgency,* some of you desperately want to envision a quick way out of this torment. Chapter 16 talks about *impeachment* and all that. Of course much or he speculation may seem quaint, by the time you read these lines.

to full strength and vigor recently, in a new kind of society. One that innovated creative ways to practice an art we're taught to despise: *Politics.*

Politics is a competitive process – often cutthroat – but also *cooperative* when we use it to negotiate. It is *politically* that we define policy, which can either hinder or unleash the fecundity of science, amateurism, volunteerism and philanthropy, as well as markets that address new needs through enlightened self-interest. Using many tools and a broad stance, we know how to do those things! We used to do it more.

In a later chapter – "Can We make a Deal?" – I'll go through many ways that adults *might* seek win-win solutions to our myriad problems. But I doubt that can happen right now, because our process of negotiation – politics itself – has been almost destroyed. And that happened deliberately.

Hence my combination of optimism and deep worry. I have many friends in science, engineering, activism and so on who are frenetically busy trying to save the world. We could do so much more, so much faster, except that – alas – all of our immune systems against error and our political mechanisms for problem-solving are presently *clogged*. They must be unclogged!

In order to do that, we'll have to combat monsters.

ZOMBIES AND VAMPIRES AND WERE-ELEPHANTS

The death spiral of U.S. political life has yet to see bottom. While most factual indicators suggest wary optimism about humanity's overall trajectory, our public addiction to dudgeon and fury intensifies daily. Words like "negotiation," "deliberation," and "discourse" sink into quaint anachronism alongside "phlogiston."

For those who complain of "incivility" and preach "let's find common ground," Chapter 2 of this volume explores deep, underlying currents that we – especially Americans – all share, deep roots that are seldom discussed and healthy reflexes that have been turned against us. I'd like nothing better than to apply those common values, resurrecting politics as an arena where – amid much fervent wrangling and dickering – positive-sum compromises rise to the top. Moreover, I'm known as a militantly-moderate person, a liberal-minded pragmatist reformer who sees much wisdom in Adam Smith and who willingly criticizes a sometimes obdurate far-left. My blog is called *Contrary Brin* because I'll argue with any faction, always with an eye to finding that path where all can win.[4]

But I'm now convinced the *never-negotiate* radicalism of today's mad right – promoted avidly on Rupert Murdoch's Fox News and by memes pouring from Kremlin basements, and even institutionalized *openly* by many Republican leaders – leaves us no choice. It's become a knife-fight. Any reaching out will just win us a bloody stump.

As Nobel-winning economist Paul Krugman put it, in an August 2019 editorial: "Democrats need to win elections, but all too often that won't be sufficient, because they confront a Republican Party that at a basic level doesn't accept their right to govern, never mind what the voters say."

By any factually supported metric, citizens should be taking torches to the shambling, undead shell of the party of Lincoln. Yet, over 40% of the voting public in the U.S. (and with similar waves in many other countries) has been mesmerized by bilious incantations via Internet and TV – a phenomenon referred to by uncomprehending punditry as "populism."

In fact, something similar has happened whenever some new kind of media erupted, as in the 1930s, when radios and loudspeakers seemed to amplify the human voice to godlike proportions, empowering gifted savonarolas to very nearly take over the world. Or back when printing presses poured forth hate-tracts that stoked Europe's 17th Century religious wars. Today's cunning Goebbels-equivalents have turned transformative internet technologies against us. Against the very civilization that fostered communications breakthroughs with curiosity and science. Oh, someday, these technologies, too, will have the promised net-positive effects, as happened to books and radio. But till then, we must survive a violent time, incited by tsunamis of malignant memes. And that will only happen by thwarting evil geniuses.

Hence, while this book is aimed at helping achieve outright victory for the "Union" side in this phase of the U.S. Civil War, *I am not here to praise Democrats, but to berate them.*

---

[4] Contrary Brin blog: http://davidbrin.blogspot.com/

Getting mired in trenches *while* extending repeatedly a bloodied hand of negotiation is not working. Nor am I the only one demanding tougher, more agile tactics. Presidential candidate Beto O'Rourke, as of July 2019 started using "foul language" to describe the Trumpists. (Gosh.) David Faris, author of *It's Time to Fight Dirty: How Democrats Can Build a Lasting Majority in American Politics*, says Republicans have all but destroyed democratic norms in America, and it's time for Dems to take on the mantle of procedural warfare. Faris's concepts include deliberately breaking up big states like California so that blue populations can match red citizens in "Senator Power." I have many doubts. But as Abraham Lincoln said about U.S. Grant, "I can't spare this man, he fights."

This battle can only be won with agility. With maneuver. By using the adversary's ponderous momentum against him. By appraising the advantages and weapons of those who hijacked American Conservatism, transforming it into a shambling zombie that would appall Barry Goldwater, William F. Buckley, or even Ronald Reagan. The Republican press has become a tool of foreign tyrants, casino moguls, coal barons, petro-princes, Wall Street cheaters, tabloid pimps, Mafiosi and resurgent Nazis – a cabal of forces who will end free enterprise as surely as they aim to finish off Enlightenment democracy and the impartial rule of law. Toward this goal they have refined a daunting array of effective tactics…

… that might yet be overcome and even turned to our advantage, with the political equivalent of *judo*, the art of using your opponents' own aggressive momentum against them;

– By slashing the bonds (or lies) holding *their* coalition together. (The very thing they do to us.)

– By confronting our neighbors *not* with familiar chasms, but commonalities. Things you and they both know to be true.

– By understanding how so many basically decent people insulate themselves against appeals to compassion.

– By going to the root of their own catechisms, like *Make America Great Again.*

– By making explicit what the Fox New hosts and fellow travelers never say aloud, like their open war against all fact-using professions.

– By using *outcomes* to destroy their comfy narratives – like the claim that conservatives are the *practical ones* – by proving Democrats are vastly *better against deficits,* at engendering a healthy economy and even at fostering open-creative-competitive enterprise.

– By proving there is common ground, e.g. showing your neighbors that we were *all* raised by Hollywood themes like suspicion of authority and individual autonomy, even if we disagree over *which* authorities are trying for Big Brother.

– By going directly after the two traits they find so appealing about Donald Trump: first his brash bully-bravado and appearance of macho "strength"...

– ... and second the way he enrages the same people who red-hat-wearing Americans hate most.

– By developing the one method that always corners them. A trick that makes a few opponents stop, think and reconsider... while sending the rest fleeing in panic and shame.

Oh, the list goes on and on. In this compendium, I'll shine light on not one, or ten, but as many as *a hundred memes and counter-memes, tactics and stratagems, polemical riffs and/or smart missiles* that have nearly all been ignored by our 'generals' – the candidates and consultants and commentators who we count on to confront this madness. I'll suggest ways to counter effective cult catechisms like "fake news" and "deep state" and the blatant, all-out war against every fact-using profession.

If even one of these tools or tricks winds up being used well by some effective public figure, then this effort will be worthwhile.

THE NERVE OF THIS GUY!

Who am I to lecture experienced politicians, analysts and activists, chiding them to adopt new weaponry in this fight for civilization? Well, I do have some cred. As a scientist, I serve on NASA commissions and consult[5] for many corporations/agencies about both "the future" and processes of change. My best-selling novels[6] (translated into 25 languages) include *The Postman* (filmed in 1997), *Earth*, and *Existence.* My non-

---

[5] http://www.davidbrin.com/speakerreferences.html

[6] http://www.davidbrin.com

fiction book about the information age – *The Transparent Society: Will Technology Make Us Choose Between Privacy and Freedom?7* – won the Freedom of Speech Award. *Time* Magazine listed *Earth* as one of "Eight books that eerily predicted the future."[8]

Sure, none of that qualifies me to yammer chidings and advice at experienced journalists or savvy politicos, or accomplished NGO leaders. Go ahead and be skeptical toward the importance or originality of these ideas! In fact, I'll avow that cognitive linguist George Lakoff has appraised the psychological-manipulating methods of our present Oligarchic Putsch far better than I can.[9] So I'll avoid much overlap with that sage.

Like many of you, I've spent the last quarter of a century yelling at the TV or Internet: "You fools! Don't you see that you could shoot down that BS with…" eliciting sighs from my ever-patient life partner.

I've gone beyond shouting at the TV. Many of the ideas presented here appeared on my middling-popular *Contrary Brin* site, along with guest editorials, columns, interviews and podcasts.

Still, folks kept chiding: *"Books are what you're known for, Brin. Compile your best postings. Get it out there!"*

WHAT LIES WITHIN

Well okay, my regular publishers would be too slow for this election cycle, so it seemed best to release a quick e-book touching on many topics. We'll spin from the war on science and fact (Chapter 5) to racism and immigration.

- From electoral cheating and gerrymandering (Chapters 4 & 8) to the economy (Chapter 11), to forging a big-tent coalition.
- From saving the planet to the right's obsession with *symbolism*, to gun control.

---

[7] The Transparent Society: http://www.davidbrin.com/transparentsociety.html
[8] Time Magazine, re futurist books. http://time.com/5380613/books-predict-future/
[9] George Lakoff: https://georgelakoff.com/

• From international relations and China and Russia (Chapters 9 & 18) to anti-government fetishism (Chapter 10) and our ongoing national family feud (Chapter 16).

• From "exit strategies" – Impeachment, Indictment, the 25th Amendment and all that (skip to Chapter 16, if that's all you care about) to overcoming "splitterism" (Chapter 12).

• From conspiracies (Chapter 7) … to the poison that is used to suborn so many of our leaders… to the antidote that might save them and us (Chapter 8).

• From ways we might all negotiate solutions *off* the hoary "left-right axis" (Chapter 13)… to resilience and readiness in case that fails.

• and *tactics, tactics, tactics* that might – or might not – work. But shouldn't someone at least *try some of them?*

CAVEATS

As I said, this tome largely gathers – with updates and edits – separate postings from *Contrary Brin*, so do expect both *gaps and perhaps, repetitions.* Likely a lot of the latter. Apologies for that –

– and for my inevitable failures at the ever-changing linguistic exigencies of our ongoing campaign for diversity, uplifting a crude civilization toward greater awareness, acceptance and tolerance. (See below.) I'll commit errors of terminology, especially re: this year's gender-and-category identification rules. Still, while this codger firmly rejects extrema of PC-bullying, let me avow to being an enthusiastic, lifelong fellow traveler in our unprecedented drive toward the kind of just and better future sometimes portrayed in science fiction. I mean well.

Why is so much of the 'good stuff' packed later in the book, like "impeachment" and other fierce tactics? Because I'm a pedantic twit and there's a lot of stuff about history, science and even philosophy I want to get to first. I control the order of the table of contents. You control what you choose to read.

Finally yes, while most of the issues and points raised here are pertinent to any human society, especially those upholding enlightenment values, this volume is decidedly USA-centric. In a followup, I hope to show how these themes and crimes and counter-tactics have redolence around the globe. But in Volume 1, these chapters focus on a pivotal fight for the soul of the "American Experiment."

Friends out there, root for us – we still have a flawed-if-useful role to play. But carry on, if we fail.

Oh, for those readers who like to *skim* (I can get wordy and garrulous), go to later "pause" interludes where I try to distill down to *zingers and one-liners.* Above all, these political judo maneuvers aim to use the stratagems and momentum of today's mad-right against them, helping us defend and revive the vital revolution that gave humanity its brightest hope. May some of our politician-paladins find weapons of practical value.

The first of those *pause* riffs between chapters will focus on *fundamentals* that seldom get mentioned in our insipid "Left-vs.-Right" grunting and sumo-shoving matches. Some are traits that you and I *share* with a vast majority of our fellow citizens, even many on the other side… qualities that we might use to bridge the volcanic wrath now gaping between us.

A wrath that all-too many of them have foolishly fallen for… but yes, in some cases *so have I.* And so have you.

As lusciously pleasurable as it can be, we cannot afford wrath. There's too much at stake.

In case you don't have time to read the whole book – (young folks say "tl;dr" *or* "too lazy; didn't read"*) – some of these "pause-for" sections will offer brief memes for political judo, summarizing tactics described elsewhere. They are compact, ranging from incisive to petty. If you came here for mature insights... skip to Chapter 2.*

Pause #1 for...

One-Liners, Zingers and "tl;dr" Quick-memes

I. ZINGERS & ONE-LINERS:
Meme grenades distilled from chapters.

– "**MAGA?** Okay wise guy, when do you claim America was greater than today?" Hint: when they say "the 1950s...." pounce! (Chapter 3.)

– "**Fake News problem?**" Why do no voices on the right offer to help moderates and professionals to set up an impartial fact-checking service? If all current ones are 'biased,' will you name ten eminent and widely respected conservatives to join a commission, charged with helping design acceptable and competing fact-services? What, you can't name any? (Chapter 5.)

– "**Fake News Fix.**" If you hijackers of the right won't propose august, respect-worthy American conservatives to serve on such panels, then we will. Retired justices, retired admirals, Nobel winners, or almost any citizen of Utah![10] Folks who may differ from us over markets and regulation – even about guns – but who agree that 'facts are things' and Nazis are bad... and that we need a way out of the poison fog of lies. (Chapter 5.)

---

[10] This will come up again. Utah is probably the largest concentration of RASRs – Residually Adult Sane Conservatives – who are disgusted, even outraged, by the Trumpian travesties. Outreach by moderate-liberal America would seem timely, even overdue.

– **"Deep State?"** Which seems more likely? A 'conspiracy' by ten million scientists, journalists, teachers, doctors, civil servants, FBI agents, intel and military officers? Or that just five thousand golf buddies in an incestuous CEO caste connive secretly with Wall Streeters, casino moguls, foreign despots and inheritance brats? (Chapters 8 & 10.)

– Adam Smith, the core founder of both market economics and liberalism, would today be a flaming Democrat. (Chapters 3, 10 & 11.)

– **Who's a commie?** How many times must Donald Trump hold secret debriefing sessions with communist despots – or conveniently "ex" communist dictators who grew up reciting Marx – without any reputable U.S. officials present – before you'll admit something fishy is going on?

– **Vladimir Putin** called the fall of the USSR "history's greatest tragedy." All of today's Russian oligarchs were raised reciting Leninist catechisms. The KGB transitioned without a hiccup. But you folks call them all great guys. Sure, they dropped the hammers and sickles, but surely you didn't fall for a trick of symbolism? Because nothing else changed. (Postponed for Volume 2.)

– **Wanna bet?** Oh, glaciers are advancing? Would you put an actual money wager on any of your ravings, from climate change to inaugural crowds to those mighty Trumpian accomplishments? (In Chapter 15 we'll see that demanding wagers, rather than being an immature stunt, actually works ferociously well.)

– **Wrong, almost always.** "Tobacco is harmless," "Cars don't cause smog," "No seat belts in cars!" and "Keep lead in gasoline!" then McCarthyism, Burning Rivers, the insane War on Drugs, mass incarceration and Supply Side voodoo... the list of wrong, wrong, wrong is endless. Can you offer times when the GOP was provably/decisively right? Actually, I can! A couple of times. But there's been so much more wrong. (Chapter 6.)

– **Conspiracy Theories:** show us any of the ones you keep changing and then dropping, that ever proved decisively true? There are conspiracies that pass half a dozen "sniff tests." But not many. (Chapter 7.)

– **IGUS**. The recent Whistleblower Crises revealed weakness in one of our major bulwarks of clean government, as the seventy-four Inspectors General of federal departments and agencies endure unprecedented meddling and bullying – or else mal-appointment – by Republican politicians.

In Chapters 5 and 10 we'll see how to restore autonomous oversight by bringing them all under an independent office of the Inspector General of the United States[11] (IGUS), along with other reforms including the Fact Act.[12]

– **Obamacare was the Republicans' own damn plan!** Cooked up by the Heritage Foundation,[13] it was on GOP platforms through the 90s and enacted in Massachusetts by Republican Gov. Mitt Romney.[14] Now Republicans call their own plan satanic. Which is worse? That hypocrisy? Or failure of any Democrats to mention it?

– **And by the way...** where's the alternative health insurance plan that Republicans have promised for ... what now? Eleven years? Any day now.

– **Judges and taxes?** Millions of U.S. conservatives who are ashamed of all the rest – Trumpism, bigotry, climate denialism, cheating, lies, trashing our alliances and blatant cozying with tyrants – justify their hold-my-nose loyalty to the GOP with a single incantation: judges and taxes. But if every other fruit is poisonous, might the whole tree?

– **Aren't you curious...** even a little... about those tax returns? Or Deutsche Bank funneling Trump loans from Russian oligarchs? The contents of David Pecker's National Enquirer safe ought to fill any American with flaming, nonpartisan curiosity, along with the scores of Non Disclosure Agreements (NDA) that Donald Trump openly brags about.[15] What happened to "We deserve to know!"

II. TACTICS DEMOCRATS COULD TRY... TOMORROW:

– Some congressional committee could unleash a tsunami of revelations just by offering full protection and immunity for testimony from anyone who has an NDA – or Non-Disclosure Agreement – with Donald Trump. Trump has bragged about his Great Wall of punitive-protective

---

[11] The Inspector General of the United States http://davidbrin.com/nonfiction/inspectorgeneral.html

[12] The FACT Act: http://davidbrin.com/nonfiction/factact.html

[13] See the signing ceremony, April 12, 2006, for the crowning achievement of Mitt Romney's governorship – a health insurance plan that was the template for the Affordable Care Act. The head of the Heritage Foundation crows over the role his group played in designing "Romneycare" based in the earlier Republican Party Health Plan for individual mandates and insurance buying markets or "exchanges" that originated at the Heritage think tank and that was touted as a way to use market forces to solve the problem of the uninsured. http://thinkprogress.org/politics/2010/04/10/90621/heritage-romneycare/

[14] Think Progress: http://thinkprogress.org/politics/2010/04/10/90621/heritage-romneycare/

[15] Karen McDougal released from her NDA: https://www.spin.com/2018/04/karen-mcdougal-nda-agreement-american-media/

NDAs. Shatter it and let the revelations spill. (Michael Cohen will tell you whom to approach.)

– Assume Chief Justice John Roberts will use the Court's right wing majority to uphold his clever new Roberts Doctrine of "no-interference between the legislative and executive," or non-justiciability, thus allowing GOP henchmen to passively refuse House subpoenas on lame and unprecedented excuses. They think fait accompli resistance will stymie investigation and oversight. But there›s a judo move that Schiff and Nadler and Pelosi can try. It means appealing to the Fourth Branch of government. It would work.[16]

– Immaturity alert! This one is almost... Trumpian. But imagine if one mid level Democratic politician were to hold a news conference denouncing fellow Democrats for their unsympathetic pestering of an addled-volatile old man who clearly qualifies for extra care and kindness under the Americans with Disabilities Act... I mean it. Paul Krugman and Nancy Pelosi have come close. But go all the way.[17] Close your eyes and imagine that being drawn out, again and again. Even those who don't 'get it' at first will catch on when Trump responds with volcanic fury, ironically proving it's true! What a tweet-storm that would trigger, hysteria that undermines his one pillar of support – the superficial appearance of "strength." (Chapter 15.)

– More immaturity: Bush and Trump and others on that side love to hurl nicknames. And yes, as grownups we avoid schoolyard bully ploys. Still, if you go there, I recommend using "Old Two Scoops." It's not overtly sneering

---

[16] As of pub date, October 25, 2019, it appears that civil servants are taking matters into their own hands, not waiting for Congressional subpoenas to step forward. I don't mind at all seeing some of my "judo Suggestions" bypassed in such ways. We'll be saved by heroes.

[17] In October 2019, Nobelist Paul Krugman wrote: "I don't mean that Trump is stupid; a stupid man couldn't have managed to defraud so many people over so many years. Nor do I mean that he's crazy, although his speeches and tweets – 'my great and unmatched wisdom,' the Kurds weren't there on D-Day – keep sounding loonier." Krugman adds, however, that Trump is "lazy, utterly incurious and too insecure to listen to advice or ever admit to a mistake. And given that he is, in fact, what he accuses others of being – an enemy of the people – we should be thankful for his flaws." Well… we'll see. The same week, on Saturday Night Live, Weekend Update host Michael Che voiced (brilliantly) a meme I had been spreading about a new and clever way to deal with the weird-crazed phenomenon of Donald Trump. ""I don't know how to ask this, but are we sure that it's OK to make fun of this guy?" he asked. "Did you ever read Of Mice and Men? Remember how Lenny was really 'strong?' What if Trump is really strong? I've got a cousin who is also strong. And he loves alligators too, but we don't make fun of him." https://www.alternet.org/2019/10/paul-krugman-trumps-mental-deficiency-may-actually-save-us-from-disaster-as-he-keeps-sounding-loonier/

or mean or obscene. But it mocks the pompous preening of a narcissistic character trait – emblematic of aristocracy – that even the reddest booster can't defend.

III. WAGER DARES FOR TRUMP:

Hey you major public figures or late night hosts: instead of reacting every week to the next distraction outrage, then the next, try openly and repeatedly challenging Donald Trump to:

– accept a medical exam by skilled doctors he can't control,

– prove his "stable genius IQ" with a panel of simple tests applied by professionals chosen randomly,

– waive IRS privacy rules enough for them to at least say publicly whether or not there's an audit,

– roll dice and randomly pick any week's top five accusations of "fake news" for a jury of respected Americans to audit in detail (see Chapter 5). Or even randomly chosen Americans.

– prove the birther thing, at long last. That Obama's parents planted – all the way from Kenya – birth announcements in Hawaiian newspapers, or to golf less than Obama. Or to pay the money he owes every city where he held a rally.[18] Make that a money bet, right now,

– or swear never again to be alone with foreign despots without trusted American witnesses present.

It's not that any one such demand will be transformative, or even become an actual wager – none of them will (for reasons given in Chapter 15). Alas, no Democratic politician or pundit seems to understand the power of repetition and persistent hammering, despite having witnessed Trump use that method to great effect.

IV. WAGER-DARES FOR OTHER REPUBLICANS:

A bit different, these in-yer-face challenges are for your confederate cousins. Demands for real-money bets will send most of them backpedal-

---

[18] Minneapolis mayor: We saw Trump stiffing cities for his rallies, so we told him to pay up.https://www.washingtonpost.com/opinions/2019/10/12/minneapolis-mayor-we-saw-trump-stiffing-cities-his-other-rallies-so-we-told-him-pay-up/

ing. Or else (rarely) persuade one to resume viewing at facts as real things. (See Chapters 5, 11, 13, and especially 15). And yes, some of these will be repeated, later in the book.

– How many Trump appointees and associates started out described by him as 'great guys,' who later 'betrayed' him? I bet it's more than any ten other presidents. Whatever the anecdotal merits or turpitudes of any particular case, will you admit it proves he's a lousy judge of character?

– Put money on military readiness. Which political party generally leaves U.S. defenses, alliances and resilience in better shape than how they found them? Which party nearly always leaves the American military worse off than before they took over? (And yes, it is the GOP. See pause#10.)

– Quick, name a Republican top leader between Reagan and Ryan who was mentioned at the 2016 Republican National Convention. Neither Bush president, nor Cheney, Rumsfeld, Powell, Hastert, DeLay, Romney, McCain... not even mentioned. All "ancient history." But if you disavow those past Republican administrations, then where is your party's credibility?

– I bet you can't name a fact-profession not being warred upon by Fox & Accomplices. Even one. (Chapter 5.)

– Name one Supply Side "economics" prediction that ever came true. That tax cuts for the rich would be invested in R&D and new factories? That they result in increased revenue and reduced deficits? That they achieve anything other than asset bubbles, collapsed money velocity and skyrocketing wealth disparities? Name one reason we should trust a supply sider with a wet match? (Chapter 11.)

– The rate of change of the rate of change of debt was positive (toward reckless acceleration) during almost every year of every Republican administration (post Eisenhower). It was negative (braking the rate of deficit growth gradually toward prudence) in every year of every Democratic administration (post Johnson). How does that fit the GOP's last ditch justification... that they are the prudent, pragmatic ones? (Chapter 11.)

– Across the last 25 years, the GOP either controlled Congress, or else could thwart it, for all but two. Care to name any positive accomplishments? Not wars or tax gifts to the rich, but major adjustments to law or even major de-regulations? (Chapter 10.)

- And again and again. Put money on Trumpian lies for any given day. Pick at random day in the near future.

V. SLIGHTLY LONGER MEME BOMBS: Also in chapters, with longer summaries.

- **What if Obama did it?** "WODI" can be effective. Every day, your "ostrich" Republican shrugs aside some antic that would have sent them ballistic, if done by Clinton or Obama. A decent bar bet would be to say in advance "Next Thursday let's try out WODI on that day's Trump travesty." It only works on a gal or guy who has a shred of remaining honesty or honor.

- **Clinton or Obama-related "investigations"** - after a quarter of a century and half a billion dollars - and never a stonewalled refusal of testimony - congrats. You proved a husband fibbed about some adult-consensual (while still inappropriate) infidelity and the wife was caught using the same sort of somewhat improper email system as Colin Powell, Dick Cheney, John McCain, Mike Pence, George Bush, Ivanka Trump and Jared Kushner. That's it. After 25 years without proof, where's your cred?

- **Answer both right and left critics of Pax Americana.** If the U.S. had behaved like all other empires and imposed mercantilist trade patterns after WWII, then America would have no debt today. Its cities would gleam and factories hum. The country would swim in gold...but hope and prosperity in the larger world would be ruined by the same short-sighted greed that brought down Babylon, Persia, Rome, Pax Sinica, Pax Britannia etc. And when we finally fell, it would be in a tumult of well-deserved wrath. But we didn't do what all those empires did. We did something very different. (Chapter 9.)

- Mitch McConnell's declaration that no judges should be appointed or confirmed in an election year, then chortling he'll pass anyone nominated by Trump in 2020... a perfect example of how one complaint - or a few - can be shrugged off as whining. But a concerted campaign of mockery....[19]

- Offer an amnesty for Americans now enslaved by blackmail. It's speculative! Perhaps no one will step up... or perhaps too many to count... in which case it's unlikely, amid a tsunami of revelation, that our scheming

[19] Old fashioned terms like honor, courage, dedication, devotion, integrity, etc. These are core values for a lot of people. And they await rescue from hypocrites who have stolen them.

enemies will survive. As we'll see in Chapter 8, the long range victory condition for our kind of civilization is a future world that's filled with open-fair competition, calm negotiation, but above all... light.

* DON'T FOR A MINUTE THINK WE'VE FORGOTTEN...

That's but a sampler list, offered for those who find an actual book "TLDR."

For the rest of you, hang in there. Chapter 15 will dive into the effectiveness of wager-demands, even – especially – when the other side weasels and refuses to bet! The tactic corners them anyway, by their own macho standards. It destroys the illusion of macho "strength." And there will be other distilled "meme bomb" collections, especially near the end of the book.

Finally... here's a challenge that I'll reiterate many times – in chapters 6 and 12 and 13 – aimed at every dogmatic purist out there:

Are you actually asserting that you are absolutely 100% right, with no margin of error?

And yes, this question can bedevil purists of the left as well as the right. Dig it (and this is good news!) Your enemies are likely no more than 99% wrong! Possibly as little as 90%. Moreover, have you the character strength to sift through your opponents' maelstrom of "wrongness" for those slivers where they actually have a point?

We'll come back to this. It's not just about being the mature person. Entering and understanding your adversary's head is a key ingredient that Sun Tzu recommended... for achieving victory.

Before getting to practical methods, any "judo" manual explores what's most important. Understanding your adversary. And yourself.

Chapter 2

Below the Surface. Underlying beliefs that most of us share

This phase of the U.S. Civil War was not of our choosing. But we've been complicit. First, by accepting many indolent assumptions, then by ignoring history.

Take the lesson of the *Greatest Generation.* As we'll see in Chapter 3, our Roosevelt-era parents and grandparents overcame a mélange of would-be plutocrats, populist tyrants and communist commissars to craft a social contract that unleashed a confident, burgeoning middle class, spectacular universities and science, vast infrastructure and entrepreneurship – plus a too-slow but ponderously-growing momentum toward justice.

That social contract was so successful that we forget how rare and special it all was! Our parents were *so* successful at crafting a flat-fair society that we members of the Boomer Generation largely assumed (and still assume) that age-old cheater plagues like *oligarchy* and *feudalism* – dominant across nearly all of the last 6000 years – were banished for good.

They weren't. Today's worldwide attempted *oligarchic putsch* – propelling America back into Civil War – is both lethally dangerous and boringly predictable. As Hannah Arendt taught, evil can be oafish and banal, while also feral-canny. But one thing villains are instinctively good at is setting decent people against each other.

So let's dig down to undercurrents that most of us share. Our enlightenment experiment is founded on some notions and practices that were never extensively practiced till recently – *common threads that are masked by our dismal obsession to couch everything in left-right terms.*

For example, if pressed, most Americans would avow:

– that liberty is desirable;

– that men and women of goodwill should negotiate in good faith – either directly or through representatives – each giving a bit in order to achieve positive-sum20 outcomes;

– that leaders are *not* the same thing as the state; they can and should be frequently replaced;

– that the rule of law must be applied evenly, fairly and transparently... though we can also change faulty laws – fairly and transparently;

– that money and power often corrupt, and it can happen from any direction;

– that a mature/sincere person should at least consider the foremost – even sacred – tenet of science: *I might be wrong*;

– that prejudices believed by our parents – and those clutched by us today – *might* be disproved by facts, at which point it's time to let them go;

– that expertise and intelligence don't guarantee wisdom, but knowledge and skill merit respect;

Moreover, if you couch it right, you can also get folks across a wide-spectrum to admit:

– that competition and cooperation are *not* opposites. Humans are inherently competitive beings and competition engenders creativity... but competition is nearly always wrecked by *cheating*, unless we *cooperatively* come up with rules and referees to keep it fair;

– that whatever is not explicitly forbidden – via duly deliberated laws that can always be questioned – is automatically allowed;21

– that most 'liberal' endeavors – at least those aimed at uplifting children – need little more justification than "stop wasting talent";

---

[20] No concept is more urgently important than that of *positive-sum* versus *zero-sum* (or even negative-sum) thinking. It is the underlying principle of our civilization, distinguishing it from all others. And it is not my purpose here to explain it. Try Robert Wright's wonderful book *Nonzero: The Logic of Human Destiny.*

[21] A vast proportion of complex human cultures, perhaps a majority, taught: "whatever isn't expressly allowed is assumed to be forbidden." Picture a cop demanding: "Who said you could do that! Show me the permission!" You and I assume – if there's no apparent way we're hurting or bothering any people or interests, or imposing any burdens – that we can reply: "Who am I hurting? Show me where it's disallowed!"

It's a safe guess that you'd credit yourself with holding all those views… while denying that your opposition-neighbors do. But try asking: Aren't *they* just as likely to claim that *you* don't?

In fact, all of the nostrums listed above are fundamental to our new kind of society, though you've likely not seen them expressed that way. Which is the point here. The first step in bridging our chasm is to escape loaded terminology.

EVEN MORE BASIC THAN THAT

Now let me surprise you by saying *other themes* run *deeper* than those above, distinguishing America and its allies from the rest of human history. For starters, *can you name any other society that raised its own children to relentlessly criticize their own tribal elders?*

The way that you - yes, you - have a powerful reflex to criticize?

A relentless stream of propaganda has poured from the indoctrination system known as *Hollywood*, pushing themes you agree with! Doubt that? Quick then, can you name a popular film you've enjoyed, across decades, which did not promote the following?

Suspicion of Authority

Tolerance

Diversity

Personal autonomy and individuality

Eccentricity

Above all, *suspicion of and resistance to unfair authority figures*. These are the very traits that enable and empower *criticism,* of the sort that you - as a politically active person - apply to your nation and its mistakes. It's all part of a critical self-improvement campaign that enabled us to thread (sometimes just barely) a minefield of potential disasters across the last century, achieving many kinds of progress. It is also the trait that - despite every effort of the oligarchs - may yet win us the stars.

Right now you may be simmering, offended by the notion that you imbibed such values from movies, novels and songs, instead of inventing them yourself. Even worse, the effrontery to suggest that your opponent-neighbors might share those same deep reflexes.

Get over it! We don't have time for self-indulgence. Nor is this the place to explore philosophical implications of such a strange propaganda campaign, so unlike the mythologies of any prior culture. Though elsewhere I've called it *The Dogma of Otherness.*[22] What matters now is the calamity that's befallen us! Because these memes, which underlie much of our success and our strength, *are now being used against us.*

Suspicion of Authority (SoA) is reflexive in *both* liberals and conservatives. Both denounce Orwellian plots against freedom and light. But they part company over *which* groups aim to be Big Brother.

– Conservatives fret about power grabs by *snooty academics* and *communists* and *faceless government bureaucrats.*

– Liberals see cabals of secret-conniving *billionaires* and *racists* and *faceless corporations.*[23]

But when you put it that way, isn't the answer *Duh?* All power centers are inherently dangerous! At various times, cheaters and would-be tyrants used corporate, or bureaucratic-socialist, or owner-elite centers of power... and if you've spent time at any university, you saw mini-despotisms in many departments. Exploiters and cheaters will fester and plot wherever they feel they can. It's why we finally invented habits and tools of accountability.

Ideally, we'd warily guard each other's backs, with liberals grudgingly admitting "all right, I am more worried about plutocrats, while you fear bureaucratic excess. Tell you what. I'll listen to you a bit if you'll listen to me."

Ideally. I've seen it happen! Though not in 21st Century America. Alas, that synergy shatters amid re-ignited civil war, when each side tells its partisans that freedom can be harmed *only* from one direction. This *political fused-spine disease* leaves us unable to turn our heads. A form of tunnel vision, it's one reason we get trapped into grunting sumo-shoving, instead of thinking two or three dimensionally... helping our neighbors do the same.

If these matters truly interest you, I recommend a brief Socratic *questionnaire on ideology24* that might reveal added dimensions. I promise

---

[22] "The Dogma of Otherness," in *Otherness,* by David Brin, 1994. http://www.davidbrin.com/otherness.html

[23] And yes, I suppose – with some reluctance – that makes me a 'liberal."

[24] Questionnaire on ideology. Try it! http://www.davidbrin.com/nonfiction/questionnaire.html

you won't view the hoary-insipid-lobotomizing "left-vs.-right axis" the same way again.

Our key point here is simple. *The putsch-masters need us at each other's throats, so they exploit the most inherently American meme – SoA – getting us denouncing each other as authoritarian elites!*

This book offers many ways to thwart them. The best and most honorable approach? Get our cousins and fellow citizens to admit:

Yes, we share the same instincts and underlying fears.

We differ over particulars.

Might there be some way we both are right?

And perhaps both wrong?

EXAMPLES OF WRONG

Oh, I clearly believe one side in our current culture battle is *wrong far more often* than the other. I will prove it, in Chapter 6. Still, there's a habit of *obstinacy* that is all-too humanly shared also on the left.

Example: we all know how American conservatives spent decades ignoring human-generated Climate Change, sneering at the leading role that conservation must play in resolving this peril. Refusing to let efficiency and sustainability become urgent projects, they pray instead to the "problem-solving magic of markets," the way natives of Rapa Nui beseeched big statues to restore their ravaged isle.

But it's arguable (elsewhere) that the Left has its own incantatory nostrums, e.g. rejecting any role for nuclear power, which helped lift millions out of poverty worldwide without adding appreciably to greenhouse emissions. Three generations have seen high benefit-to-harm ratios from fission reactors. Despite Chernobyl and other scary cautions. Despite pollution that – while frightening – has always proved containable. (This outcomes-ratio stands, astonishingly, even if you include Hiroshima and Nagasaki.) Yet, liberals won't even debate adding carefully designed, next-generation nuclear plants to our toolset for crossing a potentially Earth-killing Greenhouse Gap.

Did you fume at one paragraph while nodding at the other? Step back. Can you see a common reflex? To ignore contrary evidence and automatically say no? These "opposite" party lines share an underlying trait – a reflex to prefer distrust over the can-do spirit of modernity and science.

Only dig it… liberals *can* be argued out of their reflexes. Conservatives can too… but not during any phase of our 250 year civil war.

SEZ YOU! EVERYTHING IS RELATIVE

Alas, the honorable approach won't work if anyone using it is already an "enemy." I'll return often to the mad-right's *all-out war on facts and all fact-using professions,* a vendetta that diverts the SoA reflex of red Americans toward smartypants "elites" – the scientists, journalists, teachers, doctors and "deep state" officers –who stand in the way of oligarchy's rule. We'll get to that in Chapter 5.

But here we're exploring our neighbors' underlying assumptions. And the strongest – that they almost always fall back upon – is: *Everything's a matter of opinion.*

Let's say you gather powerful evidence to support your argument – e.g. regarding climate change. Nowadays, your links are instantly canceled with counter-links, and outraged opponents denounce any claim you make for 'credibility.' If you cite specialists, that only makes you a lackey to authority. And don't you know that "experts" are all conformist lemmings? Every fact-checking service is a would-be Orwellian Ministry of Truth.

As Thomas Paine put it, in *The American Crisis*: "To argue with a man who has renounced the use and authority of reason, and whose philosophy consists in holding humanity in contempt, is like administering medicine to the dead, or endeavoring to convert an atheist by scripture."

But then, that too is citing an authority.

I'll offer several ways to fight these well-tuned defense mechanisms. But only a few of them are potent enough to overcome the final bastion[25] of defensive relativism, one that our parents and grandparents knew all-too well:

---

[25] "Don't waste time trying to convince Trump supporters he's repugnant" by Colbert I. King https://www.washingtonpost.com/opinions/dont-waste-energy-proving-trumps-racism-get-him-out-of-the-white-house/2019/08/16/89883596-bf95-11e9-a5c6-1e74f7ec4a93_story.html

"Oh yeah? Sez you!"

THE PENULTIMATE CURRENT

And some things flow even deeper, below conditioning and culture, to a level that's biological.

Elsewhere, I've both spoken26 and published papers27 about the very worst and most damaging *addiction* to vex humanity – especially America – a plague of self-righteous indignation. Each year, evidence accumulates that sanctimony-rage is a *physically* addictive state, flooding the body with endorphins, serotonin and the kind of pleasure rush that draws many people to return – relentlessly – to this voluptuous high. The high of feeling so, so wrathfully *right.* Each of us, if we are honest, can look in a mirror and admit there's truth to this.

That doesn't make it wrong to be indignant! Often, only outrage can stoke enough courage and drive to fight a foe who flat-out deserves it. Heck, this volume is propelled by my own righteous anger over what's been done to a nation, world, species and children whom I love. I'm furious!

But we're supposed to be the calm, rational, sapient ones, able to *choose* when the self-righteous rush may take us… and when to say "hold, enough." Above all, self-control may let you do as Sun Tzu recommends, controlling *your* passion, while letting the enemy's draw him into errors.

THE ULTIMATE APPEAL OF DONALD TRUMP

I won't quibble with George Lakoff's diagnosis of Trumpism. Lakoff is correct that many "red" Americans – yes, even deeply religious Christians – admire a man who is opposite-to-Jesus in every way, because he projects confidence ("I am the chosen one"[28]) and an appearance of macho strength.

Trump's bravado – absent any sign of past physical or moral bravery – is that of a 7th grade playground bully. Perhaps some followers look back fondly on that time of life, when nerdy guys weren't successful or attractive

---

[26] See a talk on "The addictive plague of getting mad as hell." http://tinyurl.com/wrathaddicts

[27] And the scientific background to Indignation Addiction: http://www.davidbrin.com/nonfiction/addiction.html

[28] "I am the Chosen One." From Forbes: https://www.forbes.com/sites/lisettevoytko/2019/08/21/i-am-the-chosen-one-trumps-religious-comments-enrage-critics/#5d17f9406393

to women. Lakoff says it's the *symbolism* of confident strength that counts over reality. (We'll discuss Republican symbol-obsession in several places.) I don't disagree, though I suspect that something else is even more important to them.

Despite his dismal record at governance, a myriad character faults and his endless spew of lies, Donald Trump delivers on one vital count. *He enrages the very people his followers most hate.*[29]

Recall our discussion above, about *suspicion of authority* (SoA.) Each of us worries about one or another variety of scheming elites. But as commentator Thom Hartmann put it: "When liberals talk about 'elites', they mean rich people. When conservatives talk about 'elites', they mean smart people."

Okay, that's a self-flattering meme. And it should terrify us all.

---

[29] In popular parlance The goal of the administration is to "own the libs."

Go find these elsewhere…

Pause #2 for…

Political tactics & reforms that I *won't* be talking about… much.

One criterion decided what I chose to include in this book: is the idea already well-explored elsewhere? I don't have time for that and it's not what you came here for. But I should provide some links. Concepts for political reform range from the pragmatic and doable all the way to absurd distractions.

At the better end: Equal Citizens[30], a democracy reform and advocacy group headed by Lawrence Lessig, has campaigned hard against cheats like gerrymandering and voter suppression (which we'll view from different angles in Chapter 4). Equal Citizens persuaded the state of Maine to institute RC voting – or preferential balloting[31] – a system that has been used by us super-wise and forward-thinking science fiction folks for the Hugo and Nebula awards for four decades; it is nationally standard in Australia and some other nations. They are very happy with its ability to give due attention to third parties while also preventing spoiler outcomes. Ranked Choice/Proportional Voting doesn't always come down to the best candidate. But it will always prevent the worst from happening – .e.g. a horrible monster squeaking by with 40%, though hated by a divided 60%. The present U.S. system is especially insane at parsing out front-runners in a crowded field. Is a candidate who got a whole 16% in a field of ten or twenty truly the "front-runner" ahead of rivals who got 15%, 14%, 12% and 12%? Does that let a fringe constituency control the divided majority? RCV could be even more important when the public is faced with difficult, complex ballot propositions, as occurred in Britain, with Brexit.[32]

---

30 Equal Citizens: https://equalcitizens.us/about-equal-citizens/

31 https://equalcitizens.us/new-hampshire-house-election-committee/?

32 http://davidbrin.blogspot.com/2019/03/a-process-matter-that-is-actually-life.html

Of course including a "None of the above" category would likely bring many non-voters to the polls.

Also aimed at pragmatic and even more imminent reform, former Senate candidate Stacy Abrams's initiative[33], Fair Fight 2020[34] (See also Chapter 4) will concentrate on preventing voter suppression in battleground states ahead of the 2020 election. Yes, donate. But a few of you should recall the Freedom Riders of long ago and consider taking part in person. (I will offer some potential things you can do that are more... well... unusual.)

Gerrymandering and all that? Sure, lots of folks are discussing that. But I feel I have some original things to contribute. So there's a whole chapter.

The Electoral College. Is there a problem? Yessirree Bob. Out of the last five U.S. presidential elections, the Republican candidate only won the popular vote once, but got into office twice more due to squeaker/cheated Electoral College wins.[35] See a fun, informative and interesting graphic-based tutorial about how the Electoral College warps the public will.[36] And see one of my own missives[37] on this perennial vexation, posted right after Donald Trump's "victory" in 2016. (There will be more in Chapters 4 and 12.)

Still, raving against the Electoral College is a perpetual drain around which reform concepts plop and swirl and never die. A lot of them propose Constitutional Amendments, which will happen perhaps after the Second or Fifth Coming. Others would try to get around that obstacle by kludging and getting all states to sign on to a "National Popular Vote"[38] bill that would guarantee that state's presidential electors to the candidate who receives the most popular votes across all 50 states and the District of Columbia. It has been enacted into law in 16 jurisdictions with 196 electoral votes nearly all of them "blue" states.[39] Which makes it pretty obvious

---

[33] From The Hill: https://thehill.com/homenews/state-watch/457233-stacey-abrams-to-launch-program-combatting-voter-suppression-in

[34] Stacy Abrams's initiative, Fair Fight 2020 https://fairfight.com/fair-fight-2020/

[35] The one other time this happened was the greatest cheat of all, the "Tilden-Hayes Compromise" of 1876 that led to the premature end of Southern Reconstruction and enforcement of rights for freed slaves, leading to a century of Jim Crow and crisis.

[36] https://thenib.com/the-electoral-college-isn-t-working-here-s-how-it-might-die?t=recent

[37] http://davidbrin.blogspot.com/2016/12/too-fast-all-weird-electoral-college.html

[38] National Popular Vote. https://www.nationalpopularvote.com

[39] (CA, CO, CT, DC, DE, HI, IL, MA, MD, NJ, NM, NY, OR, RI, VT, WA). https://www.nationalpopularvote.com

(a) that blue citizens want to fix a blatant problem, and (b) that this prospect has Republican strategists rubbing their hands with glee. "It's a trap!" shouts Admiral Ackbar.

Even if it weren't a trap, it is a potential disaster in other ways, unless accompanied by Ranked Choice balloting. But sure, go read about it elsewhere. The idea's being widely discussed... and hence won't be, in this volume.

- A solution that I used to favor was for all states to end (as two have done) "winner takes all" allocation of that state's electors and instead divvy them up according to the popular vote within the state. It seemed a more fair approach, and my proposal remains (some say) worth looking at. But the method generally on the table - choosing electors by congressional district with two at-large going to the state's overall winner, still gives a huge advantage to red states, who inherently have many more senators... and hence more such at-large electors. But Larry Lessig is already on this - See The Equal Protection argument against "winner take all" in the Electoral College.[40]

- Lately, there have been storms of discussions about **"faithless electors,"** and not only those who might turn away from their pledged candidate on the basis of conscience. In a time that's increasingly paranoid and near civil war, there's also been talk about how a Republican controlled state legislature might get away with appointing its own slate of electors if - say - the voters of Wisconsin choose a Democratic slate at the ballot box. Paranoid or not (and would those state assembly members have houses to go home to, before that night was out?) these fantasies aren't, alas, entirely science fiction anymore.

- Let me slip in a **crackpot Electoral College idea** of my own. In wake of the November 2016 plunge into weirdness, I wrote[41] to a few millionaires suggesting they do something historic. Simply rent a luxury resort somewhere and announce that: For one week, only Electors will be allowed to enter (other than secured hotel staff). They will get transportation reimbursed and all meals and amenities on the house. There are no conditions. They are

---

[40] The Equal Protection argument against "winner take all" in the Electoral College. https://medium.com/equal-citizens/the-equal-protection-argument-against-winner-take-all-in-the-electoral-college-b09e8a49d777#.lqpgxh89y

[41] http://davidbrin.blogspot.com/2019/04/the-magic-folks-who-can-save-us-though.html

not required to deliberate or talk to each other. But if a quorum shows up, it is within their power to call it a "college" and discuss whatever they like.

No coercion, suasion or influence. Just a place to spend one week in luxury, and experience being - briefly - the 538 most important people on Earth. Oh, the howls it would have raised! So? We are long past the horse and buggy limitations that prevented this, in the 18th and 19th Centuries. Would a quorum have shown up? Well, well. Think about it for next time.

And yet, although the Electoral College is getting lots of attention, that just shifts my focus elsewhere.

The inherent Republican advantage in the Senate is discussed a lot. (And it certainly pertains to the Electoral College!) Take the fact that California's 38 million citizens get the same representation in that august body as 400 thousand in Wyoming. And why are there two Dakotas? Because Republicans in the late 19th Century saw they could anchor that sparsely populated prairie in with four senators, rather than two.

David Faris, author of It's Time to Fight Dirty,[42] suggests two responses, one implausible and the other astonishingly easy to do, if Democrats retake power in Washington. (1) break up big blue states into many smaller ones? Not likely and each tit would just lead to a tat (like four Dakotas).

But Faris's second idea - admit Puerto Rico and District of Columbia as states - is eminently do-able, possibly just with majority legislation in Congress. I'd have just one small demand to make before bringing Puerto Rico in.[43] But great. The neo-Confederacy made this a knife fight, assuming that America would not learn. Though course the real solution to the GOP's advantage in the Senate is to convince voters in currently "red" states that they've been betrayed by the Party of Putin. That it's possible to be down-home, sons and daughters of big sky country... and still participate in a nation of science and equality and the future.

---

[42] "It's Time to Fight Dirty," by David Faris. https://www.amazon.com/Its-Time-Fight-Dirty-Democrats/dp/1612196950

[43] Think it through. A bill to grant Puerto Rico statehood *without* a referendum by PR citizens? No! Have the referendum require a *two thirds* majority – or at least 60% of PR citizens – for passage, because it is understood that statehood is *not revocable* later, via say *PRexit*. We fought a civil war over secession. So once you are in, you're in, our fates forever joined! If you do choose to join, bienvenidos amigos! But no take-backs.

Other Faris proposals that might be passed by a Democratic Congress and signed by a Democratic president include doubling the size of the House of Representatives. (It is entirely within their right, instantly re-empowering millions, especially of urban citizens, while bringing representatives closer to constituents.) If nothing else, all their congressional gerrymanders would be messed up...

...and "packing" the Supreme Court - or rotating members through a much larger High Court of Appeals. While the motive is based upon a treasonous calamity - the spectacular partisanship and oligarchy-representing nature of today's conservative court majority - this is a road that's both strictly legal, and truly risky. A last resort.

And it is discussed by many scholars elsewhere. Hence it's not my department.

You came here for the unusual.

Now the first of many chapters extracted from postings at Contrary Brin. This one, from April 2017[44], has been heavily edited for use here.

Chapter 3

Profiles In Judo Invoking The Greatest Generation, Jonas Salk, Adam Smith, MLK, Lincoln… and AOC.

The most frustrating recent example of "blue polemical stupidity" is failure to answer MAGA… or the slogan "Make America Great Again."

A few have tried, using sumo-style opposition, like: "America's already great!" Oh, that's a fine counter-slogan, helping our side grunt and shove back at those who demean the nation. But it achieves nothing to undermine MAGA's power with red masses. It does no judo.

MAGA implies a clear notion of some much better time in the past. So ask a judo question: When do you envision that America had its "great" golden age?

Odds are, they'll blink in surprise, having never been asked… then stammer something about *the 1950s.* It sure seems that MAGA folks are referring generally to the era of the Greatest Generation (GG) – the boomers' parents – who overcame the Depression and crushed Hitler, contained Stalinism, built a booming market economy and middle class, got us into space, built vast infrastructure and systems for education and health, while too-gradually-but-deliberately, taking on many long-standing prejudices and injustices they inherited from *their* parents and a thousand other generations.

---

44 "Those were the days... When was America 'great'?" http://davidbrin.blogspot.com/2017/04/those-were-days-when-was-america-great.html

So let Republicans proclaim the 50s! Draw them onto that limb. Get them to charge ahead with oversimplified/romantic notions of a bucolic, better era. This is what judo is for.

Yes, the GGs had greatness. Oh, but there's a funny thing about those folks in the World War II generation. They voted high taxes on the rich, and the rich patriotically paid. They admired labor unions. They respected teachers and other professionals. They built spectacular universities and infrastructure. Above all, that clade of Americans had one *favorite living human*, a man venerated by his people, by his fellow citizens. Ask your MAGA cousin who that most-adored 20th Century American was.

The New Lords have spent millions and decades portraying Franklin Delano Roosevelt as satanic. While invoking nostalgia for the "great" American era of the 1940s and 1950s, their propaganda sweeps aside one fact – that every notable aspect of that period was *Rooseveltian*. A time when – I reiterate – unions thrived, the rich paid taxes, science was admired, and moving forward was in our blood.

Oh, you sour boomers, don't you dare invoke the Greatest Generation! They were union men, Democrats mostly, held no truck with foppish billionaires, preferred facts over assertions, built giant projects, crafted strong alliances to give the world its first general peace and… oh, yes, can I say it again? Their favorite living human was FDR.

And do you know who followed Roosevelt in that slot? Who was the most-admired American during the 1950s, even more popular than the moderate, FDR-like Dwight Eisenhower? It was a fellow named Dr. Jonas Salk, whose team effort used science and immunization (yes, vaccines) to end a terror that haunted every parent in America. Look it up. The most admired American, in an era that did possess a kind of greatness, at least in potential.

IF NOT THAT GENERATION, WHEN?

Oh, they were far from perfect, my parents and their friends. Their faults were monumental! In fact they were "great" – above all – by overcoming some (not all) of countless ways the fifties etc. sucked![45] Above all, they emulated the American Founders, and soldiers of a righteous, abolitionist blue Union and others who pushed our fine Experiment forward by *not* wallowing in nostalgia. Moreover, they raised us to launch from their shoulders, mightily amplifying their accomplishments with creativity, science and rising compassion, while overcoming many of their mistakes and blindnesses. Becoming… greater. And later generations – millennials, Xers etc. – are better still, generally wiser, nicer, calmer, smarter – the best thing we boomers ever did.

No, fanatics, you don't get the Greatest Generation, who would be appalled by your vague shrill MAGA wails. You must flee from their Rooseveltian era, in search of your earlier "great" time!

How about *farther back?* Here's a candidate period – admired by the alt-right and Fox – that's lauded in a song you might recall:

"Mister we could use a man like Herbert Hoover again!
Didn't need no Welfare State.
Everybody pulled his weight.
Gee our old LaSalle ran great.
Those were the days!"

Is it 1929 then, that folks at Trump rallies yearn for? Surely oligarchs financing the movement would love to crank-back before FDR. And yet, forget 1929. We all know that's not it.

It's 1861, only this time a confederacy that's victorious. Plantation lords and their fervid vassals and foreign backers finally overcoming the blue forces of science, facts, equality, industry, accountability, abolition and progress. And let's admit that during this round of civil war (see Chapter 14), with help from a Russian rising czar, the Confederacy took Washington.

Alas, amid dullard ignorance of real history, they ignore the only place where oligarchy's victory can take us all. To Paris, 1789.

---

[45] "Was 1957 America Better Than Today?" I answer right wing adoration of the 1950s. http://davidbrin.blogspot.com/2011/10/was-1957-america-better-than-today.html

THE ANSWER TO "SOCIALISM!"

Time and again, Blue Leaders have acquiesced to a re-framing of terminology on the political landscape. Fleeing "liberal" into "progressive" for example, then seeing that term equated with "communist."[46] Of course it's all ironic, in an era when GOP leaders are in bed with avowed communist dictators and Lenin-raised "ex"-KGB agents who openly mourn the USSR.

A huge and recurring liberal mistake is getting lured into expressing *hostility to the markets, enterprises and small businesses and startups* that generate the wealth we then use to make things better for all children. Where do the taxes come from that pay for their favorite programs? We'll get to that *apparent* contradiction in the next section, and later in Chapter 11.

First, of course the Republican Party plans to use "socialism" against democrats.[47]

A few nationally prominent Democrats, for example rising star Rep. Alexandria Ocasio-Cortez, have edged toward powerfully invoking the Greatest Generation (GG) with the "Green New Deal."[48] Later I'll list 31 reforms that Democrats and decent independents *all want,* belying press-incited calumnies about 'bitter division.' (Chapter 12.) In fact, most items on that list would be covered by saying:

"Let's bring back much of the social contract that served the white working class so well, in the 40s and 50s! High wages, a rising middle, strong union protections, low wealth disparity, much less cheating-influence by aristocrats, cheap college tuition... infrastructure!... investment in science and so on. Only we'll update all that to include all races and genders! And yes, while mobilizing against the most deadly enemy threatening our world – looming environmen-

---

46 Back in the 1970s I founded *UCSD Liberals and Progressives,* till frustrated by that campus's Marcuse-left, who took joy from Nixon and sorrowed at the "system's" success at nailing him for crimes.

47 "Is Socialism Still An Effective Political Bogeyman?" https://fivethirtyeight.com/features/is-socialism-still-an-effective-political-bogeyman/

48 "When Representative Alexandria Ocasio-Cortez of New York and Senator Edward Markey of Massachusetts introduced their Green New Deal proposal in February, they chose language loaded with nostalgia for one of the country's most transformative historical moments, urging the country to undertake "a new national, social, industrial and economic mobilization on a scale not seen since World War II and the New Deal era." https://www.nytimes.com/2019/09/18/opinion/climate-change-mobilization.html

tal disaster. And expand the greatest generation's signature program – Medicare – to at least cover all children till age twenty-five.

"You'd seriously oppose that? The Greatest Generation is spinning in their graves. You aren't worthy to mention them!"

Oh and let's be clear – someone please say it aloud – that Dwight Eisenhower made AOC's 'socialism' seem tame.[49]

WHO IS BEST FOR 'FREE ENTERPRISE'?

Now let's swing from socialism to its purported opposite – enterprise capitalism.

Today's Blue-Left keeps getting suckered into ceding territory to the Right, allowing them to style themselves as the best friends of creative market economics, the generator of most of the wealth they hope to tax. Among the 2020 candidates, only Elizabeth Warren seemed to grasp what the word "liberal" generally meant, for the last 250 years. She laces her calls for social reforms with *this will actually help a competitive market economy to thrive!*

In fact, across more than 5000 years of recorded history, far more open-flat-fair-competitive-creative enterprise systems were wrecked by *oligarchy* – by cheater kings and owner-lords and monopolists – than were ever harmed by moderate, democratic socialism (e.g. Canada or Sweden) or even by murderous Stalinists. Uber-rich cheaters must be denounced as the *enemy of enterprise*. Which is exactly what Adam Smith said.

Adam Smith? The fellow whose *Wealth of Nations (1776)* is routinely misquoted by the social darwinist right? Yes, the same sage whose *The Theory of Moral Sentiments* demanded that society's duty lay in uplifting the poor and enhancing opportunities for talent to thrive. In fact, as I'll expand in Chapter 11, Democrats should *reclaim Adam Smith as one of their own*,[50] the core founder of liberalism. (If you actually read him,

---

49 "Accusations of Socialism" http://davidbrin.blogspot.com/search?updated-max=2019-04-20T12:29:00-07:00&max-results=20

50 "Liberals, you must reclaim Adam Smith." http://davidbrin.blogspot.com/2013/11/liberals-you-must-reclaim-adam-smith.html

you'll understand.) See the point made by *Evonomics* publisher Steve Roth.[51] We'll return to Smith several times.

If done right, this could overturn the "libertarian problem" dissected later in the book. But foremost the lesson is: *don't cede any territory to the noxious, undead mad-right. Especially not the territory of healthy market enterprise, which actually does much better*, as a matter of measurable outcomes,[52] *across the span of Democratic administrations.*

In a reflex that's encouraged by both left-wing academics and giggling rightist propagandists, young liberals today spurn "capitalism" as a whipping boy term that loses all meaning, though flat-fair-competitive-accountable market enterprise has been the cornucopia goose that's laid our golden eggs, including the confidence to go after ancient crimes like racism and sexism. Yes, there are problems with capitalism! Karl Marx described inherent contradictions that can – unless countered by enlightened rules and referees – lead to the *collapse* of flat-fair-creative competition.

This was the point when the American Founders seized and redistributed up to one third of the land from lordly grandees. Or take the Progressive Movement circa 1900 whose anti-trust laws shattered a then-looming Gilded Age oligarchy, restoring some competition to American markets. It had to be done again in the 1930s and 1940s, resulting in the flattest and most vibrantly entrepreneurial society and fastest-rising middle class the world ever saw (shocking Marxists!)

Those on the right who scream hate at the word "regulation" are as unwise is the left's reflex to despise "competition." What works is *Regulated Competition*. And we'll get into that later.

HATING ON FDR… FROM THE LEFT?

Finally, I expect some of our allies on the far-left to rage at my extolling Franklin Roosevelt. As if even mentioning Adam Smith didn't cause apoplexy! (That ain't nothing. Just wait till we get to Chapter 12: "Unreliable Allies.")

---

[51] "It's Simple! Concentrated Wealth and Inequality Crushes Economic Growth More billionaire dollars, slower growth. Full stop." http://evonomics.com/its-simple-yes-concentrated-wealth-and-inequality-crushes-economic-growth/

[52] Comparing economic *outcomes from Democratic vs. Republican administrations:* http://davidbrin.blogspot.com/2014/06/so-do-outcomes-matter-more-than-rhetoric.html

By today's standards, FDR was bigoted and made some howling-awful decisions, amid a sea of good ones.[53] The same could be said of LBJ. And don't you think *they* would have recanted those mistakes, if informed by the moral advancements we've made since? Dig it. What's the best that any leaders or citizens can hope for, from posterity?

To be judged as much better than their times. That he or she could see needles had to move, and strenuously helped move them. That they built platforms from which later heroes might climb further. It's why we (largely) forgive the faults of Washington and Jefferson. It's what Martin Luther King *said* of Johnson and Roosevelt... and it's what we now say about King, knowing many of his then-hidden personal flaws.

Anyone condemning them, while ignoring all their good, should read Frederick Douglass's eulogy of Abraham Lincoln. Especially the last paragraph of this excerpt:

> "I have said that President Lincoln was a white man, and shared the prejudices common to his countrymen towards the colored race. Looking back to his times and to the condition of his country, we are compelled to admit that this unfriendly feeling on his part may be safely set down as one element of his wonderful success in organizing the loyal American people for the tremendous conflict before them, and bringing them safely through that conflict. His great mission was to accomplish two things: first, to save his country from dismemberment and ruin; and, second, to free his country from the great crime of slavery. To do one or the other, or both, he must have the earnest sympathy and the powerful cooperation of his loyal fellow-countrymen.
>
> "Without this primary and essential condition to success his efforts must have been vain and utterly fruitless.[...]
>
> "Viewed from the genuine abolition ground, Mr.b Lincoln seemed tardy, cold, dull, and indifferent; but measuring him by the sentiment of his country, a sentiment he was bound

[53] I am of an ethnicity that suffered because FDR made moral and practical mistakes, and I grew up with Japanese-Americans whose parents endured Manzanar. Still, our parents all knew that every alternative to Roosevelt – across the face of the Earth in those days – would have been worse.

> as a statesman to consult, he was swift, zealous, radical, and determined."

May you be eulogized so fairly… but ultimately so well.

From The Transparent Society ...

Pause #3 for...

The Garden of Openness An Allegory About Courage And The Enlightenment[54]

Ancient Greek myths tell of a farmer, Akademos, who did a favor for the sun god. In return, Apollo granted the mortal a garden wherein he could say whatever he liked, even about the mighty Olympians, without retribution. Inspired by this tale - the earliest parable about Free Speech - citizens of Periclean Athens used to gather at the Academy to openly debate issues of the day.

Now the fable of Akademos always puzzled me at one level. How could a mortal trust the storied Greek deities - notoriously mercurial, petty and vengeful - to keep their promise? Especially when impudent humans started telling bad Zeus jokes? Apollo might set up impenetrable barriers around the glade, so no god could peer in. But Akademos would have few visitors to join him, cowering under sunless walls.

The alternative was to empower Akademos with an equalizer, some way to enforce the gods' promise. That equalizing factor could only be knowledge. But more about that in a moment.

How did the Athenians fare in their real-life experiment with free speech? Alas, democracy and openness were new and difficult concepts. Outspoken Socrates eventually paid a stiff price for candor in the Academy. Whereupon his student, Plato, took paradoxical revenge by denouncing openness, calling instead for strict government by an "enlightened" elite. Plato's advice served to justify countless tyrants during millennia since.

---

[54] Excerpted from David Brin's nonfiction book – *The Transparent Society: Will Technology Make Us Choose Between Freedom and Privacy?* http://www.davidbrin.com/transparentsociety.html

Now the democratic vision is getting another trial run. Today's "academy" extends far beyond Earth's major universities. Throughout the world, millions have begun to accept the daring notion that disagreement isn't toxic. Free speech is increasingly seen as the best font of criticism – the only practical and effective antidote to error.

Let there be no mistake; this is a hard lesson, especially since each of us would be a tyrant if we could. (Some with best intentions.) Very little in history – or human nature – prepared us for the task ahead, living in a tribe of ten billion equal citizens, each guided by his or her own sovereign will, loosely administered by chiefs we elect, under just rules that we made through hard negotiation among ourselves. Any other generation would have thought it an impossible ambition – though countless ancestors strove, getting us to the point where we can try.

Even among those who profess allegiance to this new hope, there is bitter struggle over how best to resist the old gods of wrath, bigotry and oppression – spirits who reside not on some mountain peak, but in the heart of each man or woman who tries to gain power at the expense of others. Perhaps our descendants will be mature enough to curb these impulses all by themselves. Meanwhile, we must foil those who rationalize robbing freedom, claiming it's their right... or that it's for our own good. In other words, we still face the same dilemma that confronted Akademos.

According to some champions of liberty, shields of secrecy will put common folk on even ground with the mighty. Privacy must be defined by rules or tools that enhance concealment. One wing of this movement would create Euro-style privacy commissions, pass a myriad laws and dispatch clerks to police what may be known by doctors, corporations, and ultimately individuals. Another wing of Strong Privacy prefers libertarian techno-fixes – empowering individuals with encryption and cybernetic anonymity. Both wings claim we must build high walls to safeguard every private garden, each sanctum of the mind.

This widespread modern myth has intuitive appeal. And I can only reply that it's been tried, without even one example of a commonwealth based on this principle that thrived.

There is a better way, a method largely responsible for this renaissance we're living in. Instead of trying to blind the mighty – a futile goal, if ever there was one – we have emphasized the power of openness, giving free citizens knowledge and unprecedented ability to hold elites accountable. Every day, we prove it works, rambunctiously demanding to know, rather than trying to stop others from knowing. (Isn't it far easier to verify that you know something, than to verify that someone else is ignorant?)

It's called accountability – a light that can shine even on the gods of authority. Whether they gather in the Olympian heights of government, amid the spuming currents of commerce, or in Hadean shadows of criminality, they cannot harm us while pinned by its glare. Accountability is the only defense that truly protected free speech, in a garden that stands proudly, with no walls.

=======

I've had more feedback and intense discussion over ideas in The Transparent Society than from any of my novels, though of course there's overlap. Conversations whirl around purportedly "prophetic" notions like cop-cams, citizens counter-recording the police, face recognition systems, online narrow-minded idea-ghettos and rumor memes being used against us, along with many other topics. And yes, I still believe, more than 20 years later, that our only way to navigate this mine-field remains the tool that got us this far. Light.

Light that shines upward: sousveillance. Light that holds all elites accountable – both those we fear and those we like – and a little for each of us to endure, as well, in exchange for all the good it delivers. Like cleansing evil. Like empowering our markets and science and democracy and justice. Like freedom.

Oh, the need is more critical than ever, as tools of surveillance ever more serve cabals of the mighty. In some parts of the world, the path lies wide-open for Orwellian, top-down control, but there's still time to bring balance to this force. It's why so many of the proposals in this volume ultimately distill down to ways we can accomplish one thing. Use light to save this great experiment...

...and turn it into a civilization that's worthy of that name.

Quis custodiet ipsos custodes?

LIFE OR DEATH FOR THE GREAT EXPERIMENT

"Our trouble is that we do not demand enough of the people who represent us. We are responsible for their activities. . . . we must spur them to more imagination and enterprise in making a push into the unknown; we must make clear that we intend to have responsible and courageous leadership."
– Eleanor Roosevelt, Tomorrow Is Now (1963)

This one merges a posting about electoral cheating[55] with three others about the most egregious examples... gerrymandering[56] (with a surprising solution[57]), rigged voting machines and voter ID laws[58]. That makes for a long Chapter! But you'll find some unusual and practical ideas here, I promise.

Chapter 4

End the Cheating First

> "The arc of American history reveals an unmistakable pattern. Whenever privilege and power conspire to pull us backward, we eventually rally and move forward. Sometimes it takes an economic shock like the bursting of a giant speculative bubble. Sometimes we just reach a tipping point where the frustrations of average Americans turn into action....The oligarchs and plutocrats would like nothing better than for the rest of us to give up and drop out. That way, they get it all. But we never have, and we never will. Preserving and expanding democracy has been America's central project since its founding. It's an unending fight. And no matter how bleak it may look, we will never stop fighting."
>
> – Robert Reich[59]

Let's talk about how Fox News owner Rupert Murdoch – and his minions and overseas allies – achieved their impressive run, taking al-

---

[55] "End the cheating..." https://davidbrin.blogspot.com/2018/07/end-cheating.html

[56] "The (almost) full story on gerrymandering" http://www.davidbrin.com/nonfiction/gerrymandering.html

[57] "The 'Minimal Overlap' one-page solution to gerrymandering. http://davidbrin.blogspot.com/2017/09/the-minimal-overlap-solution-to_24.html

[58] "Voter ID Laws: Scam or Accountability?" http://davidbrin.blogspot.com/2014/10/voter-id-laws-scam-or-accountability.html

[59] https://readersupportednews.org/opinion2/277-75/58607-it-may-feel-like-the-worlds-ending-but-america-has-reason-to-hope

most absolute power in the United States. The Republican Party *lost the popular vote* in ten of the last twelve congressional elections, and in all but one of the last seven presidential elections. Yet they held the Oval Office for three crucial terms and have either controlled Congress or else had the power to render it neutered for all but two of the last 24 years.

And 'neutered' was good enough! These were the *laziest* U.S. congresses in at least a century, not just blocking valid initiatives wanted by liberals and independents, or recommended by experts and civil servants, but holding incredibly few days in session. Aside from tax-cut gifts to oligarchy, they passed fewer bills (even long-stated conservative desires) than any other congresses in living memory.[60] If you set aside useless-futile and absolutely unproductive "Clinton Investigations," they issued fewer subpoenas and held fewer hearings… but set records at fund-raising. Yet they retained control over power in Washington – the power to give our republic the political equivalent of tetanus.

How do they accomplish this? By cheating, of course.

They were already very good at it by the time Newt Gingrich took the House, in 1994, but at least his principal weapon was a masterpiece of political polemic and he took charge with a popular vote majority. That all changed when Tom DeLay and Dennis Hastert took over Republican leadership. Those two (both later convicted of felonies) were joined by Boehner, McConnell, Cheney and a wave of state-level GOP secretaries-of-state, who commenced a concerted and targeted series of moves to manipulate elections, preventing the unwashed and fickle "people" from ever again prying their hands off the wheel.

We know how urgently they needed to control the Supreme Court, which has refused to intervene against the egregious treason called gerrymandering. (Future generations will remember this craven behavior in kind with the Dred Scott Decision.) Further, the Court, in a 5–4 ruling, allowed states to purge voters for a failure to vote. Combating these cheats on the ground are groups like VoteRiders that actually get on the ground – like the Freedom Riders of old – and help poor people, the old, the young, divorced women etc. to *get* ID. Any Blue Wave will

---

[60] Lazy Congresses… needs updating: https://www.thenationalcouncil.org/ambassadors-brief-e-newsletter/ambassadors-brief-august-2014/congressional-productivity-final/#foobox-1/0/congressional-productivity-final.jpg

be inadequate unless voter repression in swing districts is fought, tooth and nail.[61]

VOTING MACHINES

In 2016, just before the general election, the FBI informed top Maryland officials that the state›s voter registration platform was purchased by a Russian oligarch in 2015. It was only the latest in a series of deeply suspicious activities surrounding the machinery of voting. For decades, the companies making US electronic voting machines just happened to be owned by former GOP or Murdoch operatives. Now, without even much pretense, Russians are making their moves.

In states that have taken the threat seriously, voting machines are either fed a hand-marked paper ballot to read, or else they provide a printed receipt that the voter can inspect and drop into a separate box. Either way, all votes made in that precinct can be audited. No matter how many back doors and cheats might be built secretly into the machines or programs, no one will dare pull a major electronic switcheroo, if enough precincts will be randomly hand-counted and audited. The same is not true in many red states, where GOP-run legislatures gave voting machine contracts to a trio of companies all of whom have strong Republican Party connections, or else the aforementioned Russian links.[62] *(The address of one of those companies? ES&S: 11208 John Galt Blvd. Omaha, NE. I kid you not. John Galt Blvd.)*

Despite fierce resistance by Republican leaders like Mitch McConnell, some money has been allocated toward increased election security. Nevertheless, as of mid-2019, twelve states still include jurisdictions that use paperless electronic machines as the primary polling place equipment in at least some counties and towns – Delaware, Georgia, Indiana, Kansas, Kentucky, Louisiana, Mississippi, New Jersey, Pennsylvania, South Carolina, Tennessee and Texas.[63] Indiana, Mississippi, Tennes-

---

[61] And I will repeatedly remind you that previous, victorious get-out-the-vote drives, in 1992 and 2008, led to briefly joyous victories, till those roused masses sank back into torpor, in 94 and 2010. Counting on get-out-the-vote alone is a proved losing strategy. Those who deny other fronts are proved fools.

[62] Voting machines. http://www.technologyreview.com/news/506676/the-states-with-the-riskiest-voting-technology/

[63] States still resisting use of paper-auditable ballots. https://www.npr.org/2019/08/31/754412132/what-you-need-to-know-about-u-s-election-security-and-voting-machines Note while two of

see, and Texas do not appear to be taking steps to replace their paperless equipment before 2020, and some Texas counties are ignoring the national trend altogether, replacing paperless systems with other paperless systems. Of course paper receipt systems call for widespread adoption of risk-limiting audits (RLAs), considered the "gold standard" of post-election audits.

This potential theft will be exacerbated by the fact that news organizations and polling firms are cutting down on *exit polls*. Exit polling has proved to be a major deterrent to cheating, because of its high degree of accuracy.[64] In precincts that are neither exit-polled nor auditable by paper receipts anything – including skullduggery and cheating – can happen. And many folks expect that cheating *will* happen – say in Virginia or Florida – if the election is tight.

By now it's grown clear that the top job of every GOP Secretary of State in red states is electoral cheating, and they are richly rewarded, both financially and with job sinecures. These states, lacking auditable paper records, will show anomalously high Republican voting next election in targeted swing districts, especially in state assembly districts that might tip the balance of power in statehouses.

VOTER ID LAWS: SCAM OR ACCOUNTABILITY? [65]

Instead of – or in addition to – howling "racism!" how about using a principle that's beloved to all conservative lawyers and jurists? One they cannot shrug aside?

Voter ID laws[66] supposedly deal with a problem of "electoral fraud," when cheaters pretend to be someone else, casting an illicit ballot. All studies show such voter fraud is extremely rare. Of course we all know this spate of laws – mostly in "red states" – are designed as repressive measures, aimed not just at poor people who often lack clear ID, but the ill-educated, or recent citizens, or the young. They also present hardships

the twelve might be deemed 'blue," those two have long traditions of entrenched party machines.

[64] One of many potential uses for volunteers would be to serve as unpaid exit pollers for local news media. A national movement to do this could not come too soon.

[65] Based on an October 2014 posting: http://davidbrin.blogspot.com/2014/10/voter-id-laws-scam-or-accountability.html

[66] Or watch this essay on YouTube: https://www.youtube.com/watch?v=fNnVEVhDSQc&feature=youtu.be

for some women, who may have failed to re-document after marriage or divorce. Some on the left call this another front in the "War on Women."

And yet, *there is nothing intrinsically* wrong with gradually ratcheting up the degree to which we apply accountability to potential failure modes![67] For generations, we've had volunteer poll watchers. It does seem reasonable, over an extended period of time, to ratchet up a completely unbiased process for voters to prove who they are. Hence Republicans proclaim: "If you don't want voters to show ID, it's because you want to cheat."

Is there a test to nail down whether a Voter ID law aims at unbiased *accountability,* or is a blatant cheat aimed at *stealing votes* way from poor people, minorities, young folks, and women? There is.

A CRUCIAL METRIC OF HYPOCRISY: COMPLIANCE ASSISTANCE

Conservative leaders going back to Buckley and Goldwater have demanded that regulations placed on business should be accompanied by *help* complying with new burdens. It's standard dogma on the right.

And Democrats agree! Almost always, whenever new or onerous regulations are applied to businesses, there are allocations to set up offices, call-lines, visiting experts and grace periods, all with the aim of helping corporations – and the rich – to comply with the new regulations. It's called ***compliance assistance.*** [68]

You see how this applies. In red states that passed new Voter ID laws, *were significant funds allocated to help folks comply?* "Here is an onerous new burden upon the poor, women and so on – but we'll commit to assisting voters satisfy these new regulations." Real money and serious effort going to communities with poor folks, minorities, recent immigrants, women, young people – helping them *obtain the identification* they need to exercise their sovereign voting rights?

Note! Beyond voting, Just getting clear ID would help them to *stop* being poor! Boosting folks on a path to helping themselves. This should be what conservatives are for. Has this happened? Alas, such efforts are

[67] My book, The Transparent Society, is all about this. Winner of the 1998 Freedom of Speech Award.

[68] First discussed at: http://davidbrin.blogspot.com/2014/10/voter-id-laws-scam-or-accountability.html

sabotaged relentlessly. *Hardly a cent* has been allocated for compliance assistance in any of the red states that passed these new voter ID laws.

Hardly one red cent.

You liberals out there. Don't make this a matter of goody-goody preaching, or denying a long term need to ratchet up ID accountability. *Make it about hypocrisy.* The blatant lack of sincere compliance assistance provides clear proof that these are attempts to *steal elections.*

A final note on voter ID and compliance assistance. Absent government support, this is one place where proxy advocacy and *personal volunteer work* can accomplish something big. Helping people get whatever ID they need does not have to be a partisan act! But it can also make a huge electoral difference. Stacy Abrams's initiative, Fair Fight 2020,[69] will concentrate its efforts on battleground states, helping Democratic candidates establish voter-protection programs ahead of the election. And yes, a few of you should recall the Freedom Riders of long ago.

RANKED CHOICE, REFERENDA AND THE PEOPLE'S WILL

What about bypassing politicians entirely? Certainly the ballot proposition or referenda system has worked well in California and other western states that adopted the Progressive Movement's[70] agenda, more than a century ago. While foolish measures sometimes pass, and we must be wary of dumb or corrupt measures pushed by special interests, voters in those states have a good track record, in part because (unlike Brexit) citizens generally have six months or more to read arguments and watch debates.

The "Five Star Movement" in Italy has aimed to use modern social media methods to get the people engaged in genuinely productive debate… with mixed results.[71] In the nation of Estonia – sometimes called "E-Stonia" for its campaign to get all government business efficiently and openly online – many topics get heard the very week or even day that they are raised.

---

[69] Stacy Abrams's initiative, Fair Fight 2020 https://fairfight.com/fair-fight-2020/

[70] The "Progressive Movement" of that era has overlaps with today's use of the word. But we should still be wary of quick assumptions.

[71] Five Star Movement. https://www.washingtonpost.com/news/theworldpost/wp/2018/03/19/five-star/

Alas, history is rife with examples of plebiscites that were staged by tyrants to validate their own rule, or else to spur hot-tempered populism. Even when the formal processes are evenhanded, quick-polls can be dangerous. Critics of direct democracy point to Brexit and several other recent "spasm" referenda (e.g. in Eastern Europe) as examples of why a representative republic approach is needed, to both heed popular will but also curb sudden mass-impulses, using both time and cooler heads to craft sagacious legislation out of that will.

The extremum is called "demarchy," in which all matters of law are settled by rapid debate online for a couple of hours, followed by a decisive e-vote among all citizens. A chilling portrayal of this system's potential drawbacks is science fiction author Joan Vinge's *The Outcasts of the Heaven Belt.*

Some aspects of this question are immediate and pressing. Many problems with referenda might be solved with a longer discussion period and, yes, Ranked Choice Voting. Certainly, if and when Democrats take power in any state that does not already have a referendum process, they should leap, using that perhaps narrow opportunity to establish one, offering hope that any future regime of an outright cheater party (guess who I mean) can be bypassed and over-ruled by the People.

THE "MINIMAL OVERLAP" SOLUTION TO GERRYMANDERED INJUSTICE [72]

One kind of gerrymandering is embedded into the U.S. Constitution, providing 400,000 voters in Wyoming with as many senators as 34 million Californians. We discuss that elsewhere and – frankly – there's plenty of lower-hanging fruit to reform before we tilt at that giant windmill.

Gerrymandering at the level of state legislatures and Congressional districts is another matter. This outrageous cheat has reached a level of such blatancy that everyone knows American democracy has been outright stolen. As I describe elsewhere, in a much more extensive analysis

---

[72] See Addendum #1 in this volume… or "The "Minimal Overlap" Solution To Gerrymandered Injustice" http://davidbrin.blogspot.com/2017/09/the-minimal-overlap-solution-to_24.html

of gerrymandering,[73] voters in many "blue states" have rebelled against their own Democratic politicians, ending the foul practice via ballot measures. Hence, with a few dismal exceptions – like Maryland and Illinois – this cheat has become ever more associated with the Republican Party.

(See a "pause" description, after this chapter, where I describe a trick that *some of you* can do, personally and easily, if you live in a gerried district, to mess up the cheaters' plans.)

But this chapter has gone too long and there's already plenty to digest. So let's put off till Appendix 1 my unusual proposal called "Minimal Overlap" that would work smoothly and effectively based on *just three sentences.* According to one senior U.S. District Appeals Court judge, *"this could really work."* Evaluate for yourself, in Appendix 1.

For now though, the lesson is clear. The cheating must end! But it will take more than outrage to accomplish that. It will take innovative approaches to legislation and court action, in technology and citizen activism.

And we may have to shake up some of our own would-be feudal lords, who have let flatterers croon that "the mob" of free citizen voters can't be trusted. Ingrates who have benefited profoundly from the fruits of a (mostly) open-flat-fair democracy, They recite magical incantations like the *Tytler Calumny* (next) to justify cheating as necessary for the good of all, and thus invite destruction upon us all. Especially upon themselves.

For their sake (as well as the world and our children) we must stop them.

---

[73] My more extensive appraisal of gerrymandering: http://www.davidbrin.com/nonfiction/gerrymandering.html

And now another tactic to use against cheaters. One that some of you – the worst victims – can do all by yourselves.

Pause #4 for...

A bizarre – but potentially useful – tactic.

Would it shock you, at this point, to learn that I'm registered Republican? And have been for 30 years?

In fact, at a time when registration in the GOP nationwide has plummeted from 29% to 22%[74] - while 88% of remaining Republicans stay fanatically loyal to Donald Trump - I am urging a particular subset of registered independents and Democrats - who have been gerrymandered out of having a meaningful vote - to re-register, as I did, back then. As Republicans!

Will you bear with me, to explain? This book is about judo political tactics, and one tactic has real merit under certain conditions - when you've been disenfranchised by a treasonous crime against America, democracy and decency. In 2013, Salon Magazine ran my article about this tactic.[75] I'll splice in segments from that essay here, with 2019 comments. If it doesn't apply to you... and you don't know anyone to pass this trick along to... then fine. On to the next chapter.

IN GERRIED DISTRICTS IT'S ALL ABOUT THE PRIMARY, STUPID

Voter uprisings have installed impartial redistricting commissions, reforming a dozen or so blue states, but not one red state, like Texas, where gerrymandering has its Michelangelos, herding Democrats into

---

[74] https://www.facebook.com/photo.php?fbid=2818456404831428&set=p.2818456404831428&type=3&theater

[75] "A modest proposal to neutralize gerrymandering: creating "ghetto" districts for minority parties has hurt our democracy: https://www.salon.com/2013/10/20/a_modest_proposal_to_neutralize_gerrymandering/

cleverly contorted ghettos. Indeed, political handicapper Stuart Rothenberg says 211 of 234 Republican seats in the House are "safe," leaving only 23 competitive.

In fairness, some residual Democratic states like Maryland and Illinois also gerrymander da Vincis. But lately (2019), leading democrats like Barack Obama and Former Atty. General Eric Holder declared war on such cheats[76] especially in those blue holdouts. Because once they are reformed, this will be a purely Republican crime.

Now the iron law of unexpected outcomes takes hold, for gerrymandering's top malignant effect has been radicalization of U.S. politics. Having engineered for themselves safe districts where the minority party has no chance, cynical politicians rendered each November general election moot (except for state-wide or national offices). Yet, safety eluded them, as this only shifted tension to their party primary! Tea Party and Trumpist insurrections show how a district's most vociferous five percent can use primary challenges to oust established representatives or bully them into cartoonish agendas.

Now consider: Gerrymandering lumps birds-of-a-feather till each district is "owned" by one party or another. Democratic voters in a Republican-owned district - or Republicans in a Democratic-owned district - will never cast a legislature vote in the only election that matters: the majority party's primary.

Unless... you hold your nose and re-register with whatever party owns your district.[77]

This holds true whether you're a Democrat in a Republican district, or vice versa.

If your district is gerried to contain mostly Republicans, then maybe it should be represented by a conservative person! But, as someone living in the district, you deserve to have some say in which variant of conservative it will be! A Tea Party radical? A slavish oligarchy-servant, or suprema-

---

[76] The Obama/Holder endeavor: https://democraticredistricting.com

[77] Note: in some states (AL being one) you don't have to register a party affiliation to vote in their primary! Just tell them you want the other party's ballot. It does mean you have to stay in the same "lane" in any runoffs, of course. But it also means you can influence the real election without having to actually join a party you detest! And it has no effect on your freedom to choose in the general election.

cist, or Roy Moore-style pederast? Or else perhaps a genteel negotiator, like Goldwater or Buckley?

Conservative radicals will scream – Democrats who attempt this kind of judo must be aiming to sabotage the Republican primary! But any large numbers who switch will have one goal: to recover a meaningful say in a district that had disenfranchised them. To vote for candidates they disagree with less – or who at least aren't perverts or crooks. A reasonable criterion.

Does a label change your principles? Remember Republicans of yore – Abe Lincoln, Teddy Roosevelt, Dwight Eisenhower – and sign the damn card! In fact, this tactic has precedents – generations of Republicans registered as Democrats in the old-time "solid south," for exactly this reason: to vote in the primary. They can hardly complain now.

RECLAIM YOUR SOVEREIGNTY

Picture the majority party primary in each gerrymandered district becoming the de facto general election, with all voters participating. Screamers and radicals would lose potency. Representatives could no longer pick which citizens to ignore by their party registration. Moreover, if enough Democrats and independents re-register as Republicans, it will screw up their calculations, their polls, and the data they use to gerrymander! That, alone, will be citizen revenge upon a cynical political caste.

Can't stomach registering as a (pick your poison) Democrat/Republican? Get over it. Partisan labels made this mess. Grin at your friends' shocked reactions. Then recruit them, rebelling against a political scam. If fifty million Americans do this, we'll show the politicians: "you can't take us for granted, nor fool all the people, all the time."

== ==

SO WHY IS BRIN STILL REGISTERED GOP IN 2019?

Okay, that tactic seemed well-and-good back when my home (blue) state was gerrymandered. But my ploy of cross-registration became personally moot when California voters rebelled, handing district-drawing to nonpartisan commissions. Democratic politicians still fretted, because many of their personal districts were now more evenly balanced. On average, each might see only a 55% or 60% Democratic majority - an advantage, but not safety. Now they must work harder. Which had astonishing consequences.

The California experiment - including open primaries and top-two run-offs - was hugely successful. (I deem it now to have the best election laws in the nation.)[78] In heavily Democratic districts, the run-off between two Democrats produced a weird epiphany: "Hey, this district consists 1/3 of Republicans who could tip the balance in my favor against that other Democrat. Let's reach out to them!" As a result, minority-party voters got more leverage than they ever had before! Their calls get answered. Rancorous partisanship in Sacramento (on average) went down. No one expected this result, which should spread across the nation.

But then, I'm avoiding the question at hand. If it's no longer of any practical use, why doesn't David Brin change his Republican Party registration?

Um, because it still has shock value?

For balance credibility?

To show I don't give a damn about symbolism?

As a conversation piece?

Would you believe... um... laziness? Because party labels shouldn't ... and in California don't... matter.

---

[78] In part thanks to the Berggruen Institute, chaired by philanthropist Nicolas Berggruen. https://en.wikipedia.org/wiki/Berggruen_Institute

Here I risk ire by asserting that the innocents and minorities we all see suffering aren't the mad-right's main or only targets for destruction. Some of society's "elites" stand in the way, blocking a feudalist coup. These are oligarchy's enemy-who-must-be-destroyed.

Chapter 5

The War on All Fact People

I may be ostracized for saying it, but the core targets of the Fox/Putin-led oligarchic putsch aren't racism or sexism or nativism. [79]

Oh, the foremost *victims* – those most deeply hurt – are minorities, women, immigrants, non-binaries, the disempowered, millions of children and vulnerable others! To varying degrees, they are the ones suffering pain and gross injustice. And sure, bigotry's dog-whistles have incited America's worst elements into violent rage. In *The New York Times*, Charles Blow summarizes: they support Trump *because* he is mean to the people *they* like to be mean to.[80]

"Trump's own punitive spirit aligns with and gives voice and muscle to American conservatives' long simmering punitive lust. And this insatiable desire to inflict pain has particular targets: women (specifically feminists), racial minorities, people who are L.G.B.T.Q. and religious minorities in this country. In short, the punishments are directed at anyone who isn't part of, or supportive of, the white supremacist patriarchy."

Still, turn your gaze upward from pathetic Nazis and jibbering supremacists, to their masters and hypnotizing controllers. *Ponder what those masters need.* To them, bigotry is incidental – a leverage tool. Their

---

[79] I expect some to torch me as a bigot and Nazi-enabler for saying that. Others will hang around, knowing that I yearn (from the bottom of my heart) to destroy racism and intolerance! If I could reverse the male-female ratio in positions of power around the globe I'd race to press the button! Still, it's my job to notice traps and debilitating clichés. And so, I must reiterate, their paramount goal is *power*. Hence, it is not the *powerless* who the Kochs, Mercers and Putin fear most. It is those with some power to keep enlightenment values and accountability alive.

[80] https://www.nytimes.com/2019/08/21/opinion/trump-immigrants-punishment.html

bid for total power is not blocked by the powerless. But it might truly be thwarted by other, competing "elites."

Consider the bleak prospects for enlightened civilization across this current battlefield. With our elections cheat-stolen, our courts stuff-stacked with shills, millions incited into populist madness, and wealth disparities skyrocketing, just one force stands in feudalism's way. *The new lords must neutralize the counter-effectiveness of our fact-professions.* [81]

Scientists. [82] Civil servants. Journalists.

Law professionals. Teachers. Doctors.

FBI agents. Intelligence agencies. Statisticians.

Skilled labor. Law professionals. Economists…

…and yes… the U.S. military officer corps, the third best-educated and most soberly responsible clade in modern American life.

Oh, pity the poor plutocrats! Across 6000 years and almost all continents, lords had simply to snap their fingers, foreclose on poor families, and wave around swords (or wands or catechisms or writs). Nowadays, they keep getting hemmed in by nitpickers, law-followers, investigators and their ilk, armed with procedures, evidences and attention to 'rights.' No wonder a top Republican objective – voiced early in his administration by Donald Trump – is to *eviscerate 140 year old civil service protections* and put all public servants under the political thumb. [83]

You know that all of the professions listed above – and more – have been assailed for years, from daily assaults on "fake news" or "lamestream" media to climate science denialism, all the way to accusations of "deep state" conspiracy by our defenders who best understand this dangerous world, including many of our most accomplished men and women in and out of uniform. A professor at the Naval War College, Tom Nichols, wrote a book about this: *The Death of Expertise: The Cam-*

[81] The war on expertise. http://www.davidbrin.com/nonfiction/waronexpertise.html

[82] Revealed early in Chris Mooney's *The Republican War on Science.*

[83] October 12, 2019, White House Senior Advisor Stephen Miller ranted on Fox News that there's a "Fourth Branch of Government," consisting of the civil servants. A point where I agree, only I hold that civil servants have saved and protected us for 3 years. https://www.youtube.com/watch?v=1Z2-r0oh5tI&fbclid=IwAR2_LdYbRy8PEXIhgHDq39fSh10J1pk_ZBpJSL0lhNR-grt2f9CAMQIGm6Vg

paign Against Established Knowledge,[84] summarized in *Foreign Affairs* as: "*How America Lost Faith in Expertise And Why That's a Giant Problem.*"[85]

It's an all-out assault – not just on this specialty, or that one, but against every variety of folks who know stuff. Why haven't opposition politicians made this a core issue? One just as pressing as alt-right bigotry?

This isn't zero sum! Nor does this point downplay the racist poison spewing across our sullied nation. You know that nothing is more useful in combatting intolerance than the flood of *facts that disproved almost every prejudiced stereotype.* Moreover, if things go badly, all the fact folks will go up against the wall, just as quickly as the antifa or trans activists, if not sooner.[86]

> "*The point of modern propaganda isn't only to misinform or push an agenda. It is to exhaust your critical thinking, to annihilate truth.*"
>
> – Former world chess champion Gary Kasparov

OTHERS HAVE NOTICED: FACTS ARE THE ENEMY

A good start would be to emphasize that it is *all* fact professions who are targeted, and hence the very notion of fact itself. Earlier I quoted commentator Thom Hartmann, who said: "When liberals talk about "elites," they mean rich people. When conservatives talk about "elites", they mean smart people."

An editorial in the Los Angeles *Times* denounced[87] the new Know Nothing Movement, finishing wisely: "Investigate. Read. Write. Listen. Speak. Think. Be wary of those who disparage the investigators, the readers, the writers, the listeners, the speakers and the thinkers. Be suspicious of those who confuse reality with reality TV, and those who

---

[84] The Death of Expertise: The Campaign Against Established Knowledge, by Tom Nichols. http://amzn.to/2pr4k0s

[85] How America Lost Faith in Expertise Foreign Affairs, March/April 2017 https://www.foreignaffairs.com/articles/united-states/2017-02-13/how-america-lost-faith-expertise

[86] Of course these groups overlap, bigtime!

[87] "Why Trump Lies." LA Times, April 3, 2017. https://www.latimes.com/projects/la-ed-why-trump-lies/?fbclid=IwAR2w7sK8fjjd4wkpogdvUk7bcLqFkhtSGzDFc1iqYz4jU1HIAcB93e-3GE0w

repeat falsehoods while insisting, against all evidence, that they are true. To defend freedom, demand fact."

Alas, the advice was bereft of useful proposals, or anything like polemical judo.

Meanwhile, I challenge you to find a day when Donald Trump or his surrogates *weren't* attacking journalism – kettles attacking pots as "fake news." Just in August 2019 it was revealed that an operation run by conservative operatives reportedly scoured more than a decade of social media history from reporters who are seen as hostile towards Trump, in order to find potentially damaging posts that can be used against them.[88] And yes, I meant "I challenge you," because that phrase is key to a weapon too little used against the madness. I talk about wagers, especially, in this volume.

More recently, an editorial in the *Washington Post* spoke out about: "For Trump and his cronies, draining the swamp means ousting experts." [89] And all through the federal government, especially the State Department, large numbers of highly skilled pros have been leaking, then hemorrhaging away. But all of that is old news… and an ongoing – ultimately lethal – treason against the nation that (alas) we are getting used to.

My own contribution is to *dig*. Down to where the sickness has its deepest polemical roots. And as usual, it starts with something healthy… the most fundamental American reflex, taught to us in every film and story: *Suspicion of Authority*, or SoA.

Again – every citizen is convinced that some elite group is conspiring to be Big Brother! Liberals perceive plots by aristocrats, Mafiosi and faceless corporations.[90] Conservatives denounce schemes by snooty academics and faceless government bureaucrats. What few of us admit is

---

[88] "Operation Targeting Journalists Seen Unfavorable to Trump Is Allied With the White House: NYT." https://www.thedailybeast.com/operation-targeting-journalists-seen-unfavorable-to-trump-is-allied-with-the-white-house-nyt

[89] Ousting experts. https://www.washingtonpost.com/opinions/trump-is-draining-the-swamp-of-needed-experts/2019/08/08/7ec457e4-ba12-11e9-a091-6a96e67d9cce_story.html

[90] And yes, I suppose that makes me a "liberal," for now. Because *that* paranoia happens to be the one that's true. As of now.

that *any* power center could be a gathering place for connivers – including elites you happen to like.

By itself, healthy skepticism toward officious castes is irksomely *healthy*. But if manipulated just right, SoA can be used as a tool *by* conspiring elites, as we saw when Hitler diverted German populism with baseless charges of a vast Jewish conspiracy. What our more recent New Lords needed was to rouse red-populist ire toward *all smartypants elites,* diverting onto those natural foes all the attention that might otherwise notice their oligarchic putsch.

It called for spreading a series of clever memes that are *never stated explicitly*. Because if stated overtly, they are obviously insane.

> *'The rest of the world is warily watching the*
> *continuing assault on what the president*
> *calls the "dishonest media," a smear chillingly close*
> *to the Nazi-era term "Lügenpresse", or "lying press."'*
> – Gary Kasparov

ANTI-FACT INCANTATION #1: ABSURD NUMBERS

You start with the most "SoA" of the MAGA nostrums… "Those snooty (academics/scientists/journalists/teachers/deepstaters/etc.) are in a grand conspiracy against truth!" Or else: "They're all conformist lemmings, charging in the same direction, in blind obedience to habit!"

The common thread connecting those two magic spells? Every knowledge caste shares the same un-American traits that undermine their credibility: *uniformity, obstinacy* and *bullying officiousness.*

Right. Okay then, let's see. According to Google in North America there are roughly :

~ a quarter of a million professional journalists...

~ half a million scientists...[91]

~ a million medical doctors…

---

[91] We should honestly make a distinction, here. Google says there are about 6.9 million "scientists and engineers. And we all know many engineers who are reflexively and obstinately RASRs: Residually Adult Sane Republicans, only gradually letting facts drag them away from GOP loyalty.

~ a million university professors...

~ a quarter of a million military officers...

~ 150,000 economists...

~ 2.8 million civil servants at all levels...

~ 3.7 million teachers...

... almost three million nurses...

...and that just begins a long list of professions who are almost daily disparaged, as Fox and other right wing media imply – without ever saying so explicitly – that *all of them are engaged together in a deliberate conspiracy.*

What... all roughly ten *million* of them? A vast conspiracy without any leaks? Wow, that's some competence and focused determination!

Faced with that absurdity, the backpedaling begins, either by splitting off the professions, one at a time, or else claiming the real cabal is only at the *top*, with all the middle and lower ranks in ignorant, lockstep compliance to dogma. (Of course the journalists and pundit "scientists" employed by Fox are the rare free spirits.)

Well, well. Having been both a journalist and a scientist, I'll attest that *there are no more competitive humans.*[92] Anyone who knows these professions also knows that each member lives on individualist ambition to be the next one to break a big story, to topple a giant, to smash a standard assumption, or to make a scoop. When a vast majority of scientists do believe the same thing, it's not by obeisance to credentialed authorities, or some imaginary *consensus*. It's because the current *model of the world* in that particular field has survived repeated and relentless challenges! So far, that is. And not only challenges from eager young postdocs, but from a flourishing and rapidly growing community of amateur scientists.[93]

---

[92] Nearly all top scientists are eclectic – also artists or authors or musicians. Fiercely competitive "young guns" – recently tenured professors with secure funding – are most ferocious of all, seeking some paradigm to topple. Contrast this to Fox myths that scientists are wimpy lemmings, yelping around the most "consensus-accepted" theory and hugging boondoggle "grants." This includes the rich folks in weather analysis who (using the same equations and data as climate researchers) can now predict hurricane paths and transformed the old, joke of a 4-hour "weather report" into a ten day miracle of prophecy you and your red uncle rely upon. Once, the U.S. right admired science. Now it's at full tilt war. Thirty years ago, 40% of US scientists called themselves Republican, now it is 3% and plummeting. They are voting with their feet, the smartest, wisest, most logical and by far the most competitive humans our species ever produced.

[93] As I explain in this video, the 20th century's professionalization of everything served humanity well, but could not continue. That vast trend is fast being replaced by an era when hundreds of

(Today's experts have largely welcomed the amateur trend. Scientists compete with each other to get PBS shows explaining the latest discoveries! And there are now countless opportunities for citizen science[94] – ways for aficionados to get involved in projects in astronomy, biology, ecology and so on.)

Above all, theories shift and change as evidence accumulates, and those models with bad predictive records are abandoned. (Hear that, "supply side economics"?)

But sure, it's healthy for some citizens to express wariness toward that "elite." Even (ungratefully) toward all of the smartypants castes whose inventiveness and curiosity engendered way more than half our wealth. In theory, one *can* imagine a technocratic dictatorship of nerdy know-it-alls – pushy, conformist, patronizing perfessors. It's not wholly unreasonable to fret that scientists will act like old-time priests and lords and guild-masters, erecting barriers, preventing interested outsiders from joining the fun. And yes, at times we do see glimmers of old fashioned guild-protection. Still…

—

Which seems more likely? A grand 'conspiracy' of ten *million* scientists, journalists, teachers, FBI agents, professors, doctors, and intel/military officers? All those smart-but-unwise eggheads are plotting against the salt-of-the-Earth everyman?

Or that 5,000 golf buddies in an incestuous CEO caste connive secretly with parasitic Wall Streeters, casino moguls, Mafiosi, "ex"-KGB agents and inheritance brats? Oh, you never heard it put that way before?

—

Let's concede that it's not unreasonable to subject any intelligentsia to SoA scrutiny. In *Democracy in America,* Alexis de Tocqueville expressed surprised admiration that villagers and townsfolk were arguing and managing their affairs quite fine without overseers appointed from above. In his "Funeral Oration" the great Athenian champion of democracy, Pericles, said that "lack of learning combined with sound common

millions will have side avocations, wherein they are almost as capable as their day-work. https://www.youtube.com/watch?v=Zw9_Q9FzljI

94 Amateur science: https://en.wikipedia.org/wiki/Society_for_Amateur_Scientists

sense is more helpful than the type of cleverness that gets out of hand, and that as a general rule states are better governed by the man in the street than by intellectuals." Though both of these sages commended two necessary ingredients: widely open education and calm. Especially the calm that it takes to argue productively with your neighbors.

Fortunately, 'technocracy'[95] – or 'rule by the smartest' – is unlikely and impractical, for dozens of reasons. (Have you ever tried to herd cats? Now try getting ten million highly competitive, confidently curious and irksomely well-informed scientific "cats" to agree on an Orwellian agenda.)

As for *journalism*, these are the men and women who trained to ask eager questions, to probe and get exposed to diverse, opposing points of view. Sure, as individuals they can be biased! Sometimes outrageously so. There is every reason to be glad we live in a society with many, diverse media – some of them amateur – all sniffing for errors. That is the essential ethos I convey in my book *The Transparent Society.*[96] And did I mention that Suspicion of Authority is a *good* habit, overall?

But when it means hating experts *in principle and in general,* then SoA has metastasized. Gone cancerous. A good reflex, it's been turned against us.

> *"If you have the facts on your side, pound the facts.*
> *If you have the law on your side, pound the law.*
> *If you have neither on your side, pound the table."*
> – Traditional advice to new lawyers.

ANTI-FACT INCANTATION #2: EVERYONE KNOWS THAT...

The War on Expertise is insidious. It depends on some magic spells that draw their power from being *implicit* and never spoken overtly or aloud. The core meme starts with something everyone knows to be true. We all know that:

---

[95] Technocracy had some supporters during the darkest days of the Depression and as an answer to communism and fascism, as well as the apparent failure of western democracy. See the film version of H. G. Wells's "Things to Come."

[96] *The Transparent Society: Will Technology Make Us Choose Between Privacy and Freedom?* (1997), winner of the Freedom of Speech Award of the American Library Association. http://www.davidbrin.com/transparentsociety.html

Just because someone is smart and knows a lot, they aren't automatically wise.

It's true! We all know examples of intelligent, knowledgeable boneheads. In fact, that nostrum is *so* true that it thrums as a deep assumption, at the back of all our minds.

Alas, in the same way that Suspicion of Authority is wholesome – till it goes toxic – this true statement has been *twisted* into something cancerous:

All people who are smart and know a lot are therefore automatically unwise!

The first statement is true and we all know it. The second is so insanely wrong that anyone declaring it is instantly revealed as jibbering loony. And yet, the latter is now a core catechism of the Confederacy! Because they've been allowed to leave it implicit.

Don't let them! Make it clear *that's what they mean*. Or else make them deny it. Either way, you'll do major judo moves.

If "those who do not learn from history are doomed to repeat it," then we should add that "Those who have learned from history will almost certainly repeat it anyway, because bias rules over truth."
– Thad McIlroy

ANTI-FACT INCANTATION #3: CONFRONT THEM OVER FACT CHECKING

We're all frustrated by the effectiveness of the "fake news!" incantation, which should be refutable by simple tabulations of competitively verified facts. Fact-checking services are supposed to do this, yet all have failed to make a dent in the impervious wall of Confederate falsehoods and denialism, not only regarding climate change but the more than ten thousand tabulated Donald Trump lies[97].

That's because every fact-checking service is dismissed – on Fox and rightist media – as 'biased,' for the basic reason that most of the false-

[97] 10,000 tabulated Trump lies. https://www.cnn.com/2019/04/29/politics/donald-trump-lies-washington-post/index.html

hoods found by these services are Republican sourced. In the realm of "Sez you!" relativism, this is clear evidence of bias.

Alas, nearly all frustrated fact people keep playing *sumo* over this! They seem to believe if they just pile the mountain of evidence higher, *that* will finally give fact checkers more credibility. But instead, the reds only dig in. You cannot win this fight with sumo.

A far better approach? Directly challenge every high level person who repeats that accusation:

Okay, you claim every existing fact-check service is inherently biased. In that case, will you now join a bipartisan effort to design a new fact-verifying service? One you'd trust?

Challenge every Fox pundit and GOP Congressperson or factotum:

Always complaining about biased fact-checkers, why have you never offered to help set up something neutral and trustworthy? Not a policy or political body, but one (or several!) charged with a single task: helping us tell true from fake?

Will you come to a conference, next week, ready to nominate august, reputable conservative men and women to serve as co-supervisors? How about retired, Republican Supreme and Appellate Court judges? Sandra Day O'Conner? Former President Bush? Warren Buffett? Retired admirals and generals? Eminent conservative statisticians and related experts, respected by their peers and known more for quality than dogma? Do you have no such sages to propose? How can that be?

Why won't you join a non-partisan effort to help us sift truth from lies?

Yes, you've seen this recommendation earlier and will confront it repeatedly, throughout the book, because it works, and because no one tries it on the national stage.

No, the Foxites won't cooperate, for obvious reasons – above all because almost any *reputable conservatives* they name, even experts who are *partisan,* will wind up shredding the "fake news" nostrum.

Instead, Hannity & co. will rail that you're trying to set up an Orwellian "Ministry of Truth." Yes, even when you offer to help set up many *competing* fact-checking services. (See *The Fact Act* below.)

They'll squirm away. But their repeated whinnying, waffling evasion will look terrible. And that is judo.

"Our countrymen have recovered from the alarm into which art and industry had thrown them; science and honesty are replaced on their high ground."
– Thomas Jefferson, upon entering office

ANTI-FACT INCANTATION #4: APPEALING TO ANTI-AUTHORITY

Sayeth the indignant defender of individualism:

Anyone who suggests that experts in a field merit respect is declaring that everyone should bow down to experts and obey them. I won't!

Bullshit. Scientists invented "Question Authority"! Did I mention they tend to be the most *competitive* of all humans, forever going after each other like gunslingers at high noon?

Hell yeah, you should start any topic by checking with experts! Begin with a tentative assumption that they know what they are talking about. (They do, at least 90% of the time.) *Then* look for others who knowledgeably disagree! Sometimes (rarely) the dissidents prove right and experts wrong! "Consensus" in science is very real when it comes to crafting useful predictive models of the world. But go ahead and show us (with burden of proof on you) that the consensus is wrong here! Or over there! It's how science advances.

Just this, though. When most of the people who know the most about a subject are seen to agree, despite their competitiveness, then it's generally wise for *policy* to *begin* by paying heed to expert advice. Especially when our children's future is at stake, it makes sense to enact policies that follow expert advice, *while* funding research to see if they are wrong! You can – and should – do both, in parallel.

(And note that this syndrome, while less rampant than on the right, certainly festers on what we might call the far-left, among "post-modernist scholars," or else those aura-reading types who proclaim that objective reality will bend to their triumphant will[98].)

I'll go to specifics in a later section, dialing into *environmental denialism.* But it's pertinent here. When 99% of people who understand climate and weather say we're all in danger, shall we do nothing, only obstruct, at the behest of coal barons, oil commissars and petro sheiks? Shall we *both* ignore expert advice *and* defund research – the satellites and instruments and avidly competing groups – that might prove the experts wrong? Or prove them right? Because that has been the upshot of climate denialism.

COUNTER-INCANTATIONS FOR SPECIFIC MATTERS

This method is no magic bullet. In a dispute among mature or sincere minds – or even Junior High School debaters – you should seek advice from prim and reasonable logicians. I'm here to show you *weapons* against culture warriors who refuse fair argument, ways to get around their screeches and distractions. These methods won't work on the truly hate-drenched or dogmatic, but they can corner the uncomfortable ones, who chant their rightist nostrums in desperation not to see or hear what's become of them.

Here are a few more very specific examples.

Bonus counter-incantation #1: In Chapter 8 we'll talk about what it takes to run a *conspiracy*. The first rule is to limit the number of plotters in-the-know! And don't have too many lower-level henchmen, either. (These rules don't apply when you control a despotic state that easily kills whistleblowers.)

Here let me just reiterate the zinger that's boxed a couple of pages back. That you can get real mileage by mocking the notion of a "conspiracy" of ten million scientists, journalists, teachers, FBI agents, professors, doctors, and intel/military officers, when it's obvious to anyone that 5,000 golf buddies in an incestuous CEO caste can much more plausibly connive in secret with parasitic Wall Streeters, casino moguls, Mafiosi,

---

98 "Thoughts, Prayers And Rejecting Political Hobbyists," https://www.bobcesca.com/thoughts-and-prayers-2/

"ex"-KGB agents and inheritance brats. The very folks who *want* populist rallies pouring hate at both people of color and smart folks.

Bonus counter-incantation #2: Here's one cult incantation that should long ago have been answered with a judo challenge, instead of year after year of plodding-grunting sumo:

The scientists pushing Global Warming are all in it for climate study grants.

Seriously, you never realized you can judo-kill that with just four words?

Show... us... the... 'grants.'

Truly, has no one simply challenged Fox n' Pals, on-air?

Back it up! Your assistants could tabulate these 'climate grants' in a day, certainly a week. Issue a list of 'climate grants" and how they correlate with the incomes of the 98% of experts in pertinent fields, who avow that something dangerous is happening to our planet.

Show us how meteorologists, who are rich from selling forecasts to industry, need 'climate grants.' Those geniuses expanded the old two-hour 'weather report' into a miraculous ten day forecast, using much the same equations and data as climate scientists. Those flush-successful meteorologists owe nothing to measly 'climate grants,' yet they too agree Earth is in deadly peril.

Back up this 'grant-hugging' calumny on the Fox web site by next week, or admit now that you're a coward-liar.

Bonus counter-incantation #3: This one may seem old and a bit odd,[99] but for 20 years I found that it always shreds! In fact, I'm told it deeply fretted Glenn Beck, back when his favorite conspiracy-yarn rants revolved around *George Soros.*

Of course Soros is a *criminal mastermind whose NGOs suckered millions around the world into raving socialist frenzy.* Never mind that his wealth and media "empire" are minuscule compared to the triumvirate of Murdoch, Koch and Saudi co-owners of Fox. Even after Glenn Beck left TV, other rightist pundits have repeated this chant:

Soros is so scary-manipulative that he personally toppled EIGHT foreign governments!

---

[99] "David Brin's Epic Takedown of Fox's Soros-Haters." https://www.discourse.net/2014/10/david-brin-epic-takedown-of-foxs-soros-haters/

I don't recall a single major figure of the left or center who noticed this doozy judo-opportunity. Because… it's true! For once, Beck and his pals weren't lying. Their Soros rant is based on one of those truths that must never be made explicit.

In fact, George Soros did – through his NGO foundations – help topple eight foreign governments! Alas, GOP intellect has plummeted so far, since Goldwater and Buckley, that no audience member of the Beck, Limbaugh, or Fox Riefenstahl-rallies ever lifted his head to ask. "Um… Glenn? Rush? Sean? Which foreign governments are you talking about?"

Are *you* ready to ask? Here are those eight[100] nations the right credits George Soros with toppling – without ever saying their names aloud.

The communist dictatorship of Hungary.

The communist dictatorship of Poland

The communist dictatorship of Czechoslovakia

The communist dictatorship of Romania

The communist dictatorship of Bulgaria

The communist dictatorship of Estonia

The communist dictatorship of Latvia

The communist dictatorship of Lithuania

And yes, Soros considered undermining the USSR and Iron Curtain to be his life's core work, helping with the liberation of hundreds of millions and a victorious end of the Cold War. Russian President and "ex" KGB agent Vladimir Putin calls the fall of the USSR "history's greatest tragedy," and he pours special blame-hatred for that calamity at George Soros.

Others also credit Soros with this impressive (and terrifying) feat! The right-wing Heritage Foundation and American Enterprise Institute repeat the accusation, along with many GOP politicians. But… but wasn't that supposed to be Ronald Reagan?

In fact, they both share credit with Mikhail Gorbachev, and with the architect of our grand 1945 to 2000 plan, George Marshall. And hey, let's be generous and give some credit to the *people* of those nations, too.

OMG, such drivel!

---

[100] The figure should be *ten*, to include East Germany and Ukraine.

Seriously, can you see the disservice that our brightest blue pols and pundits and observers have done us, by just shrugging off these Soros rants without efficiently cutting them off, at the knees? Sure, the viewers of this crap never rouse to question the tsunami of ironies and contradictions at their Nuremberg Rallies. But far more urgently – *why does no one on the other side?*

Bonus counter-incantation #4: Of course I should reference others who are also in this fight over restoring the primacy of verifiability and accountability to the word "fact." For example, right after the 2016 U.S. election was trashed by malevolent forces, Facebook invited me to their headquarters to consult about ways to use transparency to prevent their site from being hijacked again by meme-manipulators. I can tell you now that absolutely none of my suggestions were adopted, or even closely examined. I am not encouraged.

In contrast, read about how sapient Italians have been using a two-level approach to combat the anti-vaxxer fanaticism, which had left Italy with the lowest immune-rate for preventable diseases in Western Europe:

"There are Italians who will be moved by forceful communications from a genuine expert, there are Italians who will be moved by gentle persuasion from someone who seems simpatico, and there are Italians who will be moved by government policy. And that has further implications: It means that any counter-disinformation campaign might require more than one tactic, more than one message and more than one kind of messenger if it is to succeed. In a world where conspiracy theories – medical, scientific and, of course, political – are proliferating, this is more than just a useful insight. It should be the beginning of a new way of thinking about long-term strategies to deal with disinformation more generally." – writes Anne Applebaum in *The Washington Post*.[101]

A well-reasoned approach, more mature than my radical demand for in-yer-face confrontation. But yes, by all means.

---

[101] The Washington Post: https://www.washingtonpost.com/opinions/global-opinions/italians-decided-to-fight-a-conspiracy-theory-heres-what-happened-next/2019/08/08/ca950828-ba10-11e9-b3b4-2bb69e8c4e39_story.html

'FACTS' SHOULD INCLUDE MEASURABLE OUTCOMES

A chapter about the War on Facts should include *comparison of outcomes*. After all, what could be more pertinent to the purpose of politics in a mature society? Isn't that purpose to elect statesmen and stateswomen of stature who will negotiate new laws and revised policies in good faith, based not just on theories but a landscape of changing but verifiable evidence?

Okay, that paragraph made you choke on your beverage. But after you clean up, consider: there *have been* momentary glimmers of political maturity across American – and human – history. Such beacons and the reforms they engender can make up for decades of sloth and turpitude, such as we've seen of late. Moreover, you can find some folks who are now clinging to conservatism with their fingernails – I call them RASRS or Residually Adult Sane Republicans – who yearn for such an era. They may be approachable with comparison of outcomes. I'll do this in more detail in Chapter 10 (Government), Chapter 11 (Economics), Pause#15 (Clinton-Obama Obsession) and elsewhere, especially where the topic turns to *wagers*.

But for now let's examine one more bulwark rationalization of your average Republican. One of the deepest is the truism that *Democrats are squishy-compassionate*. Therefore:

– They must be naive and inept at running a Pax Americana that can be agile and win at international realpolitik.

– Those "socialists" must do badly at encouraging growth in an entrepreneurial-competitive capitalist economy.

– They're fiscally irresponsible and will saddle future generations with outrageous debt.

– Because liberals moralize, that means they cannot be the pragmatic ones.

Would it surprise you that these truisms all run diametrically opposite to fact? Or that almost none of our side's pols or pundits have glommed onto that response?

Democratic administrations – at both the state and federal level – are almost always more fiscally responsible than Republican ones. Nearly always.[102] *Republicans are the budget busters and debt-saddlers, down the line. (Chapter 11.)*

In fact, almost every clear metric of U.S. national health, from unemployment and GDP growth to deficits and liberal desiderata, like rates of poverty or public health or childcare, do better across the span of Democratic administrations.

The states that are run by blue-squishy moralizers are nearly all in better shape than those that are red-led. And the condition of our alliances – NATO and so on – is always better when the U.S. has a high moral quotient. (That's also when we attract lots of defectors from our opponents, and nothing could be more practical than that. See Chapters 9 &14.)

Finally, a legitimate conservative gripe: All right though, there is one fundamental "red" complaint about their squishy-moralizing liberal neighbors that has credibility. In fact, it is one of the root-underlying causes of their resentment.

Liberals nag.

They're rude. They get in your face with guilt trips. Last year's progress is taken for granted without a spoonful of credit, as new issues and causes press forward. Their neighbors are called racist-sexist troglodytes and no litmus test will ever be good enough. No customs of courtesy or demure behavior will restrain or tone down the guilt trips. And there comes a point when many of our conservative neighbors shrug, asking: "Why should I try?"

Dig this well, I know which side I am on – the one that aims for a truly good and wonderful civilization, like in *Star Trek*. One where the liberal preoccupations of today are rendered moot and boring, because they were solved with compassion, generosity and fabulous innovation. So when I point out some of the underlying reactionary memes, and admit some have a point, I'm not changing sides. I'm trying to be adult.

Adults don't deny facts. Well, they're not supposed to.

---

[102] "Do outcomes matter more than rhetoric?" http://davidbrin.blogspot.com/2014/06/so-do-outcomes-matter-more-than-rhetoric.html

THE FACT ACT [103]

RESCUING THE VERY NOTION OF OBJECTIVE REALITY:

All right then. Let's suppose Brin is correct. A world cabal of elites – the stupidest and richest – have got it into their heads that they must repress democratically empowered voters (the mob) and restore a natural, pyramidal hierarchy based largely on money and inherited position... perhaps soon enhanced by technological tools of universal surveillance and even immortality.[104] They further realize that one obstacle obstructs their goal: the rule of flat-fair-transparent and accountable law, administered by faithful civil servants, scrutinized by a savvy public and informed by tens of millions of smart-knowledgeable Fact People.

The oligarchic putsch must do what we see happening before our eyes. They must wage all out war upon those fact-using professions.

Their method is the same one chosen by German aristocrats in 1930 – subsidizing a hate-drenched populist movement that spews abhorrence at vulnerable minorities, but also goes after all fact-elites. And yes, we know how well that plan turned out for the German aristocracy.

How can we fight back? Well, democracy, of course. But powerful ways must be found to combat this new Know-Nothing campaign. The theme of this book – *Judo Polemic* – may offer at least a few weapons to those paladins of press, politics and punditry who are fighting for civilization.

But for a moment *let's assume victory*. At least a partial one, in which the Confederacy and its putsch maters and foreign-despot allies get ejected from power in Washington D.C. In other chapters I offer lists of priorities! Suggestions and measures that could make a big difference.

But here, concluding our chapter on the "War on Facts," I want to present something particularly pertinent. At the request of the Internet Caucus of the 2018 California Democratic Party Convention in San Diego, California, I hurriedly drafted a piece of "futuristic legislation.

The "Fact Act"[105] would help restore access to useful and confirmable information for public officials, politicians and citizens. Rather than

---

[103] "Enact the Fact Act." http://davidbrin.com/nonfiction/factact.html

[104] "Do We Really Want Immortality?" http://www.davidbrin.com/nonfiction/immortality.html

[105] Note: This "Fact Act" is not to be confused with another bill that was somewhat less apropos: The Fair and Accurate Credit Transactions Act of 2003, an amendment to the Fair Credit Re-

establishing some suspect "Ministry of Truth,"[106] this legislation will encourage systems that use diversity, competition[107] and grownup adversarial methods, helping leaders and the public to parse lies and distractions from assertions that are supported by strong evidence.

Under the Fact Act, Congress will:

ONE: Restore the nonpartisan Congressional Office of Technology Assessment (OTA) and other advisory panels[108] that were shut down in the Gingrich/Hastert/Boehner/McConnell eras.[109] Protect the Congressional Budget Office and Government Accountability Office. Enhance Congressional staff to do needed research. Take measures to ensure that scientific processes in government agencies will be both subject to critical accountability and liberated from partisan political pressures.

TWO: Restore full funding and staffing to the executive Office of Science and Technology Policy (OTSP). This bill further requires that the President must fill, by law, the position of White House Science Adviser from a diverse and bipartisan slate of qualified candidates offered by the Academy of Science, and the Academy will choose one, if the president does not. The Science Adviser shall have uninterrupted access to the President for at least two one-hour sessions per month.[110]

THREE: Each member of Congress shall be summoned to choose, from his or her home district, two advisers, one a scientist and one a statistician, funded to counsel the member on matters of verifiable fact, and to take press or public questions referred to them by the member. They will not opine on political issues, only upon the degree to which *assertions* are supported by *factual evidence.*

Likely effects of Section Three? (a) Congress-members will no longer be able to shrug off fact/scientific questions with "I'm not a scientist." (b) Any

porting Act.

[106] That the "Ministry of Truth" Orwellian accusation will be trotted out is guaranteed; hence, it must be prepared for.

[107] This principle underlies our competitive, fact-using arenas: markets, democracy, science and justice courts. We know how to do this.

[108] Other advisory panels http://davidbrin.com/nonfiction/advisoryagencies.html

[109] Even Republican appointees on OTA kept demurring from GOP dogma, saying "That's just not true," so it was eliminated.

[110] It took Donald Trump two years to fill this post. Evidently, even far-right candidates like David Gelernter made the mistake of saying to him: «I›ll tell you, when something is clearly false.» That was, apparently, unacceptable.

member's refusal to appoint these advisers will be an implicit insult to the member's home district, implying she or he could find no one qualified.

FOUR: These congressional advisers – scientists and statisticians – shall gather in a shadow "Fact Congress" (FC) twice a year to supervise the restored OTA and OSTP and ensure nonpartisan professionalism. Eclectic diversity and potent minority input will ensure there is no "Ministry of Truth."

Without usurping Congressional authority over legislation, policy or confirmations, the FC will question top scientific appointees regarding grasp of important concepts in their field, e.g., ability to discern and clearly describe factual disputes and forecast potential policy outcomes and tradeoffs, including levels of uncertainty.

If more than one quarter of Senators or Representatives submit a question to the Fact Congress, the FC will respond with advice according to best available models. Congressmembers may bring their FC advisers to House or Senate committee hearings and may charge them to form ad-hoc shadow committees, to assist with explications of fact.

FIVE: The Fact Act will restore the media Rebuttal Rule, prying open "echo chamber" propaganda mills. Any channel or station using airwaves or accepting advertising will be required to cede five minutes per day during prime time and ten minutes at other times to reputable adversaries chosen by Competitive Argument Societies (CAS) that are approved by one quarter of the members of the Fact Congress.[111]

Example: If the 25% most conservative members of the FC approve the 'Herbert Hoover Competitive Argument Society,' then HHCAS may send a rebuttal spokesmen to MSNBC, tackling Rachel Maddow. A CAS chosen by the most liberal quarter of the Fact Congress will get rebuttal time on Fox.

Rebuttals shall feature under-banners offering links for more details... plus links to refutation of the rebuttal, or else to fact-debates offered by pairs of competing CAS.[112]

---

[111] This «one quarter» provision ensures there can be no accusation of majority bullying or «voting on facts.»

[112] Again, emphasizing the competitive nature of these measures will stymie accusations of a "Ministry of Truth" or "free speech repression."

Any channel or station not using the airwaves or accepting advertising that nevertheless engages in avid political polemic, with the intent to influence electoral outcomes, will be required to offer – at intervals – a small link in one corner, that the viewer can use (or not) to access counter-arguments, or else to track the sources of both the channel's assertions and funding.

SIX: Under auspices of the Fact Congress, Competitive Argument Societies (CAS) and other entities will be offered infrastructure and encouragement to engage in public debates over policy or else disputations over fact. Fact disputations will argue matters of verifiable or falsifiable evidence, aiming to break-down and narrow – but never eliminate – uncertainties and to target specific questions meriting further study. Amateur or non-credentialed participation will be encouraged.

SEVEN: Whistleblower protections will be upgraded to encourage early/discreet problem solving within institutions, and later (if necessary) protection of whistleblowers who feel they are unfairly repressed by their own institution. Enhancing the No Fear Act signed by President Bush in 2002,[113] the FACT Act will offer a scaled sequence of safe and secure steps that encourage first self-reform, but ultimately the adversarial discovery of cleansing truth. (See Chapters 7, 8 and 13.)

EIGHT: To encourage the establishment of a wide variety of competing, credible fact-checking services, Congress will appoint a commission of sages from all parties, starting with the former presidents and retirees from the Supreme Court and top federal appeals courts, retired flag officers, American Nobelists, along with other eminent citizens with unimpeachable reputations. Among the duties of this panel will be to issue findings when a fact-checking service is accused of "partisanship."

NINE: As empowered under the 13th and 14th Amendments, this act requires that states mandating Voter ID requirements must offer substantial and effective compliance assistance, helping affected citizens to acquire their entitled legal ID and register to vote. Any state that fails to

---

[113] On May 15, 2002, Congress enacted and President Bush signed the "Notification and Federal Employee Antidiscrimination and Retaliation Act of 2002," which is now known as the No FEAR Act. One purpose of the Act is to "require that Federal agencies be accountable for violations of antidiscrimination and whistleblower protection laws." https://www.nlrb.gov/reports/regulatory-reports-and-notices/no-fear-act

provide such assistance, in order to substantially reduce the fraction of eligible citizens turned away at the polls, shall be assumed in violation of equal protection and engaged in illegal voter suppression.

Corporations demand compliance assistance when government imposes new regulations. So, why can't poor folks get help to comply with voter ID laws? (See Chapter 4) If a state does this, then its demand for Voter ID might be sincere. Alas, not one red state allocates a cent to help poor citizens, elderly, the young, or divorced women comply with onerous new restrictions on their franchise. Most have moved to close DMV offices in counties where many Democrats live! (Why do no Democrats make this point? Opposing voter ID leaves Democrats open to accusations of excusing cheaters, but denouncing the GOP's corporate-citizen "compliance assistance hypocrisy" is a clear win.)

TEN: Congressional committees and procedures will be reformed so that members will be free to negotiate as individuals, with less power vested in the chairs or majority leaders to control legislation. Each member – whether in the majority or minority – will have authority to issue one subpoena per term, compelling adversarial testimony before a congressional committee of his or her choosing for as long as three hours. (See Chapter 13.) Thus the minority will always be able to question the party in power and small numbers of members will have some ability to investigate. These member subpoenas will have priority over those issued by committee chairs.

ELEVEN: In order to eliminate conflict of interest, the seventy-three Inspectors General of federal departments and agencies shall be brought under an independent office of the Inspector General of the United States[114] (IGUS), whose appointment must be ratified by the council of sages (see SEVEN) as well as the Senate. IGUS officers shall be commissioned, uniformed, trained and held to quasi-military standards of discretion, honesty and meticulous devotion to law.

---

[114] The Inspector General of the United States http://davidbrin.com/nonfiction/inspectorgeneral.html

TWELVE: This act directs the administration to negotiate treaties extending transparency, accountability and truth worldwide.

FACTS EXIST

Imagine you are a Jew in 1930s Nazi Germany, reading all the libels and lies spread about your people in Nazi-controlled media, unable to demand: "I want a fair trial, so I can show it's all false!"

Or you're an antebellum slave, told that your condition was "natural" because of inferior intelligence, yet forbidden even to self-educate, so you might prove that calumny wrong.

A similar world awaits all of us, if we don't step up to reinforce the marvels of open honesty and knowledge and justice that our enlightenment has achieved, so far... including especially our chance to take it much, much farther. The hard-won lesson of the last two centuries, which even many liberals don't grasp, is that *most injustices shrivel under the application of light. And light consists of photons called facts.*

Reiterating: we see zillionaire oligarchs finance relentless propaganda aimed at riling millions into hatred, and not only wrath aimed at powerless minorities. Just as dangerous is their campaign – stirring up that preexisting *SoA* reflex – of open war against "knowledge elites" – *precisely because those skill castes do have power!* Civil servants, scientists, teachers, doctors, intel agents and so can do a lot to thwart the New Lords' ambitions. All must be gelded. Broken to harness. Taught their place.

Ironically, while it's been cleverly executed so far, this *overall* plan is incredibly dumb! Whatever the putschists envision... e.g. that they'll "control" the hateful mobs they've riled... or that feudalism is the natural order... or that it's for the greater good... or smiling happily as flatterer-sycophants tell them how superior they are... whatever their rationalizations, *they have already lost,* because the ultimate thing they are warring against is called Objective Reality. And it exists.

These plotters believe in triumph of their will, empowered by mountains of lucre. Indeed, they may succeed at bringing the Enlightenment Experiment crashing into a new dark age. But the cabal leaders themselves won't benefit, nor will their scions, for one reason above all.

You see, the fact people are myriad and varied. Some of them know everything about the New Lords, including where their Patagonian or subsea or Himalayan/Siberian hideaways lie. Others know stuff about computers. About chemistry. About biology. About nukes. Hence, the stupidest thing for this deeply stupid clade of would-be New Lords to do is ignore the lessons of history. Myopic as they are, they should squint at what will be their inevitable outcome, if they insist on making all the smart people really mad.

Take some advice from Dr. Bruce Banner. You won't like us when we're mad. And that's a *fact* you can bank on.

It just ain't so.

Pause #5 for...

The Big Tendentious Lie That History Obeys "Patterns"

Part 1: "The Tytler Calumny" [115]

> "A democracy is always temporary in nature; it simply cannot exist as a permanent form of government. A democracy will continue to exist up until the time that voters discover that they can vote themselves largesse from the public treasury. From that moment on, the majority always votes for the candidates who promise the most benefits fromP the public treasury, with the result that every democracy will finally collapse over loose fiscal policy, (which is) always followed by a dictatorship."

Have you seen that incantation before, or something like it? This widely-circulated "Tytler Calumny" exemplifies how our neighbors on the right – once represented in sage debate by minds like Barry Goldwater, Friedrich Hayek and William F. Buckley – are reduced to slinging comfy, fact-free slogans. Though dubiously named for a 19th Century Englishman, Alexander Tytler, the aphorism is also attributed falsely to historian Arnold Toynbee, or Lord Thomas Macaulay, even Alexis de Tocqueville, though recent scholarship leads to a 1943 speech by one Henning Webb Prentis Jr., President of the Armstrong Cork Company.[116] It's often accompanied by another cynical feat called the *Fatal Sequence.*

---

[115] Extracted from "Is Democracy Hopeless?" http://davidbrin.blogspot.com/2012/10/the-tytler-calumny-is-democracy-hopeless.html
[116] Prentis speech. http://www.lorencollins.net/tytler.html

> **Great nations rise and fall in a 200 year cycle. The people go from bondage to spiritual truth, to great courage, from courage to liberty, from liberty to abundance, from abundance to selfishness, from selfishness to complacency, from complacency to apathy, from apathy to dependence, from dependence back again to bondage.**

Now, as one who got to "channel" and complete the future history series of science-fiction legend Isaac Asimov, [117] I admit some affection for the central character - psychohistorian Hari Seldon[118] - and the notion that history's path can be somehow be tracked, even forecasted. Indeed, some patterns exist! Take the dominance, in nearly all human societies, of armed thug gangs or cabals of owner lords or commissars, who predictably passed power on to sons who never earned any of it. It's the persistent-feudal outline that Adam Smith and the American Founders strove so hard to break. Yes, I get the pattern-seeking allure.

Consider how the Tytler Calumny appeals to vanity of the one repeating it. The sad scorn of someone who deems himself *above* the hoi polloi of mere «people.» Its blithe dismissal of any possibility that democracy can sustain itself comes despite the fact that - if you include vigorous colonial legislatures - we in North America have more than three centuries of ever-ripening success, becoming steadily mightier and accomplishing prodigious feats at the same pace that we've grown more inclusive.

The Tytler nostrum (appraised here on Snopes[119]) sounds "logical" in its smug contempt for the masses... *except that it runs contrary to actual fact.* Take, for example, when the free citizens of Athens voted against distributing the windfall from new silver mines to every citizen, instead asking Themistocles to invest it in their future. Would most kings do that? As recently as the 1990s, Bill Clinton, with Senators Tsongas (D) and Rudman (R) and others in the moderate middle used revenue from the dot.com

---

[117] Foundation's Triumph. (1999) http://www.davidbrin.com/foundationstriumph.html

[118] Isaac Asimov's series and the future-history seer Seldon inspired a wide diversity of minds, across the last half century, from Nobel Prize winning economist Paul Krugman to Osama bin Laden, though I think the former had a better idea what Isaac meant.

[119] http://www.snopes.com/politics/ballot/athenian.asp

boom to pay down the national debt. Middle class voters overwhelmingly supported debt pay-down, rather than tax cuts for themselves.

Should we be surprised? Who is more likely to have a habit of weighing the consequences of debt? Middle class citizens who must wrestle with tradeoffs and mortgages, stanching their impulses and appetites every day? Or aristocrats accustomed to indulging whims, knowing there are always more coppers, pennies, pfennigs, etc., to be squeezed from those below them on the pyramid? Are the builders of Versailles, the Schönbrunn, the Taj Mahal and the Forbidden City – palatial fripperies that impoverished their nations – entitled to lecture us about deferred gratification?

Should middle class Americans, who invested in uplifting poor children, in universities, R&D and infrastructure, all the way to endeavors that might access the vast resources of space, listen to wastrel scions chiding us from 50-room yachts, demanding that we give them more?

When Bill Clinton left office, there was no one left to block the raiders – who swarmed in to vote themselves "largesse" from the public treasury – giga-tax cuts for the uber-oligarchy that (we were assured) would be paid back within a year, by supply-side miracles! Ah. Pity that not one prediction ever made by Supply Siders ever came even remotely close to coming true. And that is ever. At any level, from the federal budget to states like Kansas, Texas and Oklahoma.

Instead, exactly as described by Adam Smith, most oligarchs did not spend their tax-cut largesse on productive enterprises or risky capital formation. With some exceptions, they predictably poured it into real estate, rent-seeking property/equities and hedge speculations that pulled cash from circulation, plummeting money velocity but boosting asset bubbles, leading to staggering deficits and the 2008 Great Recession. And it's happening again.

Dig this well, so the Tytler Calumny can die its deserved death. The middle class chose debt pay-down. The aristocracy demanded short-sighted greed or "largesse," exactly as they did in 1789 France, when the First Estate refused to help pay for the nation that benefited them. Those lords' rationalization – that they needed all the money to invest in estates and employ their tenant serfs – was the same as supply sider "job-creators" use today. Exactly the same tedious incantation.

There is wisdom in competitive-open markets and crowds! But as Chapter 11 will reveal, that is a very different thing from denouncing a liberated and empowered middle class as somehow a greedy mob. Look in a mirror.

We'll return to the Tytler Calumny later, connecting it to other tendentious mythologizers like Karl Marx, Oswald Spengler and the latest mesmerizing incantation – The Fourth Turning. For now, just be ready the next time your favorite ostrich or grouchy uncle starts reciting this poisonously treasonous nostrum, bemoaning the impossibility that democracy can survive inherent contradictions of human nature. Those repeating it deride our Great Experiment, chopping at its ankles, its morale. Lyrics pour from Fox News, co-owned by billionaire media moguls allied with foreign despots and the half of the rich who wallow in flatterers – unlike the other half, who do invest in endeavors, in philanthropy or work side-by-side with engineers.

I agree that Human Nature contains seeds of downfall. But it's not some mystical 200 year "cycle of democracy-decadence" that has no known examples from history. Rather, the almost ubiquitous pattern that proved ruinous is – I reiterate – the very one that an oligarchic putsch aims to re-establish... feudalism... letting small clades of delusional inheritance-lords rule by owner-whim.

Next we'll see why they mustn't win. Not just because they are wrong-headed and variously evil, but because they're stupid. Because they cannot see where it leads.

Allons enfants de la Patrie,
le jour de gloire est arrivé...

Fool me once…

Chapter 6

Credibility How Often the Right Has Just Been Wrong

Here I'll offer two lists concerning American conservatism. One recounts grownup and rational "conservative" stances that have always been welcome at the negotiating table. In fact we're poorer not to have such voices speaking up skeptically, even demanding accountability from… well… liberal zealotry.

The other list – alas – is much longer, presenting case after case in which conservatives wrecked their credibility by screaming against clear science, genuine progress or honesty itself. [120] In example after example, time proved them not just wrong, but calamitously and tendentiously wrong. From tobacco and smog to drug wars and gerrymandering, it's a litany our neighbors try desperately to forget.

And yes, there were *liberal errors.* Two of them on a par with any single item on the conservative list. I'll cite those also, down at bottom.

WHAT DEFENSIBLE – EVEN GOOD – IDEAS MIGHT CONSERVATIVES BRING TO THE TABLE?

In Chapters 13 & 19 I call for a Big Tent that *welcomes saner versions of conservatism*[121] – for example those reminding us that market competition is the great generator of wealth, the very wealth that then enables good things, like spending taxes to help poor kids. Indeed, before the

---

[120] http://davidbrin.blogspot.com/2017/12/the-pattern-from-jim-crow-to-smog.html
[121] http://davidbrin.blogspot.com/2019/05/crushing-crazy.html

movement was suborned by petro-sheiks, coal barons, casino moguls, mafiosi, inheritance brats, Wall Street shysters, tabloid monsters and re-branded KGB/Kremlin conspirators, there were American conservatives who held up *core conservative values (CCV)*, staking reasonable negotiating positions on:

– generating market alternatives to government solutions...

– reducing the overhead burden of excess paperwork...

– reduction in debt burdens passed to our children…

– individualism that transcends dogma or party lines…

– changing one's mind in the face of strong evidence…

– defending free trade between states and between nations…

– encouraging responsible gun ownership...

– encouraging genuine competition in flat-fair-open markets…

– encouraging fiscal responsibility with our tax dollars…

– encouraging voluntary service...

– encouraging startup entrepreneurship...

– encouraging home ownership and a rising middle class...

– investment in an educated/healthy workforce...

– investment in infrastructure...

– investment in federal R&D beyond most corporate ROI horizons...

– environmental stewardship...

– honest, long range thinking in board rooms...

– resistance to "picking winners and losers" – going there only for a clear, long range need (e.g. sustainable energy)...

– defending the right of millions to live demure lives without in-your-face shock confrontation.[122]

That list surely has our RASR friends nodding: "Okay, he gets it, somewhat." Moreover, if *you liberals* could not have compiled that list, while grudgingly admitting there's some wisdom there, then you've made no effort to understand your neighbors. You're thereby not just narrow-minded, but ill-equipped for today's struggles.

If that list were truly the essential manifesto of a sane-grownup American conservatism, there'd be room for negotiation! Indeed, we

---

[122] Referred to in the previous chapter as 'nagging.'

need for all of those imperatives to be presented cogently on the table. Only now the bad news.

Alas, out of all the goals listed above, only a bilious version of the last one remains in today's *mutant* conservatism. The rest have been functionally (if not polemically) dropped by the Republican-Confederate madness. And ironically, every item has been adopted by some or most sectors of a *liberalism* that already had plenty else on its plate. (And yes, *Democrats* did all the useful *de*-regulating, paperwork reduction, fiscal responsibility and defense of individualism; offer me wager stakes on that, please. See Chapters 8 & 10.)

Later on I will offer our Residually Adult-Sane Conservative friends a historical parallel for what they might consider trying, in order to recover those core conservative values and our respect… something the Democrats did to save *their* party, back in the "Miracle of 1947." That is, if those "sane conservatives" have guts.[123]

GOOD THINGS PROMISED... AND BETRAYED

Remember how I opened this book by citing Newt Gingrich's "Contract With America"? Have you looked again – or ever – at that masterful piece of polemical brilliance? Here are the "good parts" of that Contract the GOP never kept:

– require that laws that apply to the country also apply to Congress;
– arrange for regular audits of Congress for waste, fraud or abuse;
– limit terms of committee chairs and party leadership posts;
– ban the proxy votes in committee and law-writing by lobbyists;
– require committee meetings to be open & public;
– guarantee honest accounting of our federal budget.

Really, who could object to those items? Indeed, what could be a more powerful blow to the GOP than to remind Americans of such broken promises... and then *for Democrats to fulfill them* at long last? (While mocking the "bad" parts of the Contract that *were* fulfilled.)

Instead of railing at them uniformly, let's gall old Newt as he now sucks up to Trumpists, by reminding folks that about the quarter of the

---

[123] How mature conservatives might save US conservatism: http://www.davidbrin.com/nonfiction/1947.html

time he actually tried to get some stuff done, like negotiating some legislation and budget reform with President Bill Clinton. Imagine how that'd irk him.

Then bring in how Newt's the one who upped the savage war on facts, by dismissing the Office of Technology Assessment and other advisory boards that had an inconvenient habit of telling the truth.

SO WHAT'S THEIR TRACK RECORD?

Let's be clear. *U.S. Conservatives are in no position to lecture us,* given what they've let happen to their movement. Moreover, while conservative skepticism-toward-excess-bureaucracy is welcome, when it's sane, we need to recall how often they have been *wrong, wrong, wrong,* and again *wrong...* but want us to forget:

– Prohibition…

– Break up monopolies? Never! (And curse that class traitor Roosevelt!)

– Aid to farmers? Never! (And curse that *other* class betraying Roosevelt!)

– Tobacco? No worries... (cough)

– Acid Rain… then ocean acidification…

– Cars don't cause no smog!

– McCarthyism...

– Burning Rivers...

– Keep the lead in gasoline!

– The insane War on Drugs...

– Who needs seat belts in cars?

– Vietnam[124]...

– Resisting Civil Rights[125] and hating on MLK[126]...

– Watergate, defending Nixon long past proof of treason...

– Resisting women's rights...

– Throw into prison Vets with PTSD who get relief from marijuana…

---

[124] Vietnam was a bipartisan catastrophe. LBJ came that close to saving us from JFK's biggest mistake, then decided to stay. But there's one difference between parties *since* Vietnam. Democrats may wage war (See Chapter __), but they hate sending in whole armies. Republicans love it.

[125] Stomp flat every attempt to say Democrats are still the party of George Wallace and Republicans still the party of Lincoln. The flip is so blatant.

[126] … till suddenly you always loved him, right.

– Supply Side lies and outright theft of trillions...

– Resisting easy fixes to the ozone layer...

– Resisting mileage efficiency and safety in vehicles…

– Unleashing the surge in gambling, vice, and casino mafiosi...

– Climate change denialism and science hating...

– Claiming moral superiority while Red America scores worse in every category of turpitude, from teen sex/pregnancy/STD/abortions to gambling, domestic violence, divorce, alcoholism etc...

– *More* supply side so-called "economics"…

– Divorce was a bad thing, right? Till they realized the rate is far higher for top Republicans. *12* marriages among just Reagan, Hastert, Gingrich, McConnell, Trump…

– Most traitor spies since 1955 were Republican...

– Most child molester politicians...

– Iraq Wars, based on outright lies...

– Undermining energy independence...

– A proven track record of far worse economic outcomes[127]...

– Gerrymandering, crooked voting machines, voter suppression and other blatant cheats …

– Moscow-collusion and other blatant treasons...

– Birtherism and other hydrophobic Clinton-Obama jeremiads…

– Open war against all fact-centered professions; science, teaching, journalism, medicine, law and "deep state" public servants...

– Kowtowing to Vladimir Putin, Rupert Murdoch, Saudi princess, Wall Street parasites, inheritance brats & Trumps...

You know the list can go on and on. What kills is how blithely they shrug aside this past record, as if it bears no relevance to present credibility. But they know it does. Want proof? In the section on "Name an Exception!" I'll issue the following challenge. (And it was micro-glimpsed earlier.) But let's preview it here:

Name one top GOP leader between Eisenhower and Ryan who was even mentioned at the 2016 Republican Convention. Except for Reagan and Newt Gingrich, all were brushed under the rug, including both

---

[127] Outcomes comparison: http://davidbrin.blogspot.com/2014/06/so-do-outcomes-matter-more-than-rhetoric.html

Presidents Bush, Cheney, Rumsfeld, Dennis (convicted child molester) Hastert, Tom (convicted felon) DeLay, John Boehner and so on. That's how writhing ashamed Republicans are, of their record at governance.

But if you disavow those past Republican administrations as incompetent, Russia-hating, enterprise-destroying, warmongering liars, then where is your party's credibility? *Credibility?* What's that?

HOW CAN YOU BE WRONG SO OFTEN?

A dozen states have legalized marijuana for recreational use, and a dozen more allow prescription relief from pain, nausea and PTSD. It's a good time to wonder at the misery and lives lost to the insane "War on Drugs." Certainly, both parties initially took part in this mania that wracked our cities and sent billions into the pockets of the very worst humans. The issue isn't 'do we make mistakes?' but rather 'are we willing to let evidence of an obstinate error finally change our minds?'

I am reminded of the words of the great futurist, Alvin Toffler: "The illiterate of the 21st century will not be those who cannot read and write, but those who cannot learn, unlearn, and *relearn*."

An example that's so amusing… and biting. NPR recently reported that "John Boehner Was Once 'Unalterably Opposed' To Marijuana. He Now Wants It To Be Legal."[128] Ah, an example of Republican flexibility? Alas, read on about Boehner's close ties to a burgeoning cannabis industry. Moreover, the hypocrisy is even greater among our dear *libertarian friends*, who have long railed against the Drug War, but refuse to budge in their hate-Democrats-more-than-Republicans reflex, even after blue states have led the way against prohibition. (And are fiscally more responsible and have done more *de*regulating.)

How far back does it go? Climate denialism spews from some of the same ad agencies that promoted "tobacco is harmless," "cars don't cause smog," and "no seat belts in autos!" While waging open war on science, this cult sabotages research on whether America and our children and

---

[128] Boehner and pot. https://www.npr.org/2019/03/16/704086782/john-boehner-was-once-unalterably-opposed-to-marijuana-he-now-wants-it-to-be-leg

world are in danger from planet-changing pollution. (I'll discuss this in a soon to be released follow-up to this book.)

At age 19, I participated in the famous Clean Air Car Race,[129] which was covered every night on Walter Cronkite's CBS Evening News. Among many innovations, that transcontinental demo-rally featured the world's first hybrid car and several that disproved all the lies about unleaded gas then spread by SOBs who declared autos would shatter and capitalism collapse if lead were banned. Was our nationally viewed refutation effective? Within months after the race, a bill banning leaded gas emerged from committee, and twenty years after the U.S. banished that poison, *crime rates plummeted,* as lead-free children reached maturity with healthier brains.[130] Today bald eagles soar again, because we limited DDT. Folks eat fish caught along sweet riverbanks in downtown Pittsburgh, and every species of whale still exists… all because we acted on warnings… and no communist hell descended.

Dare we repeat that? Not a bit of the predicted communist hell descended, not even black UN helicopters. Though there *was a plague of amnesia,* as our rightist neighbors forget they were wrong about every one of those things.

See: "Toxic Sludge Is Good For You, which is a history of public relations."[131] as well as "How clean air transformed American cities."[132]

Like Supply Side Voodoo Economics… the 100% disproved assertion that giant tax gifts to the rich will get invested in productive new goods and services, rather than asset bubbles and hoard-slowed money velocity. Or that skyrocketing wealth disparities will somehow help generate a fecund, flat-fair-competitive market economy. *And if you tire of my repetition, then you don't get the main lesson of this book… that repetition is key to polemical victory!*

Do you recall when GOP masters forecast doom to the entire U.S. auto industry, if new efficiency standards were imposed? What were the

[129] Only decades later did I put together how seminal and important the Clean Air Car Race was. http://davidbrin.blogspot.com/2013/01/getting-lead-out-quirky-tale-of-saving.html

[130] See Neil Tyson's Cosmos episode about this. https://www.space.com/25579-cosmos-recap-earth-age-lead-poisoning.html

[131] Toxic Sludge Is Good For You, which is a history of public relations. https://www.prwatch.org/tsigfy.html

[132] https://www.salon.com/2019/03/17/how-clean-air-transformed-american-cities/

actual results of the Obama-Pelosi 2009 CAFÉ rules? Across-the-board improvement in our cars, which now have vastly higher quality in every category while actually *dropping* in year-adjusted price, compared to other costs of living, while saving consumers tens of billions at the pump. A win-win that the Trumpists are reversing... while liberals stupidly point *only* at the pollution aspects, instead of the big picture.

The U.S. military is made up of people who tend toward a crewcut-conservative personality. Yet, the officer corps is also *fact-centered.* The armed services were the first American institutions to realize that racism, and later sexism, simply *wasted talent* that skilled defenders could not afford to forego. Likewise, officers know that climate change is a real threat to the republic, and that foreigners meddling in our elections pose real danger, possibly at the level of war. Alas, do Republicans take the advice of soberly sagacious officers? No. The latest catechism spilling from Fox is that these men and women who serve and protect us – along with the intelligence agencies and FBI – are all conniving "deep state" enemies of Real America. [133]

I've been dancing around the big one. Climate Change. We'll get there later. But again we see that the special interests, lobbyists and ad agencies are still very much the same, using similar delaying tactics and incantations as for tobacco.

It's sad that RASR conservatives – many of whom I like – can never tabulate *how often their side has been flat-out wrong* and learn from this that they need to revise – not their best *Core Conservative Values,* but their reflexes and methodologies. And especially whom they accept as allies.

DEMOCRATS AREN'T ALWAYS RIGHT

After all of these examples, *should the conservative position always be discredited?*

Nonsense. Criticism makes us better and countless potential errors in liberal programs were detected in advance by constructively critical

[133] Again, never neglect the insipid complicity of liberals, who aren't leaping to embrace these desperately needed allies.

conservative colleagues... a help that the Republican Party *refused* during this century, under the "Hastert Rule." This led to some errors in Obamacare that had to be corrected later, again without GOP help.

An earlier point that I'll reiterate many times, aimed at every dogmatic purist out there: *Are you actually asserting that you are absolutely 100% right, with no margin of error?* Dig it (and this is good news!) Your enemies are likely no more than 99% wrong! Possibly as little as 50%, if you allow for all those shared instincts and reflexes (Chapter 2) and build common ground.

Moreover, have you the character strength to sift through your opponents' maelstrom of "wrongness" for those slivers where they actually had a point? Sure it sounds noxious, but they may be rewards! Not only will that boost your cred, when arguing with them, or convincing third parties that *you're* the reasonable one.

You may even discover one of your own errors to correct! Because – and hold on now – *you* are likely no more than 99% right! Possibly as little as 90%. And finding those errors isn't just a matter of honesty. It can help you (ultimately) to win.

Indeed, sometimes a conservative assertion proves correct! Take the greatest mistake of modern American liberalism, which badly hurt the movement, shattered the Greatest Generation's Rooseveltian coalition, and helped restart the Confederacy across America – an insanity called *desegregation by forced school busing.* It was an aggressively coercive lefty "innovation" of pyrotechnic stupidity, in which arrogant "reformers" stubbornly ignored every bit of evidence that their position was pigheaded and wrong. And above all, self-destructive. In the process, they handed the Republican Party thirty million or more formerly Democratic voters, an advantage the oligarchy has exploited, ever since.

Let me further avow (though it will cost me!) what anyone knows, who has spent time on a modern American university campus. There *are* dogmatic leftist bullies who routinely take over swathes of soft-studies departments, wherefrom they issue grand, post-modernist tracts denouncing the "colonialist" concept of objective reality. Suppressing open debate, they crow over campus-level PC victories[134] that have no pertinence or effects in the real world, but that *do* give Foxzoids plenty of ammo for hysterical finger-pointing: *"See? This is what liberals are like!"* Thanks… allies.

Universities should be places that encourage diversity, debate, and courage. For example, this article demands *affirmative action for conservatives* on college faculty.[135] "Liberal colleges are recruiting conservative professors to 'stir up some trouble.'"

While this book is 99% a tactical guide to defeating monstrous, right-wing confederatism, I am fine with inviting back to campus anyone who might talk again about those CCV values we viewed at the start of this chapter. Kewl! I love good debates. I want there to be fact-loving and cogently collegial conservative voices on campus. Alas, that the sub-species is now rare, verging on extinction. All the more reason to offer habitat and breeding grounds, free of rabid Fox disease.

Anyway, anecdotes about campus lefty-flakery have zero bearing on the vast majority of moderate-pragmatic, science and fact loving Democrats.

Sadly, "Ostrich Republicans" have one final incantation. Desperate to keep their heads buried in denial they chant: "I know my side has gone insane… but… but… but Democrats are worse! Yeah, that's the ticket! Democrats are just as crazy… or worse!"

Um… sorry, but *not.*

Ronald Reagan used to chant "I didn't leave the Democratic Party. The Democratic Party left me!" Then he proceeded to begin dismantling every aspect of the Rooseveltian social contract that the Greatest Generation – including activist young Ronald Reagan – helped to build.

---

[134] The entire "neocon" movement, which connived to justify both Iraq wars, had its roots in men like Nitze, Perle, Adelman, Wolfowitz etc., former students of a mad, ingrate-mesmerizing imperialist named Leo Strauss. When they were university professors, their views ranged from conservative to – well – unpleasantly right wing, but at least they faced arguments and reality checks by colleagues and students. But when their offices were trashed by jubilant activists, it proved *counterproductive* to chase them off-campus. Fleeing to faux academes like Heritage Foundation – echo chambers of servile oligarchic rationalization – these bright fools concocted fairy tales of prodigious insanity. We – and peoples of the Middle East – paid a steep price for those gleefully trashed offices. Congratulations on such 'victories.'

[135] "Liberal colleges are recruiting conservative professors… http://induecourse.ca/affirmative-action-for-conservative-academics/

You RASRs and ostriches out there, can you lift your head and look around? Blink in dismay and realize that *the Republican Party long ago left you*. It has left America, honesty and sanity.

Pause #6 for:

A few pertinent words from Jefferson, Lincoln and…

…and the best of all Roosevelts.

Using quotations from famous or pertinent people can at times be misleading… and it's not exactly 'judo.' Still, it can also give you nunchuks to use in a polemical knife fight.

Let's start with someone I'll return to, again and again. For the greatest polemical judo move is for liberals to rediscover a chief founder of their movement, whose deeply just and moral view of flat-fair-open competition has been mongrelized by rightist propaganda and spurned by dismal reflexes of an often ignorant left.

> *Our merchants and master-manufacturers complain much of the bad effects of high wages in raising the price, and thereby lessening the sale of their goods both at home and abroad. They say nothing concerning the bad effects of high profits. They are silent with regard to the pernicious effects of their own gains. They complain only of those of other people.*
>
> – Adam Smith, *The Wealth of Nations,* Chapter IX, p. 117.[136]

---

[136] A good source for all things adamsmithian – Http://adamsmithslostlegacy.blogspot.com/search/label/vile%20maxim

And then, alas too pertinent:

> *"To announce that there must be no criticism of the President, or that we are to stand by the President, right or wrong, is not only unpatriotic and servile, but is morally treasonable to the American public."*
> — Theodore Roosevelt

And now someone else I'll return to:

> *One thing I believe profoundly: We make our own history. The course of history is directed by the choices we make and our choices grow out of the ideas, the beliefs, the values, the dreams of the people. It is not so much the powerful leaders that determine our destiny as the much more powerful influence of the combined voices of the people themselves.*
> – Eleanor Roosevelt, *Tomorrow Is Now* (1963).

And a perfect answer to "originalists"

> *"I am not an advocate for frequent changes in laws and constitutions, but laws and institutions must go hand in hand with the progress of the human mind, as that becomes more developed, more enlightened, as new discoveries are made, new truths discovered and manners and opinions change. With the change of circumstances, institutions must advance also to keep pace with the times. We might as well require a man to wear still the coat which fitted him when a boy as civilized society to remain ever under the regimen of their barbarous ancestors."*
> – Thomas Jefferson

And getting to the "mob" rationalization that oligarchs must cheat and rule for everyone's sake.

> *"You only get 'the wisdom of crowds' if the crowd has knowledge and power. But while elites officially proclaim devotion to crowd wisdom, they obsessively dread 'mindless mobs,' who must be denied knowledge or power."*
>
> – Allen Bryan

...and what the heck? How about some (bitter) humor?

1. Arizona draws 17% of its electricity from coils arrayed around the spinning in Barry Goldwater's grave. And New York draws 7.2% of its power from William F. Buckley. They pay Rupert Murdoch to keep those old-style, intellectual and honest conservatives spinning away.

2. One fellow commented over drinks on all the hurrow over how President Obama - inexperienced amid his first months in office - bowed a bit too low when greeting the Saudi King. "You don't see the same fuss over pictures of George Bush, walking hand-in hand with Saudi princes. Heck there's even a picture of Bush actually kissing the Saudi king... on the mouth!"

To which another fellow replied: "Well... in fairness... have you seen him?"

REVISITING THE GETTYSBURG ADDRESS

Here's something to try. I've asked folks to take a minute.[137] Read again or hear a great actor speak aloud Lincoln's Gettysburg Address[138] - only this time envision he's talking to you, right now. No squinting. No adjustments or allowances for time or context. Simply talking exactly to and about us, right now. It's shockingly pertinent.

"Now we are engaged in a great civil war, testing whether that nation, or any nation so conceived and so dedicated, can long endure."

---

[137] Gettysburg riff taken from https://medium.com/@david.brin/neither-side-owns-patriotism-9cd25cdf1506

[138] https://www.independent.co.uk/news/world/americas/abraham-lincoln-birthday-gettysburg-address-civil-war-us-president-trump-a8206946.html

Amen. In this latest phase of an ongoing, 250-year-old culture war, we are struggling against real enemies of this great experiment, to ensure "that this nation, under God, shall have a new birth of freedom." ...

Moreover, if you can feel the power of the Great Emancipator pouring through you, read it aloud to that teetering RASR (Residually Adult-Sane Republican) ... and explain that yes, this is how we feel, ever more, each day in the face of soul-destroying, nation-wrecking treason by a madness that – like the 1860s Confederacy – is without any moral foundation, whatsoever. Tell your ostrich Republican friends, they need to choose sides in this potentially lethal phase of our endless Civil War.

Make no mistake. Our enemies' aim is the same as always – as Putin made clear when he laughed and told his puppet that the great "liberal experiment" was obsolete.[139] He doesn't mince words. His axis of Kremlin-KGB agents, oligarchs, Saudi princes, casino moguls, carbon barons, mafiosi, Wall Street cheaters, communist despots, Fox liars and inheritance brats – they plan to ensure...

– that government of the people, by the people, for the people, shall perish from the Earth.

AND FINALLY

... one by Alasdair Gray – relayed by my colleague, author Ken McLeod[140] – that sums everything so-concisely and optimistically, but with a slightly science-fictional flair:

"Work as if you lived in the early
days of a better nation."

And returning to the best Roosevelt...

"In the final analysis, a democratic
government represents the sum total of the

---

[139] Putin, in an interview with the Financial Times, meant a far broader definition of the term – the entire experiment in "liberal" democracy, flat-fair markets, open accountability, free speech and all the other innovations pushed by Locke, Adam Smith and the U.S. founders. Its day is done, he declared, confidently. https://www.bbc.com/news/world-europe-48795764

[140] http://kenmacleod.blogspot.com/

courage and the integrity of its individuals.

It cannot be better than they are."

– Eleanor Roosevelt, *Tomorrow Is Now (1963),*

From a posting in June 2019 – if you can believe that.[141]

Chapter 7

Oh, the Conspiracies!

Travel anywhere in the world, visit a bar, pub, barbecue or someone's house or hut – you'll find one topic easy to spark: conspiracy. No matter the nation, tribe or ethnicity, folks will quickly rail about some group grudge and how "people like me" are being put upon by conniving adversaries who are simultaneously evil and almost super-naturally clever. *The world may be filled with fools who believe the cover story. But my brave and savvy folk see the truth!*

Naturally, *those foes* flatter themselves in exactly the same way, both sides muttering fill-in-the-blanks tales, as if from a giant book of Mad-Libs. Texts from olden times reveal the same pattern. Ah, should humans be known as *Homo credens*, the credulous ape?

No wonder the age of science seems threatening to many, whose favorite fantasies might shrivel under the light of evidence. I wrote *The Transparent Society* about how open and reciprocal accountability often reveals what's true, rather than what feels so satisfying to believe.

Alas, there truly *are* conspirators in this world, flourishing wherever light doesn't shine. Moreover, they developed a great technique to distract from their own plots – they *help spread* a stinging miasma of paranoid ravings that genuine schemes can hide behind! (See it illustrated in this stand-alone scene from *Existence*.[142]) Indeed, the last thing you will contemplate is that *your* favorite conspiracy might be part of that distraction fog.

METHODS TO SIFT WHICH PLOTS SEEM PLAUSIBLE

Dip your toe. Any conspiracy theory will suck you into a vortex of evidence and "evidence" along with persuasive rants and incantations. *Who*

---

[141] http://davidbrin.blogspot.com/2019/06/oh-conspiracies.html

[142] https://www.wattpad.com/5827990-the-smartest-mob-a-chapter-from-existence

has the time? Even for ones that appeal to my ego, my prejudices, or my "side" in contemporary tiffs. Hence, I cope via a set of questions to ask, whenever some folks – especially those who are "like me" – foist their favorite Evil Plot That Only We Can See. Let's start with an example that may *infuriate* many of you.

Question number one: Have trustworthy experts already worked the case? Are they accountable, transparent, and themselves scrutinized by a variety of interests? Are they answerable to multiple, separate structures? This is, after all, one reason we set up civil service with a diversity of agencies and chains of command – then augmented that setup with a free and diverse press – then augmented *that* with a wide range of member-supported NGOs, from Greenpeace to the Electronic Frontier Foundation.

(And if you aren't a dues paying member of a dozen NGOs, each fighting for a future *you* believe in, then take another look at the hypocrite in the mirror. That method is a lazy person's cheap route to bragging rights: "I'm at least doing something." Here's how.[143])

Of course, this network of accountability systems is exactly what conspiracy believers claim *has failed.* Indeed, they hold that such a thing – accountability through competitive openness – is impossible. Certainly Hollywood portrays accountable professionalism to be nonexistent in government. Writers and directors do this often *not* to promote SoA, but for reasons of lazy plotting that I describe elsewhere.[144] And in so doing, they spread a poison.

To be clear, betrayal by governmental powers belongs way up there on our list of things to watch for! Take the way one man – J. Edgar Hoover – for decades dominated the top layers of U.S. federal criminal investigation, often deciding to pursue or quash cases at whim. Still, we have inarguably the least corrupt institutions in the history of humanity. (If you doubt that, do try slipping a fifty to that cop giving you a ticket.) So, while *Mr. Transparency,* here extols "sousveillance" and looking-back at power, I am also skeptical toward raving paranoia.

---

143 "The Power of Proxy Activism." http://www.davidbrin.com/nonfiction/proxyactivism.html

144 "The idiot plot: why films never show competence." http://www.davidbrin.com/idiotplot.html

Which is not *entirely* a symptom of the mad right! Take the lefty "Loose Change" conspiracy theory, about the 9/11 calamity – that the World Trade Center towers were deliberately demolished by explosives planted over the course of months, to distract from the *intended target,* WTC building #7. Among dozens of ways that theory is loony, explosives leave chemical residues, and the wreckage was sampled not by one agency, but scores of them plus news organizations, NGOs and private citizens. Moreover, there was no lack of available debris to analyze.[145]

Question number one allows you to deal with some, not all, of the most ridiculous purported plots – those *presuming there are no competent people in the world.* Which brings us to –

Test #2: How many conspirators are needed by this scheme? How perfect a plan and execution? Loose Change is an extremum test case for these questions. It would take dozens, even scores of the most skilled experts in building demolition to plant the required explosives, and others skilled at *hiding* charges behind walls and in stand pipes, plus dozens more providing security.[146] The entire WTC security staff must be suborned or replaced, but there's no record of such replacements. (Most died in the disaster.) That's at least a hundred henchmen, performing a task never done before amid vacuum-tight secrecy and executed with perfection never seen in any government project. Oh, plus *another* several hundred to perform the bizarre other half of this theory, faking the aircraft hijackings!

Now, you might answer: "I don't believe in the Loose Change conspiracy! Whereas MY favorite one…" Hm, well, show me even one popular conspiracy theory cult that has analyzed points number one and two? Then of course there's right wing dizziness such as the mania that swarms over the death of ex-DNC staffer Seth Rich. But we deal with Clinton-Obama tirades in due course.

In Chapter 5 we discussed ravings of a "Deep State" conspiracy among civil servants, FBI agents, the entire intelligence community and much of the senior military officer corps, in cahoots with nearly all the scien-

---

[145] Don't get me started on the "melting temperature of steel" drivel that's fountained by fools.
[146] You'd also need electronic timing and ignition systems similar to those used in nuclear bombs.

tists, journalists, teachers and so on… another case where tests #1 and #2 are devastating. Which brings us to –

#3: *Why* would the conspirators choose to do it? What would convince each and all of them to betray his or her oaths, profession, conscience and country? I'm not saying it doesn't happen! The Watergate break-ins and cover-ups involved a fair number of moderately (not very) skilled people who did it all for combinations of money, hatred, loyalty-to-a-faction and potential advancement to power.

Let me repeat: *I know there are conspiracies!* Indeed, it's laughable to ignore the most blatant one called Fox News, which openly works for a mélange of foreign billionaires, from the Saudis to Russian mafiosi, from Macao casino lords to an Australian deceit mogul. We'll get to their motives and methods in several chapters. And lest we forget, the left was rife with secret foreign agents and nasty plots, at times in the last century… and may go down that path, yet again.

Still test #3 is a potent one. In our extreme example, none of the "Loose Change" zealots offer a plausible reason why even *one* skilled person would be remotely tempted to devote immense energy and dedication to performing such a heinous act on behalf of some currency speculators, let along several hundred of our most capable public servants or officers.

Money? Please. That you would assume so speaks more about *your* inherent corruptibility, than theirs. Which brings us to a really big one –

#4: Why take the risk? Loose Change offers such a great example of every maniacally stupid conspiracy theory trait. And so, ponder a thought that would go through the mind of every skilled conspirator:

These fellows working on this evil plot next to me… any one of them could have recorded our activities and conversations. An hour from now, that fellow over there may spill it all to the FBI and the New York Times. He'll be a hero, get rewards and speaking gigs and be on talk shows forever, while the rest of us get arrested, tried and then parceled out to prisons where both the inmates and guards will make life hell for traitors and attempted mass murderers.

At which point he'd think: *"Maybe… I better be the guy who blabs first."*

Seriously, how do you stop defections? Communists were dedicated, yet we pulled in defectors all the time. ISIS and Al Qaeda are zealous, yet they leaked like sieves. Yes, you can both inspire and terrify your henchmen into mass-uniformity *if you run a powerful state like China, Russia, or Saudi Arabia or a narco-kleptocracy,* where their families can be crushed at will. But show me how that would work in a Loose Change scenario.

Seth Rich? Seriously? Show me a Democrat who can keep his or her damn mouth shut! Now show me the *dozens* who would have to be complicit, from local law enforcement to the nearby FBI bureau office, to the victim's family.

Again, I'm not saying conspiracies don't happen. But consider, the first thing any conspirator with an IQ above slime-mold does is to *establish murder insurance.* You do this by setting up delay-drops containing everything you know, to be released in the event anything happens to you. Don't these people ever watch movies?

Question #4 – is the biggie. As a society we should be making it our top transparency priority to reinforce it, by *encouraging, not punishing* ***whistle blowers.*** Elsewhere (Chapter 5) I describe ways to do this that could be entirely consistent with running a healthy and effective civil service. We should do this via both law and via private foundations that offer what I've called "Henchman's Prizes."[147]

One urgent example? It has long been blatantly clear that several of the manufacturers of *voting machines* in the U.S. have suspicious connections to both Russia and the Republican Party. Is it coincidence that in most "blue" states, the voting machines are augmented by paper ballots or receipts that can be hand counted and audited, while most red states have refused that simple confidence and security backup? As of this writing, nothing has been revealed that is prosecutable – just a stench of the sort that propels so many conspiracy theories.

But the stink got overwhelming in August 2019, when voting machines in Texas and Mississippi were caught blatantly switching votes before the voter's eyes. (See videos of it happening! [148] But don't worry.

---

[147] "Attention Henchmen! Voting Machines and Other Flawed Conspiracies." http://davidbrin.blogspot.com/2012/10/attention-henchmen-voting-machines-and.html

[148] Red state voting machines caught switching votes on camera. https://www.newsweek.com/touch-screen-voting-devices-are-automatically-changing-votes-mississippi-1456445

They'll remedy the "blatantly" part and hide it from the voter in the booth.)

Dig this about plausible conspiracies and Question #4. One rich dude might possibly *fix* voting machine treason, by offering a $5 million whistleblower prize – plus guaranteed protection and hero status – for the employee of any company who brings forth proof of cheating. If proof doesn't appear, you don't pay! (But nevertheless instill fear in those bastards.) If you *do* wind up paying, you become a hero for saving the nation. How can that not be a win-win?

The easier we make it for henchmen to defect, the fewer of them Blofeld, Dr. Evil and their ilk will be able to hire and trust.[149] And so, we come to –

#5: Who benefits? Oliver Stone slandered LBJ as the *obvious* beneficiary of JFK's murder. It sounds movie-plausible, till you realize how desperately Johnson slaved and strived (and aged), aiming to make all of Kennedy's hopes and plans come true. Alas, that included JFK's horrific-macho ambitions in Vietnam, but also – on the brighter side – civil rights, the vastly-if-still-partially-successful War on Appalachian Poverty, achievements in space and so on. Is that utter loyalty to every goal consistent with spite and conspiracy to murder? (See Bryan Cranston's film, *All the Way*.)

In fact, I've never found anyone who palpably *benefited* from the Kennedy assassination, though *revenge* is another matter. JFK had haters, ranging from Cuban communists and Cuban *anti*-communist exiles to the KGB, to the KKK, to the Mafia, to Marilyn Monroe fans… all the way to the armed, dangerously loony, individually motivated and perfectly situated expert marksman Lee Harvey Oswald.[150]

On the other hand, other conspiracies have blatant beneficiaries. Fox News has been a money machine for Rupert Murdoch and his partners (who for many years included Saudi royals). Even more important, it

---

[149] http://davidbrin.blogspot.com/2012/10/attention-henchmen-voting-machines-and.html

[150] "Who benefits" can be extended to plotters who *thought* they would benefit, but failed. Far more plausible than Oliver Stone's insipid scenario (based on zero real evidence) that JFK was about to pull out of Vietnam, consider the very opposite, that some U.S. officers saw we were heading into a quagmire and sought to eliminate the uber-macho leader who was plunging us into a devastating mess. Do I believe this? Of course not. But I can concoct paranoid scenarios far better than those going stale on our DVD shelves.

helped sustain the Supply Side "Voodoo" Economics (SSVE) cult[151] long after that madness was scientifically refuted, allowing Murdoch's pals to raid the US taxpayer time and again, for trillions. Above all, by fomenting culture war – also known as phase 8 of the U.S. civil war (Chapter 14) – Murdoch's shills have accomplished his top goal: the destruction of U.S. politics as a means for adults to deliberate policy and negotiate solutions across party lines. *Gridlock* is the goal, along with demolition of any trust between the people and the government that they own. So yes, that conspiracy passes the "who benefits" test.

Note that all five of these questions, so far, are simple and straightforward, and make demands upon the conspiracy ranters, not upon you. Which brings us to –

#6: *Who* is strenuously keeping things dark? We don't know for sure (yet) that there was direct collusion between Donald Trump and the Kremlin. But Trump's absolute refusal to allow any look into his finances, or his behaviors in Moscow, or during half a dozen secret debriefings with foreign despots that lacked any credible U.S. witnesses, show someone who is desperate not to allow light onto those topics.

Now add his obstruction of professional investigations and you have behavior that is certainly far more consistent with a conspiracy than most of the fantasies boiling around.

#7: Is there a devastating rebuttal/answer to the Conspiracy Theory? Is there a short, sharp shock that would tear it to shreds?

We already illustrated this one with a crushing example – when yarn-pinning ravers persuaded millions that *George Soros* is diabolical meddler *so powerful he toppled Eight Foreign Governments!* In Chapter 5, I posed a simple question that not a single audience member *or* Beck-critic ever asked: "Say Glenn, how about *naming* those foreign regimes that George Soros toppled?"

There's a reason Beck never said their names. Because doing so would devastate his entire conspiracy narrative beyond all hope of recov-

[151] The stunningly perfect record of Supply Side *always* being 100% wrong. http://davidbrin.blogspot.com/2010/02/a-primer-on-supply-side-vs-demand-side.html

ery. Take that example to heart. Ponder whether the next conspiracy offered to you has such an Achilles Heel.

#8: Am I doing due diligence by weighing critics of this thing and seeking smart/balanced arbiters? I can almost guarantee you aren't. Heck, I'm lazy too. Still, I offered a number of ways that our modern fact-arbitrating systems can be improved, not by ensconcing some elites to rule on Truth, but using the competitive/adversarial process we're already so good at.

I pitched some of these ideas at Facebook headquarters in 2017, when the company was panicking over its role in 2016 election travesties. Alas, soon they were smugly back to assuring "We can handle this top-down, trust us."

How's that going for you?

#9: Why should we trust *your* elites? In Chapter 2, I spoke of the central message in most Hollywood films – Suspicion of Authority, or SoA, which has amplified the conspiracy-antennae, especially in most Americans. The basic difference between a decent, rational liberal and a decent, rational conservative is *which* group they worry is conspiring to become Big Brother.

Of course, given human history, we ought to conclude that *all elites are inherently dangerous.* All will be tempted to abuse power, while rationalizing that it is for the greater good. Ideally, we warily guard each other's backs. Ideally. Our systems were set up by very clever people so that elites will *compete* with each other! In their rivalry – sometimes called *separation of powers* – we have found a way to prevent any one of them from becoming an Orwellian monolith.

So yes, examine conspiracy theories! I concoct and promulgate some, in both fiction and nonfiction. And if you'll have a look at mine, I'll have a gander at yours. It's how we managed to stay free. So far.

That synergy breaks down when – amid re-ignited civil war – one side has convinced all its partisans that freedom can be harmed *only* from one direction. I regularly make efforts to prove I do *not* have such a fused political spine – that I can turn my head. While I declare – based on mountains of proof – that today's American right has gone insane, in service to a rising oligarchy bent on re-starting feudalism…

...I often eviscerate shibboleths of a much smaller loony far-left, and urge sane liberals to be wary of those allies. (See Chapter 12 and this: The miracle and compromise of 1947.[152])

THESE TESTS ARE ONLY A START

Are there conspiracies? Of course! Our civilization is threatened by some as we speak. It is to distract from real ones that so many false imbecilities are spewed. These questions won't eliminate or parse them all. Again, I show some scary places this can lead in my novel *Existence.*

Over the long run, we must employ experts whose job it is to inspect possible crimes, both investing some trust in the skilled professionalism of our civil servants *and* striving to increase their diverse accountability, their sense that they live and work under scrutiny and light. Only with this combination of high professionalism and fierce citizen oversight do we stand a chance of navigating a bright but ever foggy era.

---

[152] The miracle and compromise of 1947. http://www.davidbrin.com/1947.html

And more pattern-seeking mumbo jumbo…

Pause #7 for…

Bad History-Patterns Part 2: Marx, Spengler and a "Fourth Turning"[153]

Earlier we looked at a silly notion that too many folks fall for – *that history runs in patterns and even predictable cycles.* We dissected the "Tytler Calumny" and the "Fatal Sequence" – touchstones of modern conservative cant.[154] Now we'll expand on that. But first let's admit *the Left can also go all teleological and mystical!*

True believers of the Right tend to clutch *cyclic* models, like Tytler's. Cyclicalists see the past as endlessly repeating some fore-doomed pattern. ("What was, will be.") Adolf Hitler adopted Hanns Hörbiger's Welteislehre or "World ice theory" as the Nazis' official cosmology, proclaiming that a series of ice moons had fallen upon Earth to smash decadent civilizations, resetting the clock for hardy Nordic folk to thrive.[155]

In contrast, Marx and most leftists saw history as something to be built upon, propelled ever upward by unstoppable historical forces. Their hypnotic forecasts about the inevitable future path of human development[156] may not have been cyclical, but they were just as tendentiously hallucinatory, built upon a series of fabulated just-so stories that were then twisted (by more ruthless men) to excuse mass murder.

Call it nostalgist-romantics versus transcendentalist-romantics. A real difference… among mad cousins.

---

[153] Partial extracts from a 2009 posting: "Contemptuous Memes Part II: "Cycles of History." http://davidbrin.blogspot.com/2009/11/contemptuous-memes-part-ii-cycles-of.html

[154] Tytler and the Fatal Sequence. http://davidbrin.blogspot.com/2012/10/the-tytler-insult-is-democracy-hopeless.html

[155] By the way, this utterly smashes the incantation that "Nazis were a phenomenon of the left." As if that catechism weren't already demolished by the Night of the Long Knives and by the support given Hitler by Junkers caste German aristocrats, who thought they could control a populist monster.

[156] See this illustrated in the Strugatski Brothers' famous, Soviet era science fiction novel "Hard to be a God."

Oh, it may be that many *dynasties* grew decadent and foppishly failed over a roughly five-generation time frame (though tell it to the Plantagenets, or to Venice). Even so, the overall cultures of which they were part tended to go on over much longer time scales. Indeed, the West at large only "fell" once. And then, only if you ignore the whole eastern half of the Mediterranean.

History is rife with disasters! The non-cyclical causes vary. UCLA's Jared Diamond wrote in Collapse: How Societies Choose to Fail or Succeed.[157]) that nations often toppled into ruin by ignoring their own damage to the ecosystems supporting them, as when poorly drained irrigation transforms fertile ground into deserts. More generally, the great historian Arnold Toynbee's twelve volume Study of History (1934-61) presented the trajectories of 26 civilizations which he saw arising when «creative minorities» inspired unprecedented effort to solve difficult challenges. Societies fail, in Toynbee›s view, when the creative minority wanes or loses society›s support. Notice that both failure modes are consistent with the culprit I most blame – incestuously inbred, critic-suppressing, opportunity-stifling oligarchy.

But teleology fetishism keeps swarming over us. Almost a century ago, all the chattering classes were abuzz over Oswald Spengler's book, *The Decline Of The West*, which claimed that the First World War was sure evidence of Western Civilization's imminent collapse from senescence and decadence. Oh, sure, in Spengler's time the faults and contradictions of nationalism, capitalism, oligarchy and primitive economies failed to cope with an onrushing tide of powerful technologies and rising mass-expectations. The world did spiral into hell across the first half of the Twentieth century. But there was nothing *decadent* about how western democracies dynamically bounced back, smashed Hitler, then chose Marshall's path of steady strength and development-through-trade, as a strategy for dealing with communist expansionist empires. If decadence consists of getting 90% of world's children into lit homes with schoolbooks, exploring the solar system and the cell and the atom, purging ourselves of many age-old prejudices, liberating education, loosening the guild-constraints on expert

---

[157] "Collapse: How Societies Choose to Fail or Succeed." http://www.davidbrin.com/nonfiction/collapse.html

knowledge and accomplishing more than all other societies, combined – well, then here's to decadence!

It's easy to laugh at Spengler now. (Spengler also said that "optimism is cowardice." What a maroon.) Though one does feel a chill in the air as, periodically, our country and civilization toys with cowardice and rejection of progress. Contempt for the Masses combines with our human propensity for pattern-recognition, as we sometimes cry "Aha! I see what's happening!"[158] Ironically it's many of those who just a while ago proclaimed *"morning in America!"* – who now nostalgically grouse: *"we're past our prime."*

CYCLES OF GENERATIONS?

The latest cyclical pattern making the rounds? It mixes the usual pessimist-determinist view with dollops that are oddly hopeful and even quite rousing. My friend, international economic pundit John Mauldin, is (in his words) *"a huge fan of the work of Neil Howe. His book The Fourth Turning, has turned out to be stunningly prophetic. Uncomfortably so. A roughly 80 year cycle has been repeating itself for centuries in the Anglophile world, broken up into four generations or turnings. We have begun what Howe calls The Fourth Turning."*

First, I'm unimpressed with this cult classic. My own record,[159] back around 1980 predicting the fall of the Berlin Wall, a false Fukayaman "end of history," then a hyped-up tussle with macho Islam, followed by a fast-rising China – is inarguably far more specific and far better than Howe and Strauss. Heck, many of my Science Fiction writing colleagues have done better, too.[160]

To be clear, there *are* enticing patterns in *The Fourth Turning*, e.g. the roughly eighty year (a human lifetime) span separating the American Revolution from the Civil War, then to the Depression/WWII crisis, then the one supposedly sweeping on us now. All true! But does a pattern make cause-and-effect? According to Strauss & Howe, in each case (1) "Heroes"

---

[158] And – mea culpa – I have my own schtick, portraying Rupert Murdoch as Jefferson Davis.

[159] One of four "World's Best Futurists." https://theurbandeveloper.com/articles/five-worlds-best-futurists plus TIME Magazine listed Earth as one of "8 books that eerily predicted the future." http://time.com/5380613/books-predict-future/

[160] SF gets no respect!

stoically and courageously resolved the emergency, then strove to raise their kids in security *they* never knew. A security that turned the next immediate clades into (2) a stifled, silent generation (e.g. kids of the 1940s and 1950s), followed by (2) rebellious, individualist, transcendentalist egomaniac "prophets" (the Boomers), followed by a "nomad" generation (Gen X, including its first president, Obama) which grew up under chaotic home lives...

...followed by another «hero» generation, that will presumably fix the mess created by us boomers.[161] "The Baby Boomers will still be tearing and screaming at each other, when they are hobbling around retirement homes." And yes, that's one diagnosis I think Strauss & Howe get spot on.

Why, if I acknowledge a pattern, do I diss the pattern-explainers? Because *patterns are just stories, till subjected to the critical-adversarial appraisal of science.* Because Strauss & Howe are doing what humans do; we look for and then find (voila!) exactly the 'cycles' that we seek. When an ancient oracle (on rare occasion) correctly forecast an empire's fall, was it because of truth hidden in tea leaves or the flights of birds? A statistical fluke? Or self-fulfilling?

Far more important are those great warnings – many of them from science fiction – that have helped forestall the very danger they point at. It's exactly the role for a "creative minority" that Toynbee prescribed, and a topic I explore at length elsewhere. See: "George Orwell and the Self-Preventing Prophecy." [162]

No, what tars fellows like Strauss & Howe – aside from guilt-by-association with their biggest fan, Steve Bannon[163] – is that their cyclical *determinism* portrays at least 16 generations of English speakers as programmable

---

[161] Hard to do, if this crisis involves nuclear weapons, designer bugs and ecological collapse. How much better to avoid the 'crisis' altogether, which we seemed on track to do, before it was deliberately provoked and engineered.

[162] "George Orwell and the Self-Preventing Prophecy." http://www.davidbrin.com/nonfiction/1984.html

[163] Steve Bannon's fetish for the "Fourth Turning" disturbed Straus & Howe. But this is what you get with magical pattern incantations. Asimov's "psychohistory" inspired Paul Krugman and great visionaries and sages... as well as Osama bin Laden and Shoko Asahara, but Isaac never claimed a god's eye view. What merits inspection – and derision – is Bannon's openly-stated goal to *provoke* the Great Crisis, whether or not it would have happened without his treasonous oligarchic putsch. (It likely would not have.) But it gets better. By fashioning himself in the pattern of his look-alike – Martin Borman – Bannon made himself an object of intense hate from the very same young generation that he (a typically sanctimonious boomer) hopes to spur into becoming heroes! Ironies are nested there, at least three-deep. https://ieet.org/index.php/IEET2/print/12778

Skinner pigeons, not loosely knit creatures of a self-organizing pack. No, apparently we're herd beasts, bound by the exact topography of this decade's rigid migratory path.

They ignore (among many things) that it's a vast population of Boomers and Gen-Xers in the civil service, sciences, professions and officer corps who are holding things together, in the age of Trump. *We already have heroes.* Hence, the patterns they describe aren't America.

They do fit the Confederacy.

SOME PATTERNS, NO CYCLES

Oh, ironies pile upon ironies. For example, there is zero evidence that the West or America would be in "crisis" today without deliberate, malign aggression by forces external to our enlightenment experiment, tearing us down from our 1990s zenith. Steve Bannon brags about this, roaming the globe, setting fires and encouraging fascist populisms in countries from Hungary to Thailand. And yes, his targets for roused fervor against the West's incipient utopia are – I'll avow – some fellow grouchy, self-indulgent boomers.

Do I hold out hope for ultimate rescue by Millennial and Generation Z "heroes"? Sure. Those whom I have met are better, smarter and nicer than anything. Heroic courage remains to be seen. (See footnote 163.)

But in fact, I deem illusory "cycles" far less rewarding than the notion of "attractor states"... or pitfalls that seem relentlessly to pull in cultures, because of repetitive traits in human nature. Oligarchic feudalism is one such attractor. (Find exceptions: agrarian societies that avoided this trap. I can name only eight, and just three of any importance.) Another attractor is fear-driven tribal xenophobia. Machismo is one more. Put a dozen or so of these together and you start getting a really good picture of our tragic history. And yes, because these themes keep recurring, matters can thus look a bit cyclical. But that's like saying the fundamental reason that a car moves is because the wheels turn.

Leadership also matters. Athenian democracy did not fail till Pericles died, and then just barely. Moreover, that is where miracles keep happening to America, which keeps finding *new* attractor states.... bad presidents are followed by good ones, citizenship triumphs (barely) over anomie and cynicism, and seminal decisions transform the world.

Above all, even if there are cyclical 'wheels' that take us round and round, we are the new beings that our parents – and their parents – strove to build. And so maybe we... or our kids... can learn to steer.

This Chapter began in 2008 as a posted danger-warning[164] to congressfolk who were newly elected that year, but it grew in scope and universal relevance. In fact, I've felt guilty for not pushing the alert harder. It is my chief reason for putting together a collection and book. And yes, it segues directly off the previous chapter on conspiracies.

We all think we have the world sussed, seeing things that others don't. As an author of techno-thrillers I'm pretty well-informed about dangers looming ahead. But our biggest threat may be as old as civilization itself.

Chapter 8

Poison and Antidote – Blackmailers, Henchmen and Whistleblowers

Dear newly minted representative or official, freshly arrived in Washington D.C.,[165]

I want to talk to you about a terrible danger – and opportunity – that crosses party lines. We'll be dealing with traits like *honor* and *pragmatism*, *cynicism* and *patriotism*, *cynical self-protection*... and *courage*. While negotiating the ethical and political minefield that is Washington, always remain wary of a particular worst-case scenario... one that can systematically undermine even the most well-meaning public servants.

A LITTLE BACKGROUND

All of you enthusiastic neophytes to national power – this may be the very moment for a little protective paranoia. Always remember that

---

164 "Political Blackmail: The Hidden Danger to Public Servants." http://www.davidbrin.com/nonfiction/blackmail.html

165 Note that government officials are far from the only people available as targets! Anyone in command of critical infrastructure is on the list. Power plant operators. Commercial IT providers. Website gurus. News organizations. Indeed one of the most chilling predictive novels of science fiction – The Cool War, by Frederik Pohl, foresaw an attrition campaign of reciprocal sabotage that could – short of nuclear conflict – grind all sides down to poverty. Highly recommended. The book, not the war.

some powerful people will see you as a threat to their interests. Some of the more unscrupulous may seek to neutralize that threat, using classic methods, known across history. One of the most basic ancient techniques – going back to biblical times – has been *entrapment* and *blackmail*.

Remember the U.S. Marine guards at our embassy in Moscow, some decades back? It all started when a few boys – lonely and far from home – were invited to party with some local "students." A little alcohol, then sex with local hookers... were followed by a drug high or two... and a few lewd pictures... then some incriminating ones...

At any point, early on, those young men could have saved their own lives and served their country, simply by turning themselves in. The first to do so might even have saved his career. Others could have escaped with minor punishments. Instead, alas, they let themselves be blackmailed, by gradual stages, into doing the KGB "just a couple of harmless favors"...

... *relatively* harmless, at first. Xeroxing a few embassy visitor lists. Penny-ante stuff. Only then, the Soviets had *real* dirt on the poor fellows. Proof of espionage that could produce real prison time. And meanwhile the girls and drugs kept coming. Plus flattery. («You are special, James Bond types – above normal loyalties and laws." Very similar patterns of ego-milking helped to suborn the Walkers and that dismal FBI agent, Hanssen.) Soon, those marines were trapped. Fully in the pockets of their nation's enemies, they were betraying really harmful secrets.

DO YOU DOUBT IT STILL GOES ON?

Security experts and intelligence agents know all about this process, which has been used by kingdoms, empires, syndicates and unscrupulous groups since time immemorial. Indeed, all through World War Two and the Cold War, it was a key job of counter-intelligence professionals to watch carefully for hints of *subornation*. They collected and correlated patterns of travel, or unaccountable wealth, or crony-favoritism, keeping a wary eye open for anything consistent enough to merit closer scrutiny.

So now? Does it really matter that our roster of "enemies" has changed a bit? The KGB is "gone." But there are others – some of them heirs of past enemies, employing the very same agents and methods – who do not want our civilization to thrive. Or who would influence our top decision-makers in order to be better parasites. Anyone who thought this classic danger ended with the Cold War has to be titanically naive.

Moreover, consider this: *Bribery is actually far less efficient and reliable than blackmail!*

If you bribe an official or legislator or bureaucrat, they may demand more next time. Or else say "I helped you enough this year." But *blackmail puts them in your pocket for good.* It transforms the relationship, making him or her less a business associate and more the blackmailer's personal servant.

Has this scenario already been in play, among members of the present ruling caste?

Of course, the imagination can run wild – colored by your degree of paranoia and your personal politics. (How else would you explain some decision patterns, in recent years, that seem relentlessly to benefit just a few hostile interest groups, over and over again, at great cost to the general commonwealth? Always start by listing the big winners.) [166]

No, I won't go into detail here as to who I think may be orchestrating present day attempts at subornation. *Nor does that matter*, since no one can point to a single era of history when it did *not* happen.

We are better off assuming the tradition goes on. And that some enemies of our republic, our civilization, and the Western Enlightenment are doing it right now.

THE WARNING APPLIES TO YOU

Oh, especially you incoming Democratic lawmakers and staffers, don't be fooled by the fact that most of the known American traitors, across the last 40 years, were Republicans![167] (e.g. the Walkers, Hanssen, Manafort[168] etc.) Democrats are fallible, corruptible and human, too! In-

[166] How innocent this 2007 posting seems, posing this question as theoretical! That we are seeing this program implemented on a massive scale, in 2019, seems beyond any question or doubt.

[167] And nearly all of the *major-predator sexual perverts*, from Dennis Hastert to Roy Moore and so many of those with squelched National Enquirer articles in David Pecker's safe. That safe – plus the blackmail files of Jeffrey Epstein and his madam – constitute troves that – if leaked – might inconvenience many top players, but also offer America and the world a cleansing.

[168] Inserted during revision for the book version: convicted traitor Paul Manafort stands in here for what appear to be scores of suborned or complicit or blackmailed Republican leaders or factotums,

deed, there may be forces at work in DC, *right now*, who aim to test this methodology on the newest players in that wild and ethically-challenged town.

Even veteran Democratic representatives may need to heed this warning, because only now have they become more *interesting* targets for subornation.

Moreover, while the main topic of this open letter (and the book) is *political* subornation, can anyone doubt that even greater efforts have gone into the *commercial* kind? Rivals and predatory arbitrageurs – both domestic and foreign – have a long history of targeting human weakness in the executive suites and research labs of competitors. It ranks among the top methods for intellectual property theft

Even if I am exaggerating the current extent of suborned betrayal within the many branches and agencies, corporations and media that make up the American Establishment, this warning stands, because it will always be a danger. A peril that can turn almost any friend of our civilization into a snake, dwelling in its heart.[169]

Hence, let me offer *a little advice* to all loyal Americans – whether Republican or Democrat or independent entrepreneur – who may be embarking upon careers along avenues of power.

TAKE SIMPLE PRECAUTIONS

– **Consign yourself to live a super-clean life.** Become a personal prude. Back away from temptations, even if they take place in the apparently secure confines of (say) a billionaire's yacht or on a private estate,[170] or a royal palace in some foreign land.

Especially in those environs! Because those may be the very people who would like to "own" a representative or bureaucrat. The more flattering and friendly and ego-stroking they may seem – assuring you of secure and private pleasures – the stronger the possibility that the very

---

including (likely) a famously retired jurist.

[169] Oh, the connections I have made with my own 'chart of yarn'! I'll not publish any of that here, for many reasons, including the insurance policy of my own reveal-on-my-death cache. And because disproved libels could (rightfully!) ruin a fellow who is so rash as to to point fingers at individuals. Anyway, this book is filled with more than enough stuff to act upon, already.

[170] Was this 2007 paragraph prophetic, in light of the Jeffrey Epstein case? No. It was obvious.

walls may have cameras. Aimed in order to guarantee that you will *remain* a valued friend.

– **Hire a good professional paranoid for your staff.** Someone who knows all about these nasty tricks and who can spot bait-lures on the horizon. Likewise, have a truly wise confidant – someone not on your payroll – to whom you can turn when temptation comes your way. And don't entirely trust either of *them*.

– **Have a scenario-plan worked out, for when you are approached with *either* a potential entrapment or a follow-up blackmail threat.** Those first instants of surprise and confusion could be critical. If you are prepared (especially technologically), you may be the one to turn the tables on your persecutors... and thus do your nation a service out of all proportion to any "goods" that the bad guys have on you.

Indeed, talking this over among yourselves, you may also be well served to look into whether agencies like the FBI may offer pre-training services and even some technology, empowering you and others like you to act decisively and confidently, when and if such a time comes. (And if they don't offer such services, ask why not.)

Indeed, if you make it openly clear *that* you are wary, it may keep such plotters away.

– **Contemplate the algebra of forgiveness.** Some of you reading this may have already tumbled over the edge. It may have happened to you – some moment of weakness or falling into temptation. Perhaps even blackmail based upon *faked photos or videos,* or something you never did! (A modern problem that I discussed way back in the last century, in both *Earth* and *The Transparent Society*.)

Maybe you've been on a hellish spiral for years, hating yourself...

...or else rationalizing that you're now serving a superior side. That's what human beings often do. Even the worst traitors seldom view themselves that way. Blackmailers are often supremely good *flatterers*.

However it has come down, consider this: It's never too late to do the right thing.

Consider the following... then ponder it again. Then contemplate.

If the subornation process that I describe has been going on in a systematic and pervasive way, polluting our institutions and corrupting our trusted pub-

lic servants, how do you think history will view the first of you to show some guts? The first to stand and fight back?

If you do it with savvy and skill, somehow turning the tables on your blackmailers – as Amazon founder Jeff Bezos arguably did[171] – can you even doubt that your nation will value that service, far higher than it disdains your original, disreputable deeds?

I know I will! I'll fight for you, and so will millions of others.

– **Help foster a civilization that rewards openness and forgiveness.** This is a long term goal. But if we keep making progress toward a civilization that has a sense of proportion about lesser human failings, then we may neutralize many situations that were, or remain, "blackmailable."

Little sexual lapses should matter less than graft and treason, for example.[172] (But remember, once you are blackmailed for the one, you may then be pushed to commit the latter, and be blackmailed for *that*!)

In any event, we all need to help foster trends toward a nation and a world where people will feel safe to own up to their faults, rather than feeling terrified that their smaller slips and faults will doom their hopes. We should not be led by folks who are afraid of light.

WHISTLEBLOWERS, HENCHMEN, AND OUR ULTIMATE VICTORY CONDITION

Pausing here in this chapter's "open letter to a politician" motif, I've repeatedly hectored many of our top defenders to step back and consider what might be the long-range *victory condition* for our kind of civilization. Not just the USA, but for any species that aims for justice, integrity, progress, accountability... and the stars.

---

[171] The best recent example, though hard to emulate, was billionaire Jeff Bezos, who defied his would-be extortionists and turned the tables on them. And yes, he's the world's richest man, so it was fairly risk free. Still, it's behooved on folks like that to point out the way. There are many tales of French officials who – shown photos of their infidelity in Moscow, have snarled. *"You call zees photography? Let's try again."*

[172] For a century, prejudice against homosexuals was justified by declaring they were vulnerable to blackmail. How many decades and ruined lives passed, before the answer to that circular "logic" became obvious?

It's easy to see that victory condition if you recognize one simple truth. *All of our deadly foes, who wish us harm, are lethally allergic to light.*[173]

Bearing that universal in mind, it is clear that the long range *victory condition* for our kind of civilization is a future world that's filled with open-fair competition, calm negotiation, but above all… *light.*

Of course this relates to our current topic – blackmail and other kinds of secretive coercion. I have already spoken of whistleblower protection and rewards, in Chapter 5's section on "The Fact Act" and in Chapter 7's riff on conspiracies. We'll return to the topic again and again, because no form of *light* can be more effective than revelations from dark corners. That's why I have long urged a Henchman's Law to help protect those who do this.[174]

Moreover, *some private, patriotic zillionaire might get it all rolling by offering a set of prizes* – perhaps $5 million – for some employee of, say, a corrupt voting machine manufacturer who comes forth with proof. And if proof doesn't appear, you don't pay! (But instill fear in those bastards.) If you do wind up paying, you become a hero for saving the nation.[175]

As we go back to my "open letter," just keep in mind – light is the one cleanser that every kind of filth – in and out of our society fears most.

PICK THE ULTIMATE WINNER: CIVILIZATION

The crux? Consider again: blackmailers love to give their victims a sense of helpless isolation. But the sickness may be far more pervasive than you imagine! And spreading. For it is the nature of evil men that they are insatiable. They will keep trying whatever has worked in the past, casting their nets wider and wider, under an illusion that the good times can go on forever...

---

[173] I do not include as "foes" regular business or cultural rivals. May they compete and prosper in positive-sum ways, alongside us.

[174] https://davidbrin.blogspot.com/2012/10/attention-henchmen-voting-machines-and.html?fbclid=IwAR0BWXJYHp_Cr6w_0fpIVskBuwQL0kkBcXqCmsj-_Afo_EmfoUCPU-rugzp8

[175] Something like it was tried, briefly and without much fanfare – or enough money – in the wake of the November 2016 election. http://www.protectourelections.org/2016/11/17/one-hundred-thousand-dollar-reward-offered-for-evidence-of-election-fraud/

... until, at last, they try these tricks on people with the courage, wit and patriotism to fight back. At which point, the whole vile deck of cards may come tumbling down.

Where will you be, when that happens?

According to the algebra of redemption, *only the first to blow the whistle will be heroes*, forgiven all, rewarded with everything. After them will come the most agile rats, abandoning a sinking ship, tattling and pointing fingers in exchange for clemency...

...and the last to come out will be hung.

Again, if you are already caught in this mesh, they want you to think you are alone. But there are likely hundreds, even thousands of others, any one of whom may suddenly erupt with conscience, patriotism and courage. History shows that this kind of thing is never stable. *Either* it will result in democracy being thoroughly corrupted and destroyed... as happened many times...

... *or else* such schemes will collapse, as American and Enlightenment civilization continues its inexorable progress toward an open and transparent and accountable society. In the *first* of these two eventualities, you may thrive, having sided with the new masters. But you will know (deep inside) that you helped to end the Great Experiment. May it gnaw your guts.

But suppose what happens is the *second* outcome. (I have reason to believe it.) Then cowards who let themselves be blackmailed or cozened or suborned or bribed or flattered into treason will eventually be brought to light. And they'll be sorry.

Either way, you can see what's at stake. So be careful. Take precautions. Cut through the rationalizations. Keep your eyes open.

– Oh, one final point: If you seek the people's trust and are granted political power, that makes you a *soldier*: Live with it.

We are a civilization that's at war for its very survival. Moreover, "terrorists" are among the most pallid and laughable of our enemies.[176] There

---

[176] Comments Republican Pat Scannell, on critiquing this project: "I've always been amazed at our outsized quest for security. We won't spend $100M in civilization building efforts, but we'll spend $1 trillion in response to 19 guys with box cutters. We struggle to pay $3K/years in pre k per student, but we have no problems spending $60K/year to incarcerate them later. We lock down our schools, thinking it has made them safe from school shooters, but those efforts, like TSA, are more theater for our concerns – the generation of an artificial narcotic (and fake) sense

are worse threats to the continuation of our Great Experiment in open civilization, in science and democracy, in social mobility, in truly free-creative markets and a joyfully open mix of competition and cooperation.

None of those great things can work well in darkness, manipulated by cheaters.

Stand up. Know what the enemy can do. And deny them the power.

And now another open letter... this time an appeal to someone – some as yet unknown hero – who might use all of these lessons to save civilization.

---

of security, to quiet the cognitive discontent we have that we are insecure. Better, as Alan Watts says, to have the wisdom of insecurity, and an accurate view of balanced risks, which in the end, are far cheaper bets than the costs of trying to secure ourselves against all risks."

This recurring "open letter to a new president" continues the "algebra of redemption" theme of the previous chapter. It offers just one of a dozen ideas for how some freshly elected reformer could fulfill promises before the swirl of politics turns everything murky. This version was posted after the 2019 election of a new president in El Salvador... and I doubt he ever saw it. But I'll keep using that one as an example.

Someday, someone will have the imagination and guts.

Pause #8 for...

An Open Letter To Some New President Of A Developing Nation.

Dear President-Elect __.

Would you consider a proposal/suggestion offered by an impudent science fiction author from Upper California? You face incredible hindrances to fulfilling your vow to overcome rampant corruption, giving citizens hope and confidence in the honest rule of law. Indeed, will you bear with me when I claim that classic corruption is the least of your obstacles?

Far worse than bribery is blackmail. Whether a person was originally entrapped in some small misjudgment, or willingly did something awful, the man who is blackmailed is far easier for evil ones to control than someone who is merely greedy or venial. Indeed, there is strong reason to believe that blackmail pervades every government on Earth, and – lately – has thoroughly suborned the United States of America.

There is a way out of this! You – personally – could set an example to the world.

Declare amnesty for the first twenty men or women who come forth into the light with profound information that could transform your nation!

Yes, there must be standards. Let's say they must surrender most of any ill-gotten gains. In order for it to count, they must tell-all! Name others, including their blackmailers. There will have to be guarantees of safety, witness protection and possibly foreign refuge. Arrange these, along with safety from prosecution. Indeed, if their revelations bring down higher figures, then promise a share of any seizures!

Promise that the first who come forward - bravely - to confess and to reveal, will not be known as pardoned criminals, but as heroes.

What do you have to lose? Is twenty enough? Make it a hundred! If no one steps up, then it costs you nothing. If this unleashes a wave of pardon seekers, make sure the brave ones who step up first get special honor.

Some may accuse you of setting up pardons for cronies. But that will die down, as a tide of revelations sweep forth! Also note, you need no legislation to issue pardons... though legislation will surely follow, especially once corrupt legislators get outed.

For safety's sake, issue an Exclusion List. Ask law enforcement agencies to write down those criminals they have already built strong cases against. You can name forty men whose pardon requests will not be honored. Can you think of a better way to single them out and terrify them into making a deal?

Of course, if they see this coming, many forces will converge to prevent it, out of desperate self-preservation. You might have to craft the plan confidentially at first, then reveal it swiftly! And accompany it with a mea culpa for your own minor transgressions over the years.

Oh, this is not a new proposal. I have put it forward for many years, to no avail.[177]

But you are a special case. You are committed to eliminating the corruption that has ruined civil life in your country.

Alas, people expect - cynically - that you will just slip into a familiar pattern, either that of the sellout presidents before you, or that of Chavez, Erdogan and Duterte. There will be overwhelming pressures to go in either of those directions, so you must find something that will propel the idealistic momentum right away, and unstoppably.

This one thing would prove cynics wrong, from the very start!

I have plenty of other proposals - including a way that some leader of a developing nation might get back all the money that corruption took over-

---

[177] On blackmail: http://www.davidbrin.com/nonfiction/blackmail.html

seas to "banking havens." But this one is so simple and blatantly obvious that it needs no further explanation.

Think about how the first leader to do this will be remembered by history.

Nothing could transform your nation as swiftly and effectively as a sudden and cleansing wash of light.

There is no topic more complex – outside of biology – than international relations. The subject of "judo polemics" in foreign policy merits a book in its own right! But with this volume hurriedly gathered for U.S. consumption in the 2020 election year, I must pick and choose.

So I'll begin with the most controversial assertion of them all… that despite its many faults and some real crimes, the American Peace – or Pax Americana – has overall been the most positive time for humanity since the invention of fire. Moreover, this happened as a matter of deliberate policy, crafted by some men and women who were on a par, in vision and effectiveness, with the 1770s Founders. If that era is coming to an end, then let it be judged fairly, weighing the sins alongside a cornucopia of fruits.

And in that context, let's also spend our first international chapter gazing with both awe and caution at the return and rise of Chung Kuo – the Central Kingdom.

Chapter 9

America's place in the world – Part 1: Pax Americana and the rise of China

> *It seems to me that America's objective today should be to try to make herself the best possible mirror of democracy that she can. The people of the world can see what happens here. They watch us to see what we are going to do and how well we can do it. We are giving them the only possible picture of democracy that we can: the picture as it works in actual practice. This is the only way other peoples can see for themselves how it works; and can determine for themselves whether this thing is good in itself, whether it is better than they have, better than what other political and economic systems offer them.*
>
> *The Autobiography of Eleanor Roosevelt (1961)*

In 1945, it was apparent that one nation would soon have – for the first time in history – almost total global reach and power. In somber conversation, some of that era's top minds contemplated history and the paradox of empire.

We know that power tempts and corrupts. Across almost every continent and at least 10,000 years – ever since the discovery of metals and agriculture – large men would band together with metal implements, coercing others to hand over their women and wheat. They would then assign priests and other persuaders to tell everyone it's *good* for a local lord, or king or theocrat to pass this power to his sons. It happened almost everywhere, at almost every time. We are descended from the harems of guys who pulled that off.

Nor were they satisfied with some local theft. Knights sought to be barons, barons to be dukes, dukes to be kings. If you had an empire with a nervous border, you would conquer beyond it to get a "buffer"... which then had to be protected, in turn. We can see all of these imperatives playing out in today's world, though much has also changed.

Once upon a time, there came upon the scene a clade of men and women who had just conquered the worst evil of all time. They were brilliant on a par with the American Founders and fixated on pragmatic idealism, not dogma or incantations. And now, in their hands, lay power never conceived by Alexander, Caesar or even Genghis Khan. Gazing across the litany of predictable behaviors, rationalized cruelties and stubbornly unsapient errors that we call "history," they pondered a question that was never asked before:

Is there any way we can learn from all that and make fewer mistakes, during the coming era? Pax Americana?

====

In 1999, I wrote to *Time* Magazine, nominating my own choice for "Person of the 20th Century." I asked – *how could you even consider anyone other than George Marshall?* You probably just know him for the Marshall Plan, which famously did one unprecedented thing – the victors in a vicious war spending lavishly to uplift their recent enemies. And allies. But that is just the tip of what Marshall both influenced and accomplished. I invite you to read about this stunning example of what it means to be a truly grownup human. [178]

====

Let's squint back across all those millennia at a few historical errors that George Marshall – along with like FDR, Eleanor Roosevelt, Harry Truman, Dean Acheson, Dwight Eisenhower, Cordell Hull and others – sought purposely to avoid.

If you scan recorded accounts, you'll find that most people lived in either a period of *imperium* or a period of *chaos.* Many empires were brutal and stultifying. Still, cities didn't burn very often when central authority maintained order. Most people could work, trade and raise their families in safety, under the imperial peace or "pax."

That doesn't mean such times were wise. Often, those empires behaved in smug and tyrannical ways that laid seeds for their own destruction. For example, whenever a nation became overwhelmingly strong, it tended to forge *trade networks* that favored home industries and capital inflows, at the expense of those living in dependent areas. The Romans did this, insisting that rivers of gold stream into the imperial city. So did the Hellenists, Persians, Moguls, Aztecs and every Chinese dynasty. This kind of behavior by Pax Brittanica was among the chief complaints of both John Hancock and Mahatma Gandhi. While you can grasp *why* emperors instituted such policies, it inevitably proved stupid. Capital cities flourished... till angry barbarians from the impoverished periphery poured in.

AVOIDING PAST MISTAKES... ...AND UPLIFTING THE WORLD

Upon finding itself the dominant power at the end of World War II, the U. S. had an opportunity to impose its own vision of international trade. And it did. But at the behest of Marshall and others, America became the first power to deliberately establish *counter-mercantilist com-*

---

178 "A Quiet Adult: My Candidate For Man Of The Century." https://www.marshallfoundation.org/marshall/essays-interviews/quiet-adult-candidate-man-century/

merce flows. Nations crippled by war or mismanagement were allowed to maintain tariffs, keeping out American goods, while sending shiploads from their factories to us. Each administration since Marshall's time, regardless of political party, has abided by this compact–to such a degree that the world's peoples now simply take it for granted![179]

Of course, more than pure altruism may have been involved. Democrat Harry Truman and Republican Dwight Eisenhower both saw trade as a tonic to unite world peoples against Soviet expansionism. But if you doubt it also had an altruistic motive, remember that this unprecedented regime was instituted by the author of the renowned Marshall Plan–an endeavor that rings in human memory as an archetype of generosity.

====

HIATUS FOR MEA CULPA

***Let's be clear – I'm not glossing over America's many mistakes and crimes!* From Vietnam to Mossadegh to Pinochet to the WMD scam and Trumpian monstrosities, this pax has much to atone for, as would any bunch of jumped-up cavemen with unmodified brains and hormones, who got their hands on steel and gunpowder and petroleum and nukes. But just as we ask Washington, Jefferson and Lincoln: "Were you much better than your times, and did you move things forward?" we're also behooved to look across history at every other empire that ever was, and ask critics of Pax Americana:**

"Can you name a people who were ever tempted by overwhelming imperial power, who used it with a better *ratio* of good to bad deeds?"

Talk of "ratios" will never salve the anger of a purist. Nor will the fact that your own high standards for personal and national rectitude – standards that America has *failed* – were taught by the very same Hollywood propaganda system that preaches Suspicion of Authority, tolerance, diversity, eccentricity and the glimmering notion that – some time in our children's future – there will be an adult and benign *end to all empires*.[180]

---

[179] The original version of this essay was obviously written before Donald Trump. http://www.metroactive.com/metro/11.25.09/news-0947.html

[180] "The Dogma of Otherness." from my collection, Otherness.

Still, a defense case can be argued for the world that Marshall and fellow flawed-geniuses wrought. And foremost among articles entered into evidence is the counter-mercantilist trade system they introduced, diametrically opposite to the behavior of every other imperium, leading to America not so much being *popular* as being likely – across all those centuries – the least-hated empire.[181]

====

In fact, the Marshall Plan, per se, was nothing compared to the new trading system, under which *Americans bought roughly a hundred trillion dollars worth of crap they never needed.* And thus factory workers – first in Japan and Germany, then Korea and Taiwan, then Malaysia and China and India and Bangladesh – sweated hard, often unjustly, but saw their children clothed and schooled.[182] Whereupon those kids refused to work in the textile mills, which had to move on to the next pool of festering poverty. It wasn't clean, moral or elegant... perhaps not praiseworthy! But it *amounted to a prodigious transfer of wealth* from the United States to Europe, Asia and Latin America – the greatest aid-and-uplift program in human history. A program that (again) consisted of Americans buying craploads of things they didn't really need.

Does anyone deserve moral credit for this staggeringly successful "aid program"? Perhaps not American consumers, who went on a reckless holiday, spending themselves into debt. Moreover, as the author of a book called *Earth*, I'd be remiss not to mention that all of this consumption-driven growth came about at considerable cost to our planet. For all our sakes, the process of ending human poverty needs to get a lot more efficient.

Still, it is long past time for a balanced view of the last 80 years, which have featured more rapid development and distribution of education, health and prosperity than any and all such intervals since we lived in caves. Than all eras *combined.* For the first time, a vast majority of hu-

---

[181] Least-hated empire? https://medium.com/@david.brin/neither-side-owns-patriotism-9cd25cdf1506

[182] In much the same way that my grandparents slaved in the US garment industry, and other immigrants sweated so that their highly schooled offspring would not have to... and thus the factories moved on.

mans have spent their entire lifetimes never seeing or smelling or hearing the rampages of a pillaging army, never witnessing war with their own eyes, and spent nearly all their weeks with enough to eat. Today 90% of children worldwide bring schoolbooks home to what Americans would call hovels, but with electricity, basic sanitation, a refrigerator and lights to study by. It's not uplift at a rate demanded by our conscience! But it's faster than ever happened before, and possibly in the nick of time.

Without diminishing at all from the urgent need for more advancement (much more!), some authors have dared to speak up against the notion that *gloom* is the only motivator for reform. In truth, citizens are *more likely* to invest in world-saving, if they can see that past efforts actually accomplished something. Starting with *The Progress Paradox: How Life Gets Better While People Feel Worse,* by Gregg Easterbrook, other authors such as Steven Pinker (*The Better Angels of Our Nature*) and Peter Diamandis (*Abundance: The Future is Better Than You Think*) present overwhelming evidence that there is good news to match the bad. Not only that, but that *awareness of the good that's been accomplished may help us to believe in our power to press on harder than ever, to overcome the bad.*

Yes, again it distills down to thinking *positive sum*. For a good handle on that concept, *the* central idea of our Great Enlightenment Experiment, I recommend Robert Wright's wonderful 1999 book: *Nonzero: The Logic of Human Destiny.*

JUSTIFICATIONS FOR A NEW PAX A REVIVED CENTRAL KINGDOM

And indeed, Pax Americana may be coming to a close. At least that is the notion spread zealously by a new behemoth on the world stage. Again, I have very little time or space here, but this is a volume about seeing things from different angles. And there needs to be some push-back against a meme that's going around, promulgated especially from Beijing, that the transition is wholly good and beyond-question ordained.

Dr. Wu Jianmin, a professor at China Foreign Affairs University and chairman of the Shanghai Centre of International Studies, is a smart fellow whose observations merit close attention. In the online journal *The Globalist,* Wu Jianmin's appraisal of "A Chinese Perspective on a Changing World" was insightful.[183] Still, it typically misplaced credit for the Asian economic miracle.

"After the Second World War, things started to change. Japan was the first to rise in Asia. We Asians are grateful to Japan for inventing this export-oriented development model, which helped initiate the process of Asia's rise."

In fact, and with due respect for their industriousness, ingenuity and determination, the Japanese invented no such thing. The initiators of export-driven world development were U.S. leaders in the ravaged aftermath of the Second World War. While both Japanese and Chinese mercantilists preen about their development "invention," they have frantically underplayed the extent to which this was at deliberate American indulgence.

Instead, they spread the self-flattering notion that U.S. consumers are like fatted pigs, unable to control their appetites and worthy only to be treated as prey animals. For more on this, see: "The Power of Consumption – How Americans spent ourselves into ruin–but uplifted the world."[184] And the blogged version,[185] which also contrasts left versus right attitudes toward an "American Empire." (Hint, both sides are historically ignorant and entirely wrong.)

Of course one question to arise out of all of the above is… *how could Americans afford to go on that world-building spending spree for 80 years?* How could decade after decade of trade deficits be afforded?

The answer is inventiveness. Each decade brought a wave of new industries – automobiles, jet air travel, xerography, personal photography, industrial computers, satellites, electronics, transistors, lasers, telecom, pharmaceuticals, personal computers, the Internet, e-gaming, AI and so on. Each *new* industry generated so much wealth that Americans could keep buying *older* products – toys and textiles, then cars, then computers and so on – from overseas factories… till each *new* industry also fled

---

[183] "A Chinese Perspective on a Changing World" http://www.theglobalist.com/StoryId.aspx?StoryId=8035

[184] http://www.metroactive.com/metro/11.25.09/news-0947.html

[185] "The Power of Consumption – How Americans spent ourselves into ruin–but uplifted the world." and http://davidbrin.blogspot.com/2009/11/how-americans-spent-themselves-into.html

to cheap labor and agile Asian corporations. But no worries, there was always the next thing to invent!

Which of course takes us to the central grudge in our current trade war, the spectacularly aggressive stealing of western Intellectual Property or IP.[186]

Look, for perspective, Americans were famous IP thieves in the 19th Century, and a certain amount of that is understandable! But inventiveness is the very lifeblood of the one nation that has propelled the world economy for an entire human lifetime. It is the goose that laid countless golden eggs for everyone. And while it's fine to make and sell goods in order to gather as many eggs as you can, it's quite another thing to kill and eat the goose! One word for that is greedy. Another is stupid.

TOXIC GRUDGES

Alas, there is something much worse going on than goose-cooking. We are also seeing floods of propaganda disparaging Pax Americana, justifying not only its replacement, but its violent fall. Critically dangerous, for example, is a meme being spread from Beijing that *any strategy or tactic that the PRC might use to get on top is justified by past crimes against it, like colonialism.*

Oh, the New Mandarins are doing this for their own reasons. Even without anger at oppression and corruption, a fast-rising population can get agitated by what's called the *revolution of rising expectations.*[187] It's well known that a foreign enemy can be helpful to manage domestic friction. Nevertheless, this sort of thing can get out of hand and in this particular case it needs to be nipped in the bud. Not just because trumped-up rancor might lead to conflagration. It is also based on an *absolute lie.*

Sure, many western powers behaved aggressively toward China in the 19th Century, bullying, carving out "concessions" and insulting one of the world's great peoples. Half of the responsibility falls on that era's corrupt Peiping (Manchu or Chi'ing) court, who refused to modernize

---

[186] IP theft. https://www.invntip.com/nation-sponsored-theft-of-ip/

[187] https://www.encyclopedia.com/social-sciences/applied-and-social-sciences-magazines/revolution-rising-expectations

or reform in the fashion of Meiji Japan. But that doesn't excuse Britain, Russia, France, Germany and the rest for their callous opportunism.

In any event (almost) *none of that applies to the USA!* In fact, across all 3000 years of Chinese history, China's only real foreign friend, repeatedly and by far, was America. I can prove it, with example after example. But so could anyone with historical awareness.[188] And hence I'll save that for another time...

...adding only that pointing this out is an example of *polemical judo*, an art that's not just necessary for political salvation of the United States, but possibly to prevent a ruinous world war. Lest the Beijing communist politburo miscalculate in riling up their population against us, we need to be ready to answer.[189]

"We weren't perfect, by any means. But that accusation is a flat-out lie."

---

[188] Chinese leaders and scholars are using resentment over past Western depredations like colonialism to justify ever-rising fevers of nationalism. One can understand their reasons – – a fast-developing and educated population must be distracted from their sense of being overly controlled – but the formula is dangerous. At some level, it must be answered. At the right moment, someone must ask, in as public a way as possible: "Across 3,000 years of glorious Chinese history, you accomplished many things and were – and remain – one of the greatest centers of human culture. Still: *when did you ever have a friend? An equal friend who came to your aid when you called and wasn't afraid of you.*" "As it happens, China – across its long history –only had one consistent external friend. Have you ever heard of a California city called Burlingame? It's named after Abraham Lincoln's envoy to China, Anson Burlingame, who made life hell for the British, the French, the Russians, the Japanese, endlessly hectoring them to *get out.* To give up their colonies and "concessions" and extra-territorial bullying rights. In several cases, he even succeeded at preventing some seizures, despite the Chi'ing Dynasty's apparent eagerness to do everything wrong. A bit later on, the great hero in freeing China from those Manchu overlords – Sun Yatsen – based his repeated efforts at revolution out of Hawaii and the U.S. And when he finally succeeded, Sun sent hundreds of students to America on free scholarships. Yes, there were tussles between American forces and some of the warlords who usurped Sun, But who came to China's aid against the invading Japanese Empire, at great cost in lives and treasure? And who has spent trillions buying crap from Chinese factories, providing the economic engine of all development and making cities like Shenzhen possible? Today's huge Chinese military buildup is based upon a U.S. "threat" that does not exist. That across 150 years has never, ever existed. Moreover, there is no basis for wrath at us. If you want to sell us stuff, at the cost of U.S. jobs, well that was our policy, all along. (You're welcome!) If you want our inventions, we can negotiate over that. But don't you dare pretend any moral reason to justify *hating us.* It's not fair or right. And it may help explain those 3000 years having only one friend."

[189] China's friend? This cartoon from that era may seem non-PC by modern standards But at the time it said "We are different from you imperialist fools." https://upload.wikimedia.org/wikipedia/commons/f/f8/Putting_his_foot_down.jpg

BRILLIANT... AND DECEPTIVELY CLOSE...

While we're on the Central Kingdom, I want to point to one example of state-sponsored rationalization that struck me as especially important, insightful… and ultimately just wrong. Feng Xiang, a professor of law at Tsinghua University, argues that *"AI will spell the end of capitalism."*[190]

According to Feng, first the standard Marxian cycle will return, wreaking havoc on capitalist systems with a vengeance. For lack of anti-monopoly or fairness-generating reforms (like those enacted by our parents under FDR, or by our great-grandparents under the other Roosevelt), each business cycle will result in greater wealth disparities and a narrowing of the owner-controlling caste, leading to a conversion of vibrantly competitive markets back into history's standard, uncreative oligarchic pyramid. And yes, barring imminent reform, that stupid pattern is what we see already happening, as Marx rises from the dustbin, back into pertinence.

Naturally, Professor Feng's proposed solution is also Marxist, with "Chinese characteristics." Party-guided proletarian revolution.

Second, he joins many forecasting that the coming technological obsolescence of many types of employment will break the livelihoods of hundreds of millions, if not billions. No longer able to negotiate or bargain for the value of their labor, workers will be at the mercy of the Owner Caste. And yes, ditto. Feng's prescription for a resolution is Sino-Marxist. Top-down state paternalism.

Finally, any *artificial intelligence* that gains unsupervised control over important systems may pose an existential risk to humanity. For this and other reasons, Professor Feng argues that research into AI should be tightly controlled by a benevolent socialist state.

Why am I giving space over to a communist state-servant who promotes Marxist notions that I clearly disagree with? Because it is well worthwhile reading his appraisal of looming *problems*. After which it is instructive to study his prescriptions. Because simplistic panaceas will doubtless appeal to billions, over the next couple of decades. Especially

---

[190] From The Washington Post: https://www.washingtonpost.com/news/theworldpost/wp/2018/05/03/end-of-capitalism/?utm_term=.01fa1d726f44

at a time when our own lords seem determined to follow the Marxian pattern by driving the American middle class into penury.

Oh, but it goes much farther! And you remain uninformed about all this to the peril of your country, your civilization and the fate of your posterity.[191] (Just all that, nothing more!) In fact, Feng Xiang's missive is simultaneously brilliant and stunningly tendentious – clearly a piece of state-commanded justification propaganda, of the sort that gains heat daily in Chinese media. Exactly the sort of thing that distracts the masses… and, as already said, may get violently out of hand.

At minimum, you need to grasp the polemical intent underlying Professor Feng's missive. And to see how Feng's prescriptions – issued in variants by an army of court scholars – do *not* follow, logically, from his well-described premises. In fact, I offer answers to all of Dr. Feng's assertions, and you are welcome to read them, here.[192] In another place I show why Beijing's rationalization for central planning *forever* is hypocritically the most heretically anti-Marxist position of all. [193]

Included in those links is discussion of the major question of *central planning* and whether it's possible to guide an economy from up top. (Here's another[194] on that topic.) Every king and commissar of the past believed they could command-allocate a successful economy and all ultimately failed. Using sophisticated and agile modern tools, the Japanese did take central planning to new levels of success, before finally hitting a wall that free market thinkers believe will *always* appear, whenever arrogant leaders they believe they can control super-complex, synergistic systems. (It's what we're learning about the biggest, most productive and most-complicated such system, Earth's biosphere.)

On the other hand, there is *so* much hypocrisy among supposed free market champions! The 5,000 golf buddies in America's smug CEO caste – plus their New Lord backers and Wall Street pals – *claim* to oppose central planning. But their circle-jerk connivings only shift it away

---

[191] http://davidbrin.blogspot.com/2018/06/central-control-over-ai-and-everything.html

[192] "Central Control over AI… and everything else." http://davidbrin.blogspot.com/2018/06/central-control-over-ai-and-everything.html

[193] http://davidbrin.blogspot.com/2019/08/international-affairs-and-china-redux.html

[194] More on the myths of central planning: http://davidbrin.blogspot.com/2019/07/central-planning-and-team-human-are-we.html

from openly accountable civil servants into dark crypts that are secret, self-flattering and inherently stupid.

Meanwhile, the Beijing leadership is at least open about taking central planning way beyond Japanese levels of success, crowing, "This time we have it sussed!"

With deep respect for their accomplishments, and aware that this time *might* be different, my answer is: Well, sorta… and dangerously delusionally partway.

But this is a dispute with many ramifications[195] – some of which we'll cover in Chapter 11 on Economics. It won't be settled soon.[196] At least not till we stop arguing in clichés.

IS ANYONE STILL READING?

Is anybody still out there reading at this point? This book consists of maybe 90% of judo assaults against the mad-right treason, so I doubt many conservative readers linger. And my defense of a mostly benign American Pax (while acknowledging bloody mistakes) has likely sent every liberal or leftist scurrying, amid a cloud of curses. My attempt to bring perspective will be dismissed as arrogant, jingoist, hyper-patriotic American triumphalism.[197]

But I'll persevere anyway. Heck, perhaps some friendly-insightful AI is scanning this, right now. So let me just reiterate my assertion:

Even if America is exhausted, worn out and a shadow of her former self, having spent her way from world dominance into a chasm of debt, the U.S. *does* have something to show for the last eight decades. Humanity's longest (if deeply flawed) era of overall (per capita) peace. A majority of human beings lifted out of grinding poverty. A trajectory of science and technology that may (perhaps) lead to more solutions than problems.

---

[195] "Allocation vs Markets – an ancient struggle with strange modern implications: The ancient mythology of "economic allocation" takes on strange modern camouflage… as a defense of free market wisdom" http://davidbrin.blogspot.com/2006/06/allocation-vs-markets-ancient-struggle.html

[196] At least not in a quick-impudent e-book on US political polemic.

[197] On the American right, we do have genuine triumphalists – Bush era neocons and later Bannonite imperialists – of the most shrill and stubborn type, who share my appreciation for Pax Americana… but for all the wrong reasons, as if using the same phrase to stand for entirely different things. Their era of misrule deeply harmed the very thing they claim to love.

The launching of environmentalism and many rights movements. Perhaps even a world saved.

That task, far more prodigious than defeating fascism and Stalinism, or going to the moon, ought to be viewed with a little respect, at least compared to how every other nation acted, when tempted by great power. And I suspect it will be, by future historians.

This unconventional assertion will meet vigorous resistance, no matter how clearly it is supported by the historical record. The reflex of America-bashing is too heavily ingrained, within the left and across much of the world, for anyone to actually read the ancient annals and realize that the United States is probably the *least hated empire of all time.* If its "pax" is drawing to a close, it will enter retirement with more earned goodwill than any other.[198] Perhaps even enough to win forgiveness for the inevitable litany of imperial crimes.

And so, at risk of belaboring the point, let me reiterate. *If the U.S. had done the normal thing, the natural human thing, and imposed mercantilist trade patterns after WWII – as every previous "chung kuo" empire did – then America would have no debt today. Our cities would gleam and our factories hum. The country would be swimming in gold...*

...but the amount of hope and prosperity in the world at large would be far less, ruined by the same self-centered, short-sighted greed that eventually brought down empires in Babylon, Persia, Rome, China, Britain and so on. And when we finally fell, it would be in a turmoil of well-deserved wrath.

Oh, yes. I have my nominee for the "Person of the 20th Century."

WHAT MIGHT THE FUTURE BRING?

Other nations have started viewing their time ahead as one of triumph, becoming the next great pax or "central kingdom." If that happens, (as I portray in my novel *Existence*) will they begin their bright era of world leadership with acts of thoughtful and truly farsighted wisdom? Perhaps even a little indulgent gratitude? We can hope they will at least try evading the mistakes that are written plain, across the pages of his-

---

[198] Assuming the Trump-trashed alliances and goodwill can be rebuilt.

tory, wherever countries briefly puffed and preened over their own importance, imagining that this must last forever.

But this, too, shall pass.

Where after all do universal human rights begin? In small places, close to home – so close and so small that they cannot be seen on any map of the world. Yet they are the world of the individual person: The neighborhood he lives in; the school or college he attends; the factory, farm or office where he works. Such are the places where every man, woman, and child seeks equal justice, equal opportunity, equal dignity without discrimination. Unless these rights have meaning there, they have little meaning anywhere. Without concerted citizen action to uphold them close to home, we shall look in vain for progress in the larger world.

– Eleanor Roosevelt, Remarks at the United Nations, March 27, 1958

Hey, it could happen.

Pause #9 for...

...a Daydream: What Could Happen If Adults Ever Regain Power.

It won't surprise you to know that I have wasted time that could have been spent on several novels, pounding out political and polemical essays that constitute the bulk of this work. On occasion, I crafted lists of "suggestions" for unusual measures that might help decent negotiators of all sides to work around our current gridlock. And because they were unusual – often outside the constraining "Left-Right Axis" – I've gained some following among unconventional thinkers out there...

...and no attention at all from the political or punditry caste that might get actual traction. Alas. My biggest and most lamentably futile such foray came in late 2006, after the nation soundly thumped the do-nothing-but-suckle-oligarchs congresses led by Dennis Hastert, for ten years the topmost Republican in the United States.[199] With Democrats coming into (brief) control of the Capitol, then President George W. Bush claimed he'd be open to compromise. It seemed a good time to put down my own set of proposed reforms[200]. I'll offer many of those suggestions yet again, in Chapter 13: "Can We make a Deal? What Would Adults Do?"

I've churned out plenty since, from fixes for gerrymandering and the FACT Act (Chapter 4) to overcoming a likely plague of coercion and blackmail (Chapter 8). On the very first page of this missive, I suggested learning

---

[199] Along with deservedly disgraced leaders Tom DeLay and Mark Foley, none ever mentioned again by the party they so fervently served.

[200] "You Broke It, So You Fix It: A Modest To-Do List for Congress." (2007) http://www.davidbrin.com/nonfiction/suggestions4congress.html

from the enemy, asking "Should Democrats Issue Their Own 'Contract with America'?" [201]

And in Chapter 12, I'll attempt to bridge the (factually almost-nonexistent) chasm between "liberal" and "moderate" Democrats, by listing 31 consensus goals they all have in common. Measures of basic logic, pragmatic reform and decency that are universally rejected or thwarted by a cult that's almost always wrong. (Chapter 6.)

DAVID'S SUMMER DAYDREAM

It's not yet autumn as I type this, and so I might be excused some fantasy, during summer's waning weeks. So... what if sanity prevails? Not via the violent/radical revolution that oligarchists seem intent on provoking, but yet another of those moderate-but-implacable waves of reform that swept America and much of the world several times, across the last three centuries, preserving this Enlightenment Experiment that's so worth fighting-for.

And why not? The 18th Century Founders did it. The millions who turned out, sacrificing everything at Lincoln's call did, as well, as did the Greatest Generation. Assuming we manage it again, what could such a millennium look like? Try to imagine if we rediscovered an almost extinct word – negotiation.

Oh, it's been tried. The last top Republican to use it was Newt Gingrich, in the anno mirabilis year 1995, when – amid the beginnings of our virulent madness – Newt paused to dicker with President Bill Clinton and achieved some real legislative milestones. For which Gingrich was soundly punished and replaced as speaker by Hastert, whose "Rule" combined with Tea Party primary-mania to terrorize any Republican who even thought about negotiating with any Democrat, over anything, ever.

What was "Obamacare"? Folks don't remember, but it was almost cloned from the Republicans' own health care scheme, crafted by the Heritage Foundation and pushed to reality in Massachusetts by then Gov. Mitt Romney. Barack Obama presented it thinking that negotiation might resume if he abandoned all DP ideas and started with the GOP's own damn plan. And no one showed up at the table, though they did hurl socialism jeremiads – over their own... damn... plan.

---

201 "Should Democrats Issue Their Own 'Contract with America'?" http://www.davidbrin.com/nonfiction/contract.html

But let us squint and imagine this insanity ends. That we again see "statesmen" on both sides of the aisle, like when Senators Tsongas (D) and Rudman (R) came that close to negotiating an entitlements reform package[202] that would have solidified Social Security and Medicare for two generations. (A deal that's still waiting out there, by the way.)

HOW WE MIGHT NEGOTIATE

Again, I'll offer many suggested measures and actions in Chapter 13: "Can We make a Deal? What Would Adults Do?" So for my Summer Daydream, let's stay very general and just put up a muzzy wish. Imagine the Putinists lose their grip on American conservatism, whereupon great leaders across the spectrum agree:

We have a full plate, after the laziest Congresses in U.S. history. So let's start by compiling lists of what each of us really, really wants, in order of priority. Instead of vague polemic, let's be as explicit as possible... then compare those lists!

Some items that you want will be high on my list of things to prevent! Many will result in tussles, in which we try to find common ground. Or the majority may impose its will. That's politics. Welcome back.

Only consider again those lists. Is your (say) second priority item only number ten on my list of things to thwart? Is MY number one something you might live with, if you only have to sacrifice (or delay) your item number fifteen?

Say I am a Republican of the sincere kind (a "RASR" or former "ostrich," now standing up for what Barry Goldwater would believe, if he were alive today.) You think my earnest concerns about Voter ID are exaggerated out of all proportion, but if I give way on compliance assistance - helping the poor etc. to get ID - would you give me a steady, predictable ratcheting upward of verification at the polls?

Believe it or not, this used to be normal. John Nash (subject of the film A Beautiful Mind) developed mathematical tools for it. Michael Lewis's book (and the film) Money Ball describes how trades are made in sports. Yes, "deal-making" can be nasty and cutthroat, filled with traps and betrayals,

---

202 https://www.federalregister.gov/agencies/bipartisan-commission-on-entitlement-and-tax-reform

as in the universe where Donald Trump dwells, and wants to drag us all. But at its best, it can be the very essence of "positive sum."[203]

Yes, after Barack Obama wasted eight years trying to draw opponents to a conference table, it would be rational to say "fool me a thousand times, shame on me." Like Charlie Brown getting faked by Lucy, it's natural to be wary. Still, there are ways to keep a steady bearing. To use judo effectively until...

...until our adversaries get up off the ground for the zillionth time with a fresh realization. "Huh. Maybe I'll do better if I start playing fair, looking for ways we can all win."

Of course it was all a daydream. They'll only wake up after a drubbing so huge that they abandon all the madness that Rupert Murdoch has trawled across their minds. So when we return to the topic of "What would adults do," in Chapter 13, it will be largely back to weapons and judo.

How adults and loyal Americans can first win. And then offer an open hand, with malice toward none.

---

[203] Again the core concept is described in Robert Wright's *Nonzero*. Alas, many on the right speak of rising tides that lift all boats, without even glancing at the vast majority of human civilizations, that were decidedly zero-sum. It takes effort. Design. Enlightenment.

ISSUES THAT MATTER TO FACTIONS

Let's hear this incantation the next time you dial 911…

Chapter 10

Government is the problem?[204]

In January 2017, Donald Trump's newly appointed director of the Office of Management and Budget, Rep. Mick Mulvaney (who as of September 2019 was also acting White House Chief of Staff) posted an essay that asked an amazing question:[205]

"Do we really need government-funded research at all?"

It won't surprise you that much of a chapter on the right's hatred of "government" will focus on this stunning sub-topic: that anyone – even a jibbering dogmatist – could pose such a question about tax-supported R&D with a straight face. Yep, who needs the one thing that vastly multiplied all U.S. productivity since World War II. Heck, that enabled us to *win* World War II.[206]

But let's put that particular insanity in larger context. Because, as we saw in "The War on All Fact People" (Chapter 5), there's a much larger agenda at foot.

GOVERNMENT "HELPERS"?

The hypnotic incantation that *all-government-is-evil-all-the-time* would have bemused and appalled our parents in the Greatest Generation – those who persevered to overcome the Depression and Hitler, then contained Stalinism, went to the moon, developed successful companies, built a mighty middle class and began a grinding journey toward im-

---

[204] This chapter comes largely from an essay in Evonomics circa 2016. https://evonomics.com/david-brin-ultimate-answer-government-useless/

[205] "Do we really need government-funded research at all?" https://www.vox.com/science-and-health/2016/12/21/14012552/trump-budget-director-research-science-mulvaney Indeed, ponder who would benefit from a plummet in U.S. scientific pre-eminence, and see if it overlaps with Mulvaney's and Trump's purported masters. There is no contradiction.

[206] A BBC article lists how government research enabled all of the advances that led to the iPhone. http://www.bbc.com/news/business-38320198

proved justice, all in an era of powerful unions and high tax rates. The mixed society that they built emphasized a wide stance, pragmatically stirring private enterprise with targeted collective actions, funded by a consensus negotiation process called *politics*. The resulting civilization was more successful – by orders of magnitude – than any other. Than any combination of others.

So why do we hear endlessly repeated nostrums – pushed by right-wing media and some on the left – that this wide-stance, mixed approach is all wrong? In fact, a recent Pew Poll showed distrust of government among Americans at an all-time high.[207] Ronald Reagan, the most avid and effective promulgator of this meme, famously repeated:

"The scariest words in the English language are – I'm from the government and I'm here to help."

Of course folks who clapped and cheered at that snark are among the first to demand that help, at any excuse.[208] Indeed, this general, abstract loathing collapses when citizens are asked which specific parts of government they'd shut down. It turns out that most of them like specific things their taxes pay for.

"Declining trust in government has spread across nearly all advanced industrial democracies since the 1960s/1970s," writes political scientist Russell Dalton: "Regardless of political history, electoral system, or style of government, most contemporary publics are less trustful of government than they were in the era of their grandparents." This despite the fact that we are richer and better off by almost any measure you can name.[209]

We all know that Congress polls as the least trusted institution in American life – yet, in each district, we keep re-electing our own

---

207 Pew poll on mistrust of government. http://www.people-press.org/2015/11/23/beyond-distrust-how-americans-view-their-government/

208 Red states are on-average and total far higher recipients of federally mediated transfers of wealth, contracts and assistance.

209 Russell Dalton. https://www.washingtonpost.com/posteverything/wp/2017/03/03/americans-have-lost-faith-in-institutions-thats-not-because-of-trump-or-fake-news/?hpid=hp_hp-cards_hp-posteverything%3Ahomepage%2Fcard&utm_term=.e086ffb2ad3a

crook.[210] (Though churches have also taken a steep hit, and are now trusted by much less than half.[211])

In a sense, this isn't new. For a century and a half, followers of Karl Marx demanded that we amputate society's *right arm* of market-competitive enterprise and rely only on socialist (left-handed) guided-allocation for economic control. [212] (See Chapter 9's section on central planning.) Meanwhile, Ayn Rand's ilk proclaim we must lop off our *left arm* – forswearing any coordinated projects that look beyond the typical five year (nowadays *quarterly*) commercial investment horizon. [213]

Any sensible person would respond: *"Hey I need both arms! Let's keep examining what each arm does well, revising and calibrating our knowledge of what each shouldn't do."*

Does that sound too practical and moderate for this era? Our parents thought they had dealt with all this, proving decisively that calm negotiation, compromise and pragmatic mixed-solutions work best, though preferably with a lean toward letting individuals, small groups and markets solve whatever they can. The Greatest Generation would be stunned to see that fanatical would-be amputators are back in force, ranting nonsense.

WHY NO ONE ANSWERED THE "TEA PARTY" SCAM

It still seethes, and I mentioned in several of the postings that comprise this volume – the insipid lunacy of letting crypto-confederates in the so-called "Tea Party Rebellion" get away with *hijacking the American Revolution.*

This wasn't just stupidity of course, Many liberals shy away from looking at the "Founders," for fear of being tarred with their admitted faults. Huge ones like the fact that some – Washington and Jefferson – owned

---

[210] 2019 note: The "AOC uprising" – toppling old-line liberal reps in primaries – echoes the "Tea Party" rebellion of 20 years ago.

[211] Over 700 charges – as of mid 2019 – of sexual abuse hitting just now slamming the Southern Baptist Convention. https://www.houstonchronicle.com/news/investigations/article/Southern-Baptist-sexual-abuse-spreads-as-leaders-13588038.php

[212] Guided allocation: http://davidbrin.blogspot.com/2006/06/allocation-vs-markets-ancient-struggle.html

[213] My own acerbic dissection of Rand's arguments and fiction is at: http://www.davidbrin.com/nonfiction/aynrand.html

slaves. Though others, like Adams and Franklin, were fiery in condemnation, setting alight the abolitionist movement.[214]

In Chapter 14, I talk about how the 1770s Revolution might be viewed as Phase One of our ever-recurring U.S. Civil War. But more important is to utterly demolish the propaganda that it was an uprising against taxation per se, or against "government bureaucracy." First, the complaint was "No taxation without representation," and you have only to read contemporary accounts to know how furious Americans were that some of the Empire's biggest and most industrious cities and regions had no one to speak for them in Parliament. Ben Franklin was sent to Britain by Pennsylvania primarily to persuade the Penn family to allow themselves to be taxed. They owned 70% of the land and refused. Other colonies were similarly bollixed. And by the way, this obstinacy on the part of the top 1% of 1% was similar in France, in 1789, when the First Estate utterly refused to help... and thereupon lost their heads.

Moreover, it was maritime commercial cities like Boston, New York, and Philadelphia that expressed fury at the king-crony monopolists, whose mafia protection racket forced all colonial trade to pass through their ports and docks, extorting bribes every step of the way. An oligarchy of absentee lords who owned two-thirds of all the land in the colonies and refused – under feudal privilege – to let it be taxed, as did the lords in 1789 France and our own oligarchs today.

There were other grievances in the Declaration of Independence, such as Parliament's insistence that colonies stop issuing their own money, which had kept economic activity so vigorous that there were no slums or unemployed, until the new restrictions caused a depression. And yes, there was grumbling over the law forbidding migration over the Appalachians. What you won't find in the Declaration is much of anything that at all resembles the list of grudges issued by today's so-called Tea Party, subsidized by the Koch brothers and other kingly aristocrats.

---

[214] "The musical Hamilton brilliantly allows us to own and digest, rather than just assail, the Founders and their faults. A tragic hero brought down by a sex scandal... when one of his opponents (Jefferson) had his own affair to hide. Unsavory business dealings and shady characters lurking about... accusations of double-dealing... even potentially treasonous discussions with foreign powers? All there. And all still topical. There's a smart progressive way to engage with the Founders and we need more people to wake up and use it." – Dr. Allen Bryan.

Why did no one answer the "tea party" scam to hijack the American Revolution? As I've said repeatedly: our generals in this fight – at least till recently – seem… deficient.

It is not very unreasonable that the rich should contribute to the public expense, not only in proportion to their revenue, but something more than in that proportion.

– Adam Smith, The Wealth of Nations, Chapter II, Part II [215]

COMPETITION'S CONTRADICTIONS… AND A SOLUTION

For a supposed liberal polemicist, I hang around libertarians a fair amount. And why not? Some are among the liveliest minds I know. Anyway, I'll give them this – they invite me to berate and argue with them. That's a hopeful sign. Alas, as we'll discuss in a chapter devoted to that movement, libertarians have allowed paid shills to sway them into a bizarre conversion. So I start by demanding: *Isn't libertarianism fundamentally an appreciation of competition?*[216]

I openly avow – as did that founder of liberalism, Adam Smith – that competition is the greatest creative force in the universe. Competition produced all of nature's evolutionary marvels, including us. By far the most successful human enterprise – science – is inherently adversarial as scientists go at each other relentlessly. Moreover the arts, supposedly our "highest" endeavors, are often ferociously competitive, even when they lecture us about cooperation! The core enlightenment processes – *entrepreneurial markets, science, democracy* and *justice* – all produce the modern

---

[215] A good source for all things adamsmithian – http://adamsmithslostlegacy.blogspot.com/search/label/Vile%20Maxim

[216] As we'll see later, the "C-word" – competition – is seldom mentioned at libertarian gatherings anymore. It has been replaced – after decades of subsidized propaganda aimed at that community – by another sacred touchstone: "P" for Property. Sure, property is necessary to some degree, in order to incentivize market activity and there's nothing wrong with fair rewards fostering success. But like all good things – water, oxygen, food, sex – excess concentration becomes toxic. When confronted directly about this wholesale abandonment of the C-word, in favor of propertarian oligarchy, many libertarians instantly get it and blush with embarrassment.

miracle of positive-sum outcomes that way, as companies, laboratories, politicians, attorneys and folks like you all strive to do better than your rivals, creating (however imperfectly, so far) the famous rising tide that lifts all boats. Nor is this book you are reading anything other than deeply competitive.

Yes, there are also many *cooperative* or *consensus* or even *moral* aspects... read Adam Smith's *The Theory of Moral Sentiments*, to see that "competition" does not mean "cut-throat" or the brutal image of social darwinism. Not when it's healthy. We'll get to that, further down.

Alas, competition – in nature and primitive human societies (like ours) – contains an inherent *contradiction*. A runaway process of self-destruction that historically led – nearly always – to a particular kind of calamity...

...to the *winner* turning around and *cheating!* Adam Smith saw what had happened to markets and societies for millennia. Winners are never satisfied with success in the latest market battle, with a cool product or financial or political achievement. As humans, we use any recent advantage to ensure that competitors will fail in *future* struggles. To bias the next competition. To absorb their companies. Squat on patents. Craft monopolies or cartels to divvy-up the souk or bazaar. Spy on competitors, but keep them – and consumers – in the dark. Capture regulators and politicians. Make sure the laws favor us.

> *The proposal of any new law or regulation of commerce which comes from this order, ought always to be listened to with great precaution, and ought never to be adopted till after having been long and carefully examined, not only with the most scrupulous, but with the most suspicious attention. It comes from an order of men, whose interest is never exactly the same with that of the public, who have generally an interest to deceive and even to oppress the public, and who accordingly have, upon many occasions, both deceived and oppressed it.*

– Adam Smith *The Wealth of Nations,* Chapter XI, Part III

Victory on the battlefield may have made you great, but you don't want to return there again and again for an endless series of even matches! Yet, Smith showed that's exactly what's needed! Flat-fair-open-creative competition must go on and on, maximizing innovation while minimizing blood on the floor.

There is a clear example of how we can and have tamed that old contradiction, transforming from reciprocal destruction into endlessly vigorous, positive sum competition. That example is the system of ritualized combat called *sports,* where returning weekly for relatively even matches became the core idea and keeping competition credibly fair became the ruling obsession.[217]

Smith saw how cheating by owner-oligarchs wrecked the creative effectiveness of markets – the same cheating that frustrated the American founders and propelled them to Revolution. And so – in the seminal year 1776 – Smith called for something new. A way to get the best, most creative-competitive juices flowing in the largest possible variety of human beings, while preventing many old failure modes. As in sports, competition in economics and politics and civil life can only be self-sustaining – continuing to deliver positive-sum outcomes – if it happens amid a network of transparent, fine-tuned, relentlessly scrutinized and universally enforced rules.[218]

---

[217] "The United States, by contrast, holds a reputation in large parts of Europe as the epitome of winner-takes-all capitalism, yet it operates variants of a proto-socialist model for all of its major sports. Success is hailed, yet curtailed, and failure rewarded: The worst-placed teams get the first pick in the following season's draft of new players, allowing them to restock on talent, a form of redistribution rejected elsewhere in the American economy.... American sports are not so because they like socialism–they are simply taking the best path to making money." From Sports: America's Wildly Successful Socialist Experiment. The Atlantic 2019. https://www.theatlantic.com/international/archive/2019/09/us-europe-soccer-football/598012/

[218] *Fair* competition isn't just a matter of morality. It is also the way to maximize competitive output, by ensuring that bright people and teams get second, third chances and so on. And creating ever-flowing opportunities for new competitors to keep arising from the population of savvy, educated and empowered folk. That kind of fairness requires rules and careful tending to ensure new competitors can and will always arise to challenge last year's winners. And that earlier winners can't cheat. Because... we've seen... they will.

== A "Clock" Showing What We Got ==

One of the best bits of political polemic has been the "National Debt Clock," spinning up the rapid pace at which deficits pile burdens on our children. And yes, despite Modern Monetary Theory (MMT) - the liberal attempt to out-voodoo Supply Side - debt does matter. Only note that when we had surpluses and black ink under Bill Clinton, how conveniently the Debt Clock went "out of order," rather than honestly run backward. So much for honest polemic.

Oh, how's this for an easy-quick and devastating answer to the "hate-all-government" hypnosis! I'd love to see a second "National Debt Clock" showing where the U.S. deficit would be now - likely running surpluses - if we taxpayers had charged just a *5% royalty on the fruits of U.S. federal research*!

Oh there were solid policy reasons to choose otherwise. And those reasons may be obsolete. Anyway, in an era of jibbering dogmatists, how effective such a "clock" would be. We deserve such a tasty piece of counter propaganda. (See: Eight Causes of the Deficit Fiscal Cliff.[219])

====

GOVERNMENT, COMPETITION'S BIGGEST FRIEND

Another figure who is – like Adam Smith – both worshipped and heretically misinterpreted by the right is Nobel Prize winning economist Friedrich Hayek. For all his many jeremiads against the stifling effects of excess regulation, Hayek returned to a core point that *markets work best when they have a maximum number of skilled, knowledgeable and empowered participants.* Only then can wisdom of the (broadly informed) crowd overcome the inevitable biases and incomplete pictures clutched by smaller, controlling elites. (We'll touch on him again in Pause #12.)

Ponder a moment how that outcome is diametrically opposite to the central aim of oligarchy.[220] Then consider this.

---

[219] Fiscal cliff. http://davidbrin.blogspot.com/2012/10/eight-causes-of-deficit-fiscal-cliff.html

[220] Hayek drummed hard against the foremost, inherently ignorant controlling elite – government regulators. But if pressed, he admitted the dismal record of two-score centuries of far more inbred-ignorant aristocracies. Moreover, it's doubtful that investment and resource allocation will be more "market wise" if the transparency rules of 100,000 diverse and accountable civil servants are replace by the self-justified, conniving whim of a few hundred secretive CEO/Wall Street lords.

At least half of the government 'interventions" we've seen, across the last 80 years, were aimed at uplifting countless members of disadvantaged or repressed castes high enough so they can compete.

Minorities and women who get rights can enter the marketplace as skilled, knowledgeable and empowered participants, whether as competitors or savvy consumers. Appalachian children – or those in ghettos or native reservations – who get enough food, sanitation, health care and education can enter the marketplace as skilled, knowledgeable and emboldened participants. Infrastructure helps too, bringing them water and Internet and letting them travel. Likewise research into medical or other problems that hold so many back from skillful, joyfully brash competition. Equal justice and monopoly-prevention keep competition avid. And a basic safety net encourages entrepreneurs, workers and small business owners to take risks, knowing their children won't starve and they can find their way back, in case of failure. There are second chances.

At least half of all liberal government programs need no "moral" justifications at all! The pragmatic reason – to stop wasting talent – is sufficient. It bears repeating, so here's that pro-competition criterion again:

Will this government intervention expand capability and opportunity, helping to increase the number of skilled, vigorous competitors?

Some liberal programs fail that test! Some *do* try to "pick winners and losers" without a compelling, long range need. Others *do* try to "equalize outcomes, not opportunity." Those exceptions can be scrutinized by libertarians or libertarian-minded Republicans, and fiercely subjected to criticism or negotiation by other standards. Still, the most towering hypocrisy is to reject those government interventions that Adam Smith demanded – and that Hayek often grudgingly accepted – that increase the number of capable participants in wide open markets. At least non-hypocrites would show plans for replacing those interventions with non-government ways to expand participation – to stop wasting talent – in practice, not theory.

Should much of this have gone into the chapter on Economics? Maybe. But here's where the point distills most clear. Government is a tool. It *can* be applied by the mighty against the People – and that fear is expressed in the Suspicion of Authority messages of countless Hollywood films.

Or else it can be applied as the Founders – including their mentor Adam Smith – intended, as a set of openly negotiated rules and referees that actually *help* citizens to get on with their lives and ambitions, free from the cheating and oppression that constrained all our ancestors before. The Greatest Generation crafted an equilibrium that involved a *lot* of rules and taxes! That equilibrium was an immense success and subsequent assaults upon it have resulted in horrific failures. But it's possible our ten billion highly educated and perceptive children – armed with AI modeling tools and bursting with individual confidence – may find good results with something looser.

Toward that end, there's a place for libertarians and conservatives applying pressure always to re-examine and re-justify government and its rules. But you folks must first concede the oligarchic calamity of 6000 years. You must admit the calamities you've thrust upon us. Earn back some credibility. Start by opening a book you rave about, without ever reading a word, Adam Smith's *Wealth of Nations.*

=====

Have I struck you as reticent and shy? Too demure to speak out when something bothers me? Well, I'll try to correct that. Especially regarding the innumerable times that liberal/democrat/blue leaders *fail to exploit weaknesses* on the mad right.

One of the most infuriating has been allowing that shill-for-oligarchy movement to expropriate countless virtue-symbols as their private property. We'll discuss the right's *symbolism obsession* at several points – ranging from Confederate statues and flags to ship-names to "strong father" preening. But possibly the most stunning of all failures in liberal-moderate generalship was allowing the so-called "Tea Party" to glom a *claim on the American Revolution.*

At risk of repetition, in Chapter 14 I'll show that the revolution was almost entirely a "blue" uprising and what I call Phase One of the U.S. Civil War. Crum, will anyone bother to read Jefferson's prose in the Declaration

of Independence? Or perceive why it was maritime commercial cities, like Boston, New York, and Philadelphia that expressed fury at the king-crony monopolists, whose mafia protection racket forced all colonial trade to pass through their ports and docks, extorting bribes every step of the way? Another top grievance was the oligarchy of absentee lords who owned two-thirds of all the land in the colonies and refused – under feudal privilege – to let it be taxed, as did the lords in 1789 France and our own oligarchs, today. [221]

It was a revolution against owner-caste oligarchy and cheating! Adam Smith recommended the remedy of democracy, plus openly negotiated and deliberated laws that are evenly enforced by transparently accountable civil servants. And our markets got better – more creative and productive – each time those rules were adjusted to expand our circles of democratic inclusion. Yet fools on *our* side in this latest phase have allowed that great rebellion to be hijacked by pro-aristocracy propagandists, letting stand their claim that our Revolution was against "government."

Hello?

=====

SCIENCE THIS

Let's zoom back to Mick Mulvaney's assertion – supported by far-right rationalizers like Matt Ridley[222] – that government supported science is useless and counter-productive, that the forward march of technological discovery is fore-ordained, that competitive markets allocate funds to develop new products with greater efficiency than government bureaucrats picking winners and losers, and that research without a clear, near-future economic return is both futile and unnecessary.

---

[221] Yes, lefties, the whole birth of our nation was tainted by original sins like slavery. But the Revolution *was* propelled far more by states that had banned it and ardent abolitionists like Adams and Franklin, plus other 'great men' who at least expressed hypocritical homage to getting rid of it. In Chapter 14 we'll go into why the British knew they'd get more support *against* the rebellion in the South. No, you should reclaim the Declaration of Independence for what it was – a major step forward along a terribly long and hard road.

[222] 'Worth of basic science attacked as a mere "myth" https://physicstoday.scitation.org/do/10.1063/PT.5.8146/full/

Former Microsoft CTO and IP Impressario Nathan Myhrvold issued a powerful rebuttal to Ridley's murdochian call for amputation:

"It's natural for writers to want to come out with a contrarian piece that reverses all conventional wisdom, but it tends to work out better if the evidence one quotes is factually true. Alas Ridley's evidence isn't – his examples are all, so far as I can tell, either completely wrong, or at best selectively quoted. I also think his logic is wrong, and to be honest I don't think much of the ideology that drives his argument either."

Woof. Nathan's rebuttal can be found here, along with links to the original, and Ridley's response.[223]

Expanding from Myhrvold's points, let's put all of this into *those 60 centuries I keep citing.* During most of that time, independent innovation was actively suppressed by kings and lords and priests, fearing anything (except new armaments) that might upset the stable hierarchy. In his monograph, "Entrepreneurship: Productive, Unproductive and Destructive," economist William J. Baumol tells a story widely repeated among classical sources like Pliny and Petronius, of an inventor who presented the secret of unbreakable glass to Emperor Tiberius, only to receive death, instead of a reward, because the invention was viewed as destabilizing... a tale reset in China by Ray Bradbury in "The Flying Machine." Baumol cites earlier words by M. Finley:

"Technological progress, economic growth, productivity, even efficiency have not been significant goals since the beginning of time. So long as an acceptable life style could be maintained, however that was defined (by the ruling castes), other values held the stage."

Those "other values" – critiqued by Smith– included rent-seeking, noble privilege, monopolies, cartels or (in Baumol's more modern analysis) state corporations and commissariats and organized crime. With rare exception, parasitical cheats were more privileged than competitive innovation.

Moreover, across nearly all of history, innovators felt a strong incentive to keep any discoveries *secret*, lest competitors steal their advantage.

---

[223] Myrhvold rebuttal: http://www.wsj.com/articles/where-does-technological-innovation-come-from-1447258125?tesla=y

Hence, many brilliant inventions were lost when the discoverers or direct heirs died, from Heron's steam engines and Baghdad Batteries to Antikythera-style mechanical calculators and Damascus steel – from clear glass lenses to obstetric forceps – all lost for millennia before being rediscovered after much needless pain.

History does offer rare examples when innovation flourished, with spectacular returns. In most, state investment and focused R&D played a major role: from the great Chinese fleets of Admiral Cheng He to impressive maritime research centers established by Prince Henry the Navigator, that made little Portugal a giant on the world stage. Likewise, tiny Holland became a global leader, stimulated by its free-city universities. England advanced tech rapidly with endowed scientific chairs, state subsidies and prizes.

Of course none compare to the exponential growth unleashed by late-20th Century America's synergy of government, enterprise and unleashed individual competitiveness. One result was the first society transforming itself from the feudal *pyramid of privilege to a diamond shape*[224] whose vast and healthy and well-educated middle class proved to be the generator of nearly all our great accomplishments.

This slams a steep *burden of proof* upon Mulvaney and others who assert *we* are the ones doing something wrong. Or that innovation will just zoom ahead as if by natural law. But then, their aim is *not* what they claim – to release us from thralldom to shortsighted, oppressive civil servants and snooty scientist-boffins. It is to discredit all of the modern expert castes. And by now we know why.

== What happens when regulations go stale? ==

About that thralldom to officious bureaucrats. Yes, classic conservatives and libertarians have a point – there will always be a danger that umpires may be corrupted, or for referees to get sluggish, or suborned, or to meddle unnecessarily, thwarting the whole purpose of the game. It's not wrong to focus SoA in that direction! The last generation's reforms will always need re-scrutinization. Admitted.

---

[224] For more on the diamond-shaped society. http://davidbrin.blogspot.com/2011/09/class-war-and-lessons-of-history.html

Okay then, here's a question: who actually de-regulates, when appropriate?

Ayn Rand followers howl over "captured" agencies that serve only major industry players, throttling, not fostering, creative competition. Rand's favorite examples? The railroad regulating Interstate Commerce Commission (ICC) and the market stifling Civil Aeronautics Board (CAB).[225] Alas, her followers never pause to notice what became of those bureaucratic traitors... decades ago.

Democrats banished them! Moreover, AT&T was broken up and the Internet was unleashed by legislation authored and pushed through Congress by Al Gore, two regulatory openings that had absolutely stunning market consequences.

Now add Bill Clinton's deregulation of GPS, Al Gore's paperwork reduction "reinventing government" campaign and Barack Obama's declaration that citizens may record police (and the list goes on). Whereupon one has to ask...

... where were Republicans in all this? Does anti-regulatory *polemic* matter more than effective action? Despite their railings - and holding most of the political cards for all but two of the last twenty-five years - "conservatives" never delivered major deregulation on the scale of those Democratic unleashings.[226] Except repeatedly in two particular industries - finance and resource extraction - with *historic* results they want us to ignore or forget. Please name another example.

Libertarians like their aphorism: Liberals want freedom in the bedroom. Republicans want freedom in the boardroom. We want both! Then they shrug, hold their noses theatrically and vote Republican. Sure, the GOP favors the boardroom - members of the Wall Street and CEO castes. But not competition, or entrepreneurship, or healthy markets. Or delivering even on core promises.

---

[225] Dissected in detail in "Atlas Shrugged: The Hidden Context of the Book and Film." http://www.davidbrin.com/nonfiction/aynrand.html

[226] This challenge stood the test of time, until Donald Trump began the wholesale demolition of agencies in ways that did not attempt to *change* laws, duly legislated, but by blatantly violating them. To be clear, for much of the last 20 years the Republican Party owned and operated all three branches of U.S. government. They could have deregulated by changing laws. They chose this approach, in contempt for the Founders and Adam Smith.

====

WE ARE DIFFERENT. AND DIFFERENT IS DIFFICULT

I've asserted that the Rooseveltian reforms might have been too successful. Historians credit them with saving western capitalism by vesting the working class with a large stake. Indeed, they were so successful that the very idea of class war – rampant across almost every other nation and time – seems not even to occur to American boomers.[227] But as boomers age-out, is that grand time of naïve delusion over?

Forbes in 2016 announced that just 62 ultra-rich individuals have as much wealth as the bottom half of humanity.[228] Five years before, it took 388 rich guys to achieve that status.[229] Which raises a question I'll repeat *ad nauseam* throughout this book. *Where the heck does this rising, proto-feudal oligarchy think it will all lead?*

To a restoration of humanity's normal, aristocratic pyramid of power, with them on top? Or to radicalization, as a billion members of the hard-pressed but highly skilled and tech-empowered middle class rediscover class struggle, alongside five billion angry workers? (I portray both possibilities in a near-future novel, *Existence.*) The last time this happened, in the 1930s, lordly owner castes in Germany, Japan, Britain and the U.S. used their mass media ownership to stir populist rightwing movements, hoping to suppress activity on the left while allowing business as usual. Not one of these efforts succeeded. In Germany, Italy, Spain and Japan, their pet monsters rose up and took over, leading to immense pain for all and eventual loss of most of that oligarchic wealth.

In Britain and the U.S. 1930s reactionary fomenters dragged us all-too-near the same path… till *moderate reformers* accomplished what neither Karl Marx nor the fascists deemed possible – adjusted the wealth imbalance and reduced cheating advantages, so that a rational and flat-open-fair capitalism would be moderated by reciprocal competition, un-

---

[227] "Class War and lessons of history." http://davidbrin.blogspot.com/2011/09/class-war-and-lessons-of-history.html

[228] http://www.huffingtonpost.com/entry/global-wealth-inequality_us_56991defe4b0ce4964242e09?ir=Impact§ion=impact&utm_hp_ref=impact

[229] See: The 500 Richest Individuals in 2015 and commentary. http://www.forbes.com/sites/chasewithorn/2015/03/02/forbes-billionaires-full-list-of-the-500-richest-people-in-the-world-2015/#3df88bf316e3367f7a8b16e3

der transparent rules and stimulated by investments in a healthy, educated population. None of that even slightly damaged the Smithian incentives to get rich through delivery of innovative goods and services. That brilliant, positive-sum moderation led to big majorities in our parents' middle class Greatest Generation adoring one living human above all others: Franklin Delano Roosevelt.

(Again, ask MAGA folks: *"When was America great?"* Chapter 3.)

Some billionaires *aren't* shortsighted fools, ignorant of historical lessons. Bill Gates, Warren Buffet and many tech moguls want wealth disparities brought down through reasonable, negotiated Rooseveltian-style reform that will still leave them standing as very, very wealthy people. Heck, even Glenn Beck[230] can now see where it all leads, declaring recently (in effect) "OMG what have I done?"

The smart ones know where current trends will otherwise lead. To revolution and confiscation. Picture the probabilities, when the world's poorest realize they could *double* their net wealth, just by transferring *title* from 50 would-be gods. In that case, amid a standoff between fifty oligarchs and three billion poor, it is the skilled middle and upper-middle classes who'll be the ones deciding civilization's course. And who do you think those billion tech-savvy professionals – so derided and maligned by murdochian propaganda – will side with, when push comes to shove?

It's time to look again at the most successful social compact ever created – the Rooseveltian deal made by the Greatest Generation – which we then amended and improved by reducing race and gender injustice and discovering the importance of planetary care. Throw in a vibrantly confident wave of tech-savvy youth, and that is how we can all move forward. Away from dismal feudalism. Toward (maybe) something like *Star Trek.*

This article ran originally as a special report in the January 2016 newsletter of Mark Anderson's Strategic News Service.[231]

---

[230] Re Glenn Beck http://www.nytimes.com/2016/11/27/magazine/glenn-beck-is-sorry-about-all-that.html?rref=collection%2Fsectioncollection%2Fmagazine&action=click&contentCollection=magazine®ion=rank&module=package&version=highlights&contentPlacement=7&pgtype=sectionfront

[231] Strategic News Service: https://www.stratnews.com/

A drum I have beat for ages, in speeches at agencies and companies. I pray I won't be best remembered as the Cassandra people should have heeded.

Pause #10 for...

Emergency Readiness.

Professor Peter Denning of the Naval Post-Graduate School in Monterey CA interviewed me in Communications of the ACM (CACM) about "resilience" of our critical infrastructure,[232] from the power grid and cell phones to transportation, food supplies and solar roofs, from water supplies, and transportation to the Internet. These nerve and bloodlines for society depend on reliable connections. What would happen if a massive cyber attack or an electromagnetic pulse, or other failure mode took down the electric grid in a way that requires many months or even years for repair? What about a natural disaster such as hurricane, wildfire, or earthquake that disabled all cell phone communications for an extended period?

Does this relate to polemical judo? Of course it does, since we need a functioning civilization in order to repair its politics. Anyway, candidates who talk about this will give a sober, serious impression to voters.

(Note: the matter of military readiness is deferred to volume 2. Though a consensus is growing, among military professionals.[233])

---

232 "An Interview with David Brin on Resiliency" https://m-cacm.acm.org/magazines/2019/6/236996-an-interview-with-david-brin-on-resiliency/fulltext A shortened version appeared on the IEET site: https://ieet.org/index.php/IEET2/more/Brin20171010 And I hope to post the whole thing online soon.

233 The retired Navy admiral who oversaw the mission that killed Osama bin Laden rebuked President Donald Trump for what he called the abandonment American leadership domestically and abroad in an op-ed, citing what he said he'd heard from members of the military and intelligence community. "The America that they believed in was under attack, not from without, but from within," Adm. William H. McRaven, who led the U.S. Special Operations Command before retiring, wrote in the New York Times. On the same day gen. David Petraeus calls the Syria withdrawal 'a betrayal' And former Defense Secretary James Mattis 'roasted' President Trump with merciless jibes. https://abcnews.go.com/Politics/navy-seal-commander-us-attack-trump/story?id=66370025 and https://www.npr.org/2019/10/19/771546293/kurdish-general-slams-u-s-syria-policy-gen-petraeus-calls-withdrawal-a-betrayal

Here I offer a dozen measures – some of them easy/cheap – that could improve robustness of critical infrastructures against shocks, preventing us from ever facing a "Postman" situation. And yes, I'm qualified as a physicist, electrical engineer and longtime consultant on these matters with corporations and agencies. But frankly, it's the science fiction. Of course it is.

Q: What is the difference between resilience and anticipation?

Brin: Our prefrontal lobes help us envision possible futures, anticipating threats and opportunities. Planners and responders augment these organs with predictive models, intel-gathering, and Big Data, all in search of dangers to anticipate and counter in advance. Citizens know little about how many bad things these protectors have averted. But this specialization in anticipation makes it hard for protectors to appreciate how we cope when our best-laid plans fail, which they do, sooner or later.

Resilience is how we handle unexpected contingencies. It enables us to roll with any blow and come up fighting, keeping a surprise from being lethal. It's what worked on 9/11, when all anticipatory protective measures failed.

====

What you personally can do

Other than help agitate for politicians and civil servants to pay attention, what can you do about all this? Plenty, like checking to see if your locale allows and offers the new boxes letting your roof solar power your own home. Or equipping your cell phones with apps to access mesh networks. Or just making sure your household emergency supplies are up-to-date.

One thing I've done... join CERT, the national network of Community Emergency Response Teams.[234] It's what's left of civil defense in the U.S., as Fire Departments all across the country offer 20-hour training sets that will minimally prepare you to be a (very) basic "responder." (Complete with some nifty equipment.) And if you are a therapist or ham radio operator, there are other groups for you.

---

234 Community Emergency Response Teams https://www.ready.gov/community-emergency-response-team

Also, load up on some NGOs... those activist orgs[235] who will merge your annual membership dues with millions of others to hire top pros who will then work daily as your proxies to save the world for you. And you can pick only those who are doing what you think needs doing. What a deal. I've nagged you about this before. I'll do it again.

====

Q: Let's see what anticipation and resilience look like for a common threat, disruptive electrical outages. They can be caused by storms, birds, squirrels, power grid overload, or even preventive reduction of wildfire risk. Without power, we cannot use our computers or access our files stored in the Internet. Even our best disaster planning cannot fix the disruption if infrastructure damage is severe. Yet, communication is essential for recovery. What can we do to preserve our ability to communicate?

Brin: On 9/11, passengers aboard flight UA93 demonstrated remarkable resilience when they self-organized to stop the terrorist plot to use that plane as a weapon against their country. If we want that kind of resilience to work on a large scale, we need resilient communications. Alas, our comm systems are fragile to failure in any natural or unnatural calamity. One step toward resilience would be a backup peer-to-peer (P2P) text passing capability for when phones can't link to a cellular tower. Texts would get passed from phone to phone via well-understood methods of packet switching until they encounter a working node and get dropped into the network. Qualcomm already has this capability built into their chips! But cellular providers refuse to turn it on. That's shortsighted, since it would be good business too, expanding text coverage zones and opening new revenue streams. Even in the worst national disaster, we'd have a 1940s level telegraphy system all across the nation, and pretty much around the world.

All it would take to fix this is a small change of regulation. Five sentences requiring the cell-cos to turn this on whenever a phone doesn't sense a tower. (And charge a small fee for P2P texts.) Doing so might let us restore communications within an hour rather than months.

---

235 Joining NGOs: http://www.davidbrin.com/nonfiction/proxyactivism.html

Many efforts have been made to empower folks with ad hoc mesh networks, via Bluetooth, wifi webs, and so on. None of these enticed more than a tiny user base – nothing like what's needed for national resilience.

Later news item: In August 2019 Apple announced it had shelved a "walkie-talkie" feature that would have allowed iPhone users to communicate with each other in areas without cellular coverage. Apple was working with Intel to enable iPhone users to send messages directly to other iPhone users over long-distance radio waves that bypass cellular networks. (Different from Apple Watch's Walkie-Talkie feature, which relies on Wi-Fi or cell connection.) The project is said to have been suspended in part because Apple is expected to switch from Intel to Qualcomm modems in iPhones starting in 2020. (But as mentioned, Qualcomm also has a method to bypass cellular texting.)

Q: It appears that solar power for homes and offices is at a tipping point as more people find it cheaper than the power grid. Localized solar power should also bring new benefits such as ability to maintain minimum electrical function at home during a blackout. Is independence from the electrical grid good for resilience?

Brin: It would be. One can envision four million solar-roofed homes and businesses serving as islands of light for their neighborhoods, in any emergency. But there's a catch. Under current regulations, most U.S. solar roofs have a switch that shuts down the home or business solar system when the electrical utility has blacked out. The purpose is to prevent spurious home-generated voltages from endangering repair linemen. This is a lame excuse for an insane situation. Simply replace that cutoff switch with one that would still block backflow into the grid, but that feeds from the solar inverter to just 2 or 3 outlets inside the home, running the fridge, some rechargers, and possibly satellite coms.

Just changing over to that switch would generate archipelagos of autonomous, resilient civilization spread across every neighborhood in America, even in the very worst case. A new rule requiring such switches, and fostering retrofitting, would fit on less than a page.

Across the next decade, more solar systems will come with battery storage. But this reform would help us bridge the next ten years.

Later News Item: In October 2019 California passed a law requiring all newly constructed homes to have solar roofs. That same month, several major utilities blacked out half a million customers at a time, to ensure that hot winds would not cause powerlines to spark wild fires. The combination will likely send solar installations upward dramatically. If all of the new units are better designed to provide inward power even during blackouts, then we may see this dismal fragility start to ease.

Q: What about protection against Electro Magnetic Pulse disruption?

Brin: Much has been written about danger from EMP – either attacks by hostile powers or else the sort of natural disaster we might experience if the Sun ever struck us head-on with a Coronal Mass Ejection, commonly called a solar flare. These CMEs happen often, peaking every eleven years. We've been lucky as the worst ones have missed Earth. But some space probes have been taken out by direct hits and a bulls-eye is inevitable.

The EMP threat was recognized over thirty years ago. We could have incentivized gradual development of shielded and breakered chip-sets, including those in civilian electronics. Adoption could have been stimulated with a tax of a penny per non-compliant device, with foreseen ramp-up. By now we'd be EMP resilient, instead of fragile hostages either to enemies or to fate.

Q: What about solar on the southward walls of buildings to power the buildings? Some cities are already doing this.

Brin: Sure, south-facing walls are another place for photovoltaics. But there's competition for that valuable real estate – urban agriculture. Technologies are cresting toward where future cities may require new buildings to recycle their organic waste through vertical farms that purify water while generating either industrial algae or else much of the food needed by a metropolis. With so much of the world's population going urban, no technology could make a bigger difference. The pieces are coming together. What's lacking is a sense of urgency. Pilot programs and tax incentives should encourage new tall buildings to utilize their southward faces, nurturing this stabilizing trend during the coming decade.

Q: You've also spoken about apps systems that turn your smartphone into an intelligent sensor. Can you say how this supports resiliency?

Brin: Cell phones already have powerful cameras, many with infrared capability. Soon will come spectrum-analysis apps, letting citizens do local spot checks on chemical spills or environmental problems, and feeding the results to governments or NGOs for modeling in real time. The Tricorder X Prize showed how just a few add-on devices can turn a phone into a medical appraisal device, like Dr. McCoy had in Star Trek. Almost anyone could use such apparatus in the field with little training. Take a few measurements, and a distant system advises you on corrective actions.

Infrared sensors, accelerometers, and chemical sensors could provide a full array of environmental awareness systems by turning citizen cell phones into nodes of an instant awareness network. (I describe this in my novel Existence.)

Such a mesh is already of interest to national authorities. But the emphasis has been hierarchical - authorities send public reports down to citizens after gathering and interpreting data flowing upward. The hierarchical mindset comes naturally when you are an authority with protective duties. But this can blind even sincere public servants to one of our great strengths - the ability of average citizens to self-organize laterally.

Use your imagination. The greatest long-term advantage of our kind of society is that lateral citizen networks, while occasionally inconvenient to public servants, aren't any kind of macro-threat, but will make civilization perform better. This is in contrast to despotic regimes, for whom such citizen empowerment would be lethal.

Q: Some of your proposals are less familiar. You have spoken of "all sky awareness." What is that and how does it improve resiliency?

Brin: Defense and intelligence folks know we need better 24/7 omni-awareness of land, sea and air. Major efforts involve protective services and space assets. When the Large Synoptic Telescope comes online in Chile, we'll find 100 times as many asteroids that could threaten our planet, or like the one that broke 10,000 windows in Chelyabinsk. Closer to home, dangerous space debris should be tracked round the globe.

Similar technology could improve air safety and impede smugglers by tracking both legal and illicit air traffic. For example, the cell networks I mentioned earlier could detect and triangulate aircraft engine sounds for comparison to an ongoing database, especially at low altitudes where drug smugglers and human traffickers operate, or where terrorists might attempt an attack, or detecting the path of airliners that stray, like Malaysian Air flight 370. Imagine those in peripheries like Canada, Alaska or nearby waters automatically reporting sonic booms. Among a myriad more mundane uses, these might perhaps localize incoming hypersonic weapons, of the kind announced recently by Russian President Vladimir Putin.

Sound implausible? In December 2018, a loose network of amateur "plane-spotters" managed to track Air Force One visually, during President Trump's top-secret Christmas dash to a U.S. air base in Iraq. A U.K. photographer used these clues to snap the unmistakable, blue-and-white 747 jetting far overhead.

Another method: revive the SETI League's Project Argus, aiming to establish radio and optical detectors in 5000 amateurs' back yards, spread around the world. As Earth rotates, these backyard stations would sweep the sky in overlapping swathes, sifting for anomalous signals, but also detecting almost anything interesting that happens up there. Argus failed earlier because of the complexity and expense of racks of equipment. Today – with a small up-front investment by some mere-millionaire – we could offer a small box for a couple of hundred bucks that could be latched to an old TV dish-antenna, then Wi-Fi linked via the owner's home. The dish – plus a small optical detector – could report detections in real time and any pair or trio that correlate would then trigger a look by higher-level, aimable devices.

Sure, most of the participants would think of their backyard SETI stations as helping sift the sky for aliens. So? As a side benefit, we'd become hundreds of times better at detecting almost any transient phenomenon overhead, improving both anticipation and resilience.

I can go on with a much longer list of unconventional and generally very inexpensive ways that very simple regulatory or incentive actions might transform national resilience, making society more robust to withstand shocks across the decades ahead.

Q: What about civil unrest or lawlessness if the disaster takes out or overwhelms local law enforcement? Easy to see gangs roaming affluent neighborhoods in SUVs stealing stuff and especially food, with no police to stop them.

Brin: I well understand this worry! I've written collapse-of-civilization tales. (One of them, The Postman, was filmed by Kevin Costner.) Hollywood presents so many apocalyptic scenarios, we tend to assume we live on a fragile edge of collapse. But Rebecca Solnit's book, A Paradise Built In Hell, shows decisively that average citizens - whether liberal or conservative - are actually pretty tough and dynamic. They quickly self-organize to help their neighbors. A quarter or more of citizens will almost always run toward whatever the problem is. Take citizen response on 9/11, or when disasters hit their neighborhoods.[236] See also research by Philpot et. al., showing that bystanders will intervene to try to make peace, in the presence of a conflict.[237]

If "affluent neighborhoods" want to be safe, there's one method that works over the long run... don't alienate the poor and middle class and ensure that the vast majority identify as members of the same overall tribe. As neighbors, we'll come to your defense.

Q: Anything to mitigate cyber attacks, including phishing and massive identity theft?

Brin: Sincere people across the spectrum are right to worry about companies and governments collecting massive amounts of personal data on citizens: from the ways they use their smartphones, to always-on mics at home and office (e.g. Alexa). Phishing is another example where crooks use already open knowledge about you to lure you into fatal online mistakes. We all fret about disparities of power that may lead to the "telescreen" in George Orwell's Nineteen Eighty-Four. From facial recognition to video fakery to brainwave interpretation and lie detectors, if these techs are monopolized by one elite or another, we may get Big Brother forever. There are forces in the world who are eager for this. China's "social credit" system aims to stir the masses to enforce conformity on one another.[238]

In the West, most people are right to find this prospect terrifying. The reflex in response is to say, "let's ban or restrict this new kind of light."

---

[236] Examples are innumerable, as when students in Christchurch New Zealand self-organized after an earthquake so well they ran out of tasks. Famously George W Bush's administration and Louisiana officials made it a high priority to thwart such efforts, during Hurricane Katrina.

[237] "Would I be helped? Cross-national CCTV footage shows that intervention is the norm in public conflicts." https://psycnet.apa.org/doiLanding?doi=10.1037%2Famp0000469

[238] The Chinese regime announced a new rule which requires residents to pass a facial recognition test in order to apply for an internet connection via smartphone or computer. From Dec. 1, 2019, no cell phone or landline number can be transferred to another person privately.

And that is the worst possible prescription. The elites we fear will only gain great power if they can operate in secret, enhancing that disparity, because we won't be able to look back.

Consider. It matters much less what elites of all kinds know about you than what they can do to you. And the only thing that deters the latter is what we know about them. Denying elites the power to see has never happened (for long) anywhere in the history of the world. But denying them the ability to harm citizens is something we've (imperfectly) accomplished for 200 years. We've done it by insisting that we get to see, too. If not as individuals, then via the NGOs we hire to look for us.

As I appraise in The Transparent Society, the answer is more light, not less, for common citizens to be empowered by technology to take up much of the burden of supervising and arguing and applying accountability. The more we can see the less the bad groups can hide. If we do this, we'll not only be resilient, we'll never have Big Brother.

The answer to phishing, ID theft, etc. is the same as always – to catch and deter villains, by ending most shadows for roaches to hide in.

Q: We don't know how to do this because the Internet itself is baked in a cloak of anonymity. We are not going to redesign the Internet protocols any time soon. We need more than light. Isn't the solution good locks on our databases?

Sorry, show me one time when "good locks" worked for very long. Every week, some previously "for sure" database is raided or leaks. All that needs happen is for any lock to fail once, at all, via code-breaking or hacking or phishing or human error, and the information is loose, infinitely copyable. If you base your sense of safety on secrecy, it will be impossible to verify what others don't know.

Look, I'm not saying that there should be no secrets or privacy! Our skilled protectors need tactical secrecy to do their jobs. But smaller volumes and perimeters are easier to defend and seal. It has always been U.S. policy that secrecy should bear some burden of justification and – eventually – a time limit.

This isn't the time or place to argue the point. Alas, the reflex to seek safety in shadows is so strong that folks forget how we got the very freedoms, wealth and justice we worry about losing. Not by hiding but by assertively demanding to see. What I do ask is that you squint and look ahead fifty or a hundred years, and ask what is our baseline victory condition?

Every enemy of this enlightenment, individualist, open-society experiment – every lethal foe – is mortally allergic to light. They suffer when their plans, methods, agents and resources are revealed. In contrast, we are at worst inconvenienced and – as shown by the Snowden and WikiLeaks affairs – even prodded to improve a bit. If, say in fifty years, there is worldwide transparency of ownership and power and action, then we win. We – a humanity that is inquisitive, confident, individualistic and free – simply win.

Q: These resiliency proposals all sound so reasonable. Why have they not been implemented?

A cynic would answer that there's not much economic-constituency behind resilience. No big-ticket orders. How much money is to be made from a slightly costlier home-solar cutoff switch that would feed rooftop energy to three outlets in a million U.S. homes? I spoke about backup peer-to-peer texting at a defense industry conference where a Verizon vice-president in attendance went absolutely livid. Qualcomm tried subsequently to get them – and AT&T – to try some regional experiments; might P2P texting might actually turn a profit? Alas, no one wants to risk disruption, even though this one function could knit our entire continent together, in a crisis.

EMP resistance should have been slowly woven into civilian electronics for decades. And here's a thought – maybe it has been! After all, if we had truly savvy leaders, they would want to slide this protection into place as quietly as possible. Why? Because there is a critical vulnerability window, during which those who are thinking about hitting us might strike if they see the chance slipping away. History shows that such transitions can be dangerous, as revealed by John F. Kennedy in While England Slept.

Some bright folks are paying attention. Elon Musk told me he would fix the solar cutoff problem with his Power Wall storage system, and that is the answer... in a decade. A $100 switch to allow daytime self-power would still be worthwhile till then. Another zillionaire expressed interest in the all-sky awareness project, but more for its contribution to SETI than national or world security. Membership in CERT – Community Emergency Response Teams – rises every year. And so it goes. Just way too slowly.

What matters is the very concept of resilience, which worked so well on 9/11 and at every turn of American history. The U.S. Army, till just one generation ago, based its emergency planning on vast pools of talented, healthy volunteers rushing in to fill the thin blue line. Sure, in an era of high tech and lightning reaction times, we must rely on a highly professional cadre of protectors. But the worst thing they could do is to declare "Count on us... and only on us."

No, dear defenders. We love you and thank you for your service. But a time will come – maybe soon or much later – when you will fail. And when that happens, it will be our turn – citizens – to step up.

Help us to prepare, and we won't let you down.

Where they claim they are the pragmatic and frugal ones…

Chapter 11

Economics – No, you don't get Adam Smith… and Other Rationalizations

"For as wealth is power, so all power will infallibly draw wealth to itself by some means or other."
– Edmund Burke (1780)

In August 2019 a coalition of executives representing some of America's largest companies issued a statement that redefines "the purpose of a corporation."[239] No longer should the primary goal be to advance the interests of shareholders, said the Business Roundtable. "Companies must also invest in employees, deliver value to customers and deal ethically with suppliers." The statement was signed by nearly 200 chief executives, including the leaders of Apple, American Airlines, Accenture, AT&T, Bank of America, Boeing and BlackRock.

"While each of our individual companies serves its own corporate purpose, we share a fundamental commitment to all of our stakeholders," the statement said. "We commit to deliver value to all of them, for the future success of our companies, our communities and our country."

Now of course we can all be excused some cynicism, knowing these executives owe their jobs to cartels of the biggest proxy voters. Moreover, many of them have manipulated rules of incorporation and taxation

239 "Milton Friedman Was Wrong: The famed economist's "shareholder theory" provides corporations with too much room to violate consumers' rights and trust." https://www.theatlantic.com/ideas/archive/2019/08/milton-friedman-shareholder-wrong/596545/

to keep trillions stashed outside of 'our country.' And a habit of craven kowtowing to very large, despotic foreign powers has tested every moral claim.

Still, the statement amounts to a long overdue correction of a malignant tumor-meme that infected corporate America since 1970, Milton Friedman's cant that corporate officers owe duty only to immediate value for big shareholders.[240] Everything else, Friedman soothed, from long range planning to investment, to reputation, to the good of the commonwealth that supports our people and system, would work itself out via basic market forces. Unleashed from any residual sense of complexity or duty, members of an ever-narrowing CEO caste appointed each other to boards that then set ever-escalating executive compensation packages based on quarterly stock performance.

Under sway of the ones who would benefit most, Republican Congresses not only passed Supply Side tax cuts that supremely favored the upper crust, but removed controls that the Greatest Generation had put on maneuvers like *stock buybacks,* in which companies have lately spent many tens of billions in reserves and profits purchasing and inflating their own shares in order to... you guessed it... help officers make their "Friedman goals," their magic bonus value thresholds.

Results have been uniformly disastrous, with corporate R&D and long term investment rates plummeting while executive pay, including stock and bonuses, went through the roof. So what are we to make of this?

THE BIG LIE: FISCAL RESPONSIBILITY

We'll soon see clearly that Republican administrations are always – 100% of the time – far worse wastrels when it comes to debt and deficits, a point made with emphatically clear charts, later in this chapter.

Further, when your RASR or ostrich Republican mewls about the inevitable demise of Social Security and our failure to act on that slow death spiral, you might mention how – back in 1993 when Democrats had

---

240 Friedman's cult of quarterly profit: https://www.theatlantic.com/ideas/archive/2019/08/milton-friedman-shareholder-wrong/596545/

Congress and sincere adult Republicans still existed – President Clinton fostered the Bipartisan Commission on Entitlement and Tax Reform as part of the administration's effort to promote economic growth and control the budget deficit. The purpose of the commission, chaired by Senator J. Robert Kerrey (D-NE) and Senator John C. Danforth (R-MO), was to seek bipartisan agreement on long-term *entitlement reform* and structural changes to the tax system.[241]

The resulting bill *almost passed*.[242] It would have gradually cranked up retirement age and saved trillions, in exchange for instituting health care for children and the poor along with meaningful contributions by the rich. But the opportunity was trashed, first by Newt Gingrich and then by Dennis Hastert, who worked with Fox to end all traces of adulthood in the GOP. Danforth-style Republicans are now entirely extinct.

That entitlements reform package is still out there. Fiscal conservatives could make a win-win deal. But then – as happened with Welfare Reform – a major hot button issue to rant at their base might go away! And we can't have that now, can we?

MUTANT TALENT? [243]

Why are executive compensation packages so vastly higher in the U.S. than anywhere else in the world? Even many of the smartest billionaires,

---

[241] In the 1970s capitalists were terrified by the fact the Union Pension funds seemed – if funded at projected rates – to be the main accumulating pools of capital. Indeed, by 2020 workers would 'own the means of production' that way, organically, without revolution. I believe much of the Reagan and after "revolution" was specifically targeted to end that dire 'threat.' They succeeded... and not one pundit today even remotely recalls those old worries, or sees or mentions how it was prevented, even though it was much discussed in the 1970s.

[242] https://www.ncbi.nlm.nih.gov/pubmed/7999185

[243] Other economic topics: About liberals reclaiming Adam Smith: http://davidbrin.blogspot.com/2013/11/liberals-you-must-reclaim-adam-smith.html About Smith and Friedrich Hayek http://evonomics.com/stop-using-adam-smith-and-hayek-to-support/ Recall from Chapter 9 how Americans Spent Themselves into Ruin... But Saved the Worldhttp://davidbrin.blogspot.com/2009/11/how-americans-spent-themselves-into.html Crucially, the world still needs America to keep buying, so that factories can hum and workers send their kids to school, so those kids can then demand labor and environmental laws and all that. And for that to happen, U.S. inventiveness – the golden egg-laying goose that paid for it all – must be preserved. Finally, in an economics riff that was too complex to be included in this political book, I explore how nearly all "leaders" fool themselves into thinking they can "allocate" a nation's resources better than market forces. Those in the West who most loudly proclaim Faith in Blind Markets – or FIBM – are members of a narrow, incestuously conniving CEO caste who 'pick winners and losers' far more narrowly and with far less competitive knowledge than those communist or kingly allocators of old. http://davidbrin.blogspot.com/2006/06/allocation-vs-markets-ancient-struggle.html

like Bill Gates and Warren Buffett have joined in warning that it's gone way out of hand. But those denunciations are shrugged off by the right as sour grapes.

"These CEOs and such are worth every penny!" comes the rejoinder without much or any comparative proof. Alas, while countless pundits and critics have denounced these skyrocketing compensations as immoral, what we seldom hear is the objection *put in AdamSmithian terms.* Tell me if you've encountered this:

By the very notion of capitalism, when pay for a service goes way up, it should draw in talent from elsewhere, competing for the greater rewards. Many of society's brainiest and best would drop other pursuits to go into management and finance, till the available talent pool (supply) reaches saturation with demand. Competition then brings pay levels back to equilibrium.

Yet they keep climbing into the stratosphere. Your assertion amounts to a repudiation of the market economics you claim to believe in!

It's a different and in some ways better argument than the moral ones offered by Gates, Buffett and every decent person. Alas, Oligarchy's shills have a counter:

"Market forces won't bring down prices if the commodity is super scarce. These are mutant-level geniuses! No would-be competitors drawn in from other fields can possibly grasp or perform on those mountaintops."

Ah, good one. But in this back-and-forth we get the last word:

So today's hand-over-fist U.S. corporate execs are like mutant NBA basketball stars? Each worth whatever the team can possibly afford? But... um... aren't those sports stars subjected to the most intense scrutiny, tracking and performance metrics of any humans on the planet? Their "mutant" status is verified analytically...

...which is the last thing that most CEOs today want. In fact, a great many writhe to avoid performance appraisal, issuing excuses and distractions that would embarrass any ball court prima donna.

This calls for an experiment! Let's see how Boeing and other manufacturing firms do, if they go back to promoting top officers from among the best engineers who actually build stuff?

On that note, I recommend a 1954 Hollywood movie – with William Holden and Barbara Stanwyck – called *Executive Suite,* which illustrates how we're not the first to face these issues, with more and more boardrooms taken over by financial wizards instead of folks who came up delivering the goods and services the company is all about. Notably the Chinese – for all their faults – draw most of their ruling officials from a cadre of skilled managers who had been engineers. And you can tell that's doing well by them.[244]

> *"All for ourselves and nothing for other people, seems, in every age of the world, to have been the vile maxim of the masters of mankind. As soon, therefore, as they could find a method of consuming the whole value of their rents themselves, they had no disposition to share them with any other persons."*
> – Adam Smith

THAT VOODOO THAT YOU DO

You've seen this before and will several more times in this collection of essays. For decades we've been subjected to cult incantations like the Laffer Curve[245] and Supply Side "economics" that foretold a spectacular – nay miraculous – outcome: that huge tax cuts for the rich would prompt recipients to invest heavily in R&D, product development and new factories! (Thus increasing the "supply" side of the supply-and-demand curve, get it?) Moreover the ensuing boom in stimulated economic activity would result in increased revenue for the treasury, *even at the lowered tax rates!* And hence, supply side promised almost instantly *reduced* federal and state governmental deficits.

Prime the pump with a gusher of red ink… and soon you'll be swimming in lovely black ink surpluses! It's not surprising that this alluring

---

[244] My rascally-impudent suggestion that could save America in dozens of ways. Ban the undergraduate business major. Let folks come back for a masters after they've spent some years creating and delivering goods and services. There, I said it.

[245] In fact, there are levels at which the Laffer Curve is true! If you tax everything, business will halt and you'll get nothing. So? The 1980s incantation was that the curve was always in the overtaxed, business suppression zone. No proof. None. And subsequent experiments – at the extreme in Kansas during 2015-2018 – showed diametrically opposite lessons.

theory was tried once. Is it shocking that we bought it again and again? And again, when it never once delivered? Among my top five *demands for a wager,* listed elsewhere in this book, is this one:

Can you name even one Supply Side prediction that ever came true? In science, or indeed most fact-centered professions, repeated failure to predict outcomes is deemed a likely sign of flakery, if not flat-out dishonesty. Hence the war on fact professions.

Evonomics.com – the smartest site online for economic/social analysis – aims not at opposing free markets, but *saving* them from the oligarchy disease that ruined flat-fair-creative competition in every past civilization. No online site discusses Adam Smith more often.[246] (My own Evonomics page is here.[247]) Take for example, Steve Roth's essay "Capital's Share of Income Is Way Higher than You Think,"[248] which dissects how almost half of the market income arriving at U.S. households is received just for being wealthy – owning stuff – and not either *work or active investment.*

Oh, there are exceptions! Many of the recent tech zillionaires – who spend their days happily working alongside engineers and creative types – recycled their extra cash into R&D, new ventures, new goods, services and productive capacity, even daring exploits in accessing the resources of space! That's exactly what the mad right said would happen with Supply Side. (Moreover can you guess which way those long-ROI, risk-taking, tech-savvy caste of investors lean *politically?* With a few exceptions, like Peter Thiel, they are mostly Democrats,[249] or independents who agree that markets must be regulated to reduce the age-old enemy of enterprise –cheating.[250])

---

[246] Except, of course, scholarly sites dedicated to the study of Adam Smith! https://evonomics.com

[247] "Best-of-Brin" essays about the world, economics, politics and philosophy at the Evonomics site. http://evonomics.com/author/davidbrin/

[248] From Evonomics: http://evonomics.com/capitals-share-of-income-is-way-higher-than-you-think/?utm_source=newsletter_campaign=organic

[249] My anecdotal assertion. But I'll consider sincere offers of wagers. While Wall Streeters & oil-guys are "risk-taking" they remain short-ROI and hostile to science.

[250] *"Ironically, Smith's epic work The Wealth of Nations, which was first published in 1776, presents a radical condemnation of business monopolies sustained and protected by the state, in service of a lordly owner-caste. Adam Smith's ideal was a market comprised of small buyers and sellers. He showed how the workings of such a market would tend toward a price that provides a fair return to land, labor, and capital, produce a satisfactory outcome for both buyers and sellers, and result in an optimal outcome for society in terms of the allocation of its resources. ... He made clear, however, that this outcome can result only when no buyer or seller is sufficiently large to influence the market price–a point many who invoke his*

But as for the vast majority of Supply Side largesse recipients, they aren't looking for risk or to sweat hard on some new venture. When they get a sudden burst of income, most of the rich plant it where Smith described aristocrats always pouring their excess wealth, into passive rent-seeking – or *rentier* – properties with safe or seemingly-guaranteed return. Of course this inflates asset values, not just stock equities but also real estate, even art. (Recent mass-purchases of rental properties by rich families have priced young first time home buyers out of the market.)

Beyond asset bubbles and expanding wealth disparities, perhaps the worst effect is *plummeting money velocity,* a measure of how often each dollar gets spent. Now there are times – e.g. during high inflation – when you want MV to go down! But generally speaking, a dollar paid to a bridge repair worker, say during an infrastructure campaign, will get spent immediately at the grocer, whose employees spend quickly for their own needs, and so on, hence high "velocity" for that dollar, which gets spent and taxed many times. But when rich folks get a lot richer – even good guys like Buffett – not very many of those dollars go to workers at the yacht factory. (The aspersion that Supply Side is "trickle down" aims in the right direction, but doesn't do justice to this travesty.) Again, most of that extra income goes into passive rentier investments that send Money Velocity crashing.

Indeed, MV *has* crashed, even as deficits and debt go through the roof with every double-down we've seen on Supply Side voodoo. And yes, I will gladly make this a *wager* as described in Chapter 15.

Now let me be clear yet again. *I want competitive-flat-fair-creative markets to work well.* I know where the taxes come from that pay for liberal programs that uplift poor children, so they can then innovate and compete, in a virtuous cycle never before seen in human annals. But there are reasons why oligarchs, Laffer cultists and other fanatics had to change so many rules to get those gushers flowing into aristocratic maws. Because the Greatest Generation knew better. Massive stock buybacks etc. were banned! And if you wanted tax relief to help you to invest in long ROI product development, or factory equipment, you took generous de-

---

name prefer not to mention. Such a market implicitly assumes a significant degree of equality in the distribution of economic power–another widely neglected point." – from David C. Korten's book, When Corporations Rule the World.

ductions specifically targeted for those things! Moreover, when the state invested in your workers' sanitation, health and children, plus the R&D and infrastructure that maintain a forward moving civilization, you saw that as ultimately beneficial to your shareholders… and everyone else.

So, again… name one reason we should trust a supply sider with more than a wet match?

However beautiful the strategy, you should occasionally look at the results.
—Winston Churchill

AGAIN, CRISES OF CAPITALISM

Let's get back to the Business Roundtable's revised notion of corporate duty, rejecting Milton Friedman's at-best-myopic commandment to fixate solely on quarterly share price. Fine, thanks BR. It's now recommended that companies also invest in employees, deliver value to customers and deal ethically with suppliers. I would certainly expand that customer service goal to *thou shalt fulfill what the company exists for!*

If it's widgets, take pride in those widgets. And if you've branched from widgets into cloud based AI, doesn't it make sense to prioritize doing *that* well? Sure, this desideratum overlaps with customer service. But sometimes your vision will stretch beyond what customers currently desire. It should.

Many times in this volume I recommend getting a better than clichéd notion of what Karl Marx and Marxism (seldom the same) were about. Remember when it seemed that both were consigned to history's dust-bin? Well, old Karl's tracts are flying off the shelves now, on university campuses and in worker ghettos around the globe. And the smarter billionaires are starting to notice. They'll consider what kind of society could serve their enlightened self-interest over the long run. In my novels, *Earth* and *Existence,* I forecast that some members of a world aristocracy might even hold conferences about it, and perhaps we are seeing crude, preliminary signs.

"It's not whether we should be capitalist or socialist. It's how do we make sure that capitalism is working the way it has in the past," said top investor Alan Schwartz at the recent Milken Conference,[251] warning of "class warfare." He noted that salaries and wages as a percentage of the economic pie are at a postwar low of 40%, prompting a "throw out the rich" mentality that would require some form of income redistribution to head off.[252] The rise of inequality is discussed in great detail – and placed in historical context – in Thomas Piketty's tome, The Economics of Inequality, as well as in *Capital in the Twenty-First Century*, where Piketty notes, "At the heart of every major political upheaval lies a fiscal revolution."

Mega investor Ray Dalio warns that unless the American economic system is reformed "so that the pie is both divided and grown well" the country is in danger of "great conflict and some form of revolution that will hurt most everyone and will shrink the pie."[253]

Later in this chapter we'll see those charts I promised, revealing how Republicans are vastly *worse* regarding *debts and deficits*. But let's start with the one below, which repudiates every claim of the Supply Side cult. It shows how U.S. *wealth disparity* underwent steady decline under Rooseveltean social-economic arrangements, as the share owned by the bottom 90% rose steadily compared to the portion held by the top 0.1%, all of it accompanying rapid GDP growth and scientific/technical advancement. This ongoing augmentation of the middle class shattered every pr ediction made by Karl Marx, making his followers look dimwitted…

---

[251] https://www.latimes.com/business/la-fi-milken-conference-ray-dalio-20190502-story.html

[252] "Throw out" is of course a euphemism for what folks risk, if they let disparities reach levels of 1789 France or 1917 Russia. And those thresholds are closer than most think.

[253] Ray Dalio. https://www.barrons.com/articles/billionaire-ray-dalio-income-inequality-education-u-s-at-risk-51554468777

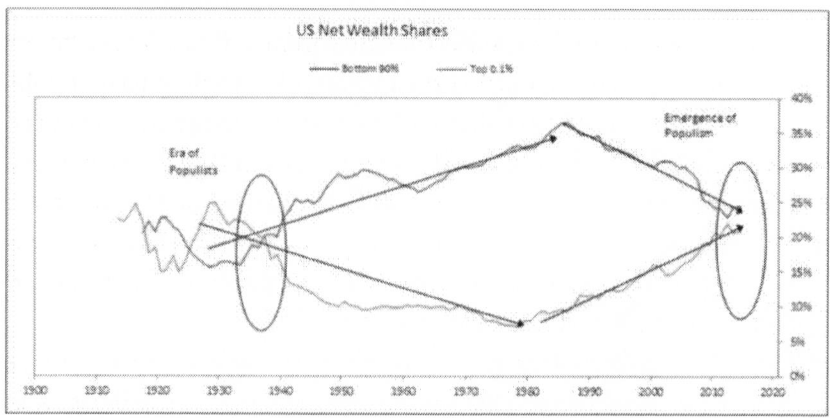

... that is, until the Reagan era's reversal of post-WWII tax, regulatory and labor policies weakened unions while undermining investment in infrastructure and R&D, pouring wealth instead into the "job creators" – an "investor class" whose behavior began mirroring every anti-competitive, "rentier" syndrome described by Adam Smith, in *Wealth of Nations.*

Even more ominous, resurgent Marxists are now nodding and grinning, diagnosing the Greatest Generation's experiment – in flat-fair-competitive-creative market enterprise bolstered by a vigorously progressive nation – as mere a historical blip, temporary aberration that no nation could sustain, as top oligarchs manipulate the system toward self-destruction, in patterns that exactly follow Old Karl's forecasts, in *Das Kapital.*

Maintaining a civilization of empowered citizenship and fair-competition is a dilemma summed-up by famous historians Will and Arial Durant, in The Lessons of History:

> *"...the unstable equilibrium generates a critical situation, which history has diversely met by legislation redistributing wealth or by revolution distributing poverty."*

"Redistribution" is one of those words that can trigger apoplexy and get you called all sorts of names. But it's exactly what the poorest two-thirds across the globe will demand, when they see that they can double their book wealth just by transferring title from say the 50 wealthiest families. It might happen quicker than you think, in a fit of fervent politics, without even needing guillotines. And would that be the end of the world for hundreds of millions of entrepreneurs and business owners, inventors and regular capitalists? Their chief concern won't be to protect the uber-most lords who are striving daily to make Marx's final scenario come to life. Their aim will be to prevent the revolution from radicalizing and crushing market enterprise, altogether.

Again, take a "redistribution" example that few ever discuss, but I mention in several places – when the American Founders (hardly viewed as the most radical of socialists) seized and parceled out up to a third of the land in the former colonies, an act of redistribution that makes FDR look like a minnow. And it was matched later by the taking of "property" from Southern slaveholders and redistributing that ownership to… well… to those freed people themselves. Oh there are precedents. And each time, market enterprise survived.

The lesson? Moderate resets don't have to be the end of the world. But worlds *can* end if you greedily defer all moderate resets, tempting fate by tempting mobs.

== IT'S MADE OF PEOPLE! ==

Amid all the talk about the potentially dangerous or useful AI (artificial intelligence), it's good to remember we've done it before. Our towns and nations have extensive, independent memories and lifespans longer than we mere workers in the hive. Sometimes (not always) our teams and committees have far greater competence and intelligence than any one member, achieving wondrous accomplishments. The *corporation* was formed to encourage risk-taking investment by limiting shareholder liability, but it also turned into a way to get some of those e *pluribus unum* synergies via cohesive group intelligence. Oh yes, we already have some experience with "smart artificial entities."

No, I am not a supporter of the *Citizens United* ruling, by which a rightwing-biased U.S. Supreme Court allowed oligarch shareholders to funnel

unlimited democracy-warping dollars through corporations they control. Still, when we discuss the pros and cons, I see parallels in this history with the more recent debates over AI. I recall how early science fiction tales portrayed robots as malevolent *Frankenstein* monsters, till Isaac Asimov proposed that robots were tools that might be constructed to be safe and useful, just as knives have handles. His famous "Three Laws of Robotics" comprised an early attempt at a positive sum formula, aiming to get much of the good while taking sapient care to minimize the foreseen bad. (Of course many of his tales, and mine, are about the unforeseen.)

You see the parallel here. Corporations are effectively robots with countless humans – and now other entities – operating limbs and busy hands, brains and (hopefully) hearts. We know that such artificial constructs can be like any other machine, they're either beneficial or a hazard. Those odds shift under the influence of both *transparency* and *rules*. Rules that might distill down to *Hart's Laws of Corporatics:*[254]

1) A corporation must not harm real people, or the world, or local systems they depend on. (Don't make us sorry we chartered you.)

2) A corporation must act to fulfill its transparently specified charter, as long as doing so does not violate the First Law. (We chartered you for a reason. That's what you exist for.)

3) A corporation must act to insure its continued viability and make profit, as long as doing so does not violate the first or second laws.

(Note that limited liability corporations, until not very long ago, had to be chartered by specific acts of state legislatures, specifying duties and even life spans.)

If an actively vigorous and well-informed citizenry – through their honest and capable representatives – chooses to transparently negotiate wise definitions of "harm" and chartered purpose, then we may have come full circle back to the declaration issued by the Business Roundtable in 2019. If you ask me, it'd be not a moment too soon.

---

[254] Source: Larry Hart, a valued member of the *Contrary Brin* community, with input from Alfred Differ.

===

NOSTRA CULPA

In May 2018 a petition[255] was sent to the Chairman of the U.S. Senate Committee on Banking, Housing, and Urban Affairs by 36 eminent retired general and field officers in the U. S. Armed Forces, along with retired civilian leaders from the National Security Council; the Departments of State, Treasury, Defense, Justice, Commerce and so on. Were these sage protectors concerned about foreign despots? Terrorists? White and blue collar criminals? Drug lords?

As it happens, all of the above are empowered and enabled by secret-anonymous shell corporations. And surprise, the leading nexus of these dark dens is not Switzerland, or the Cayman Islands. It is the state of Delaware. Followed by many others of these not-so-United States. From that petition:

"The U.S. remains the easiest place in the world to set up an anonymous shell company according to an academic study from the University of Texas and Brigham Young University.... These companies have put Americans at risk and worse – criminals enjoy the benefits of strong investment returns and total secrecy here in the U.S. Drug cartels and human trafficking operations have long understood the benefits of corporate secrecy to launder money from criminal enterprises. More recently, anonymous companies are implicated in terror financing, fraudulent contracting with our military, and even sanctions evasion."

These eminent leaders added: "As we ratchet up sanctions against hostile nations, it is telling to note that the Iranian Government previously skirted our sanctions for years by utilizing a web of shell companies, including some registered in the United States, to buy a skyscraper on Fifth Avenue in Manhattan."

---

[255] A petition was sent... https://thefactcoalition.org/wp-content/uploads/2018/05/20180531-National-Security-BOT-Support-Letter-Senate-Final.pdf

Read the letter here, and spread the word.[256] No, this Congress won't do anything to benefit the nation, humanity or the future. But tracks and seeds can be laid.[257]

We will return again and again in this book to my principal theme, conveyed back in 1997's *The Transparent Society.* There is no ingredient to our Enlightenment more absolutely necessary than light.

"Most 'Wealth' Isn't the Result of Hard Work. It Has Been Accumulated by Being Idle and Unproductive. It's time to call the housing crisis what it really is: the largest transfer of wealth in living memory."[258]

OUTCOMES? LET'S COMPARE ACTUAL OUTCOMES

Should economics be treated like any other science, with confident theories tested by experimental evidence? Comparing predictions with outcomes?[259] Lenin thrashed till his death over contradictions between Marxist theory and actual events. Mao dealt with inconsistencies by killing them. Orwell showed us how tyrants adjust "truth" to match theo-

---

[256] https://thefactcoalition.org/wp-content/uploads/2018/05/20180531-National-Security-BOT-Support-Letter-Senate-Final.pdf

[257] This is reminiscent of the "Helvetian War" that I described in my 1989 novel EARTH. Only I never expected "Helvetia" to stand for America.

[258] Evonomics: https://evonomics.com/unproductive-rent-housing-macfarlane/

[259] The following is from a 2012 blog, linking to other, earlier comparisons of outcomes: http://redgreenandblue.org/2012/09/19/david-brin-the-gop-wont-run-on-their-record-they-run-from-it/ "Since 1960, Republicans have controlled the White House 28 years, and the Democrats 24. And in those years, Democratic administrations have created 42 million jobs, and Republican ones 24 million jobs. This, according to a Bloomberg analysis of BLS data, is a devastating set of numbers – and by the way, the stock market has performed better during Democratic tenures as well, as another Bloomberg analysis showed that returns on investment under Democrats have done about nine times better than under Republicans. "But let's assume you folks are members of that dying race, wonk-citizens who are moved by facts. Try this explication of economic growth vs. debt under the two parties. Do you still believe (against all evidence) that the GOP is the way to fight the deficit? Or unemployment? In modern times every Democratic presidential administration left office with a lower unemployment rate than when they took office. But only one Republican Administration has managed this accomplishment. That fact is basic. Devastating. Absolutely verified and true. Ask your adamant-ostrich friends to name one unambiguous statistical metric of national health that went up as a direct result of Republican rule. They cannot. So, what is the GOP sales pitch? It amounts to *" Okay we're terrible! Insane and corrupt. But Democrats are worse! So hire us again, no matter how awful we were!"*

ry. From Goebbels to Murdoch to Trump, the notion has been "repeat something truthy-sounding incessantly and get rallies chanting it. Sheer will can triumph over mere data." (You can see why the fact professions are inconvenient.)

Earlier in this chapter we dealt with one major modern falsehood – Supply Side so-called "economics," which has the startling 0% successful forecast rate. But here it's time to reveal a different a calumny... and a calamity. The calumny – an outright lie that Americans are all taught to believe for all their adult lives – is the *Republican claim that they are pragmatic and frugal, while Democrats are wastrels.*

Our calamity is the absolute refusal of any Democratic politician or liberal or moderate pundit to hammer that lie, then pound it again, and again until it shatters.

Want that hammer? Okay, buckle up. Here it is:[260] The crucial *second derivative of debt*[261] is the *pace* at which the *rate-of-change* of the federal debt is itself *changing...* either accelerating toward fiscal disaster or braking away from it. That measure was positive (toward accelerating debt) during almost every year of every Republican administration since Eisenhower.

In stark contrast – that crucial metric is always negative (deceleration) every year of every Democratic administration. Let that sink in, because it is diametrically opposite to rhetoric that's become "truthy" in our minds.

Why is the second derivative of debt more valid than – say – looking at just the size of this year's budget deficit? Because our fiscal situation carries momentum from actions taken three to five years ago, even a decade. Stepping on the brakes does not instantly stop your hurtling car – it *decelerates* your rush toward that cliff. Hence, the second derivative tells you – almost instantly – whether an administration is at least *trying* to be fiscally responsible.

---

[260] Updated from "Do Outcomes Matter More Than Rhetoric?" http://davidbrin.blogspot.com/2014/06/so-do-outcomes-matter-more-than-rhetoric.html

[261] In calculus lingo, the *first derivative* of national debt is the total *deficit*. The second derivative is how that deficit changes, year to year.

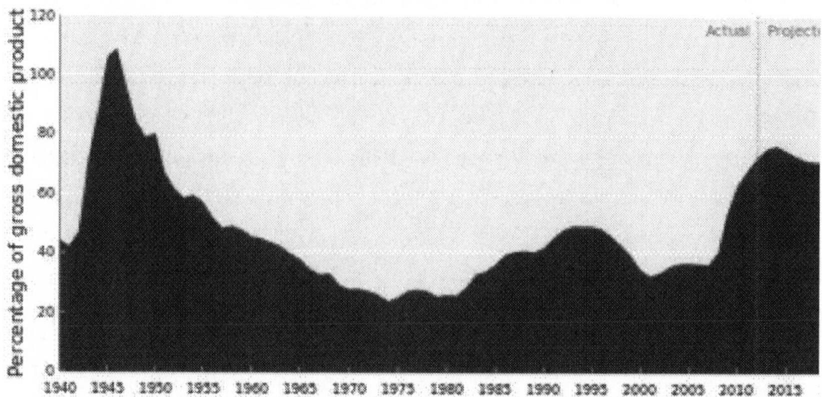

Examine the second derivative of debt in this 2015 chart of the U.S. federal deficit as a fraction of U.S. GDP. Wherever the curve is seen *turning*, go ahead and guesstimate a rough *center* to that stretch of curve. Of course there are bumps, so a little subjective smoothing is called for. But if, across any three to five year span, the center point of your curve lies *above*, then the arc is swinging toward up-vertical and *debt is on a worsening track.*

If the center of a curve is *below*, there's an improving trend. Decelerating deficits curve back down, even toward surplus. Think *convex* versus *concave.*

Recall: GOP administrations began in 1969, 1981, 1989, 2001 and 2017. Democratic ones in 1977, 1993 and 2009. Now draw your curves. It truly is amazing! Here's a marked-up version of that chart, as I posted it in 2015.

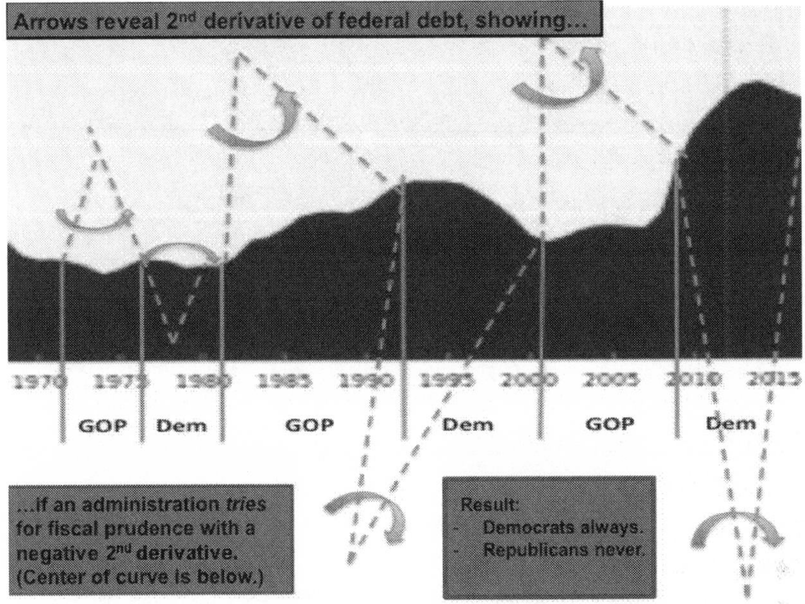

The illustration above was revealing when I published it, late during the Obama Administration. Let me reiterate. The rate of change of the rate of change of debt was positive (toward reckless deficits) during almost every year of every Republican administration (post Eisenhower). It was negative (building momentum toward prudence) in *every* year of every democratic administration (post Johnson). Now add in this bald-faced fact – that Bush Administration accounting tricks kept costs of the Afghanistan and Iraq Wars "off the books" for half a decade, letting them slam the formal deficit just when economic mismanagement sent the economy into hell, leaving behind a mess that included hyper-velocity debt. In other words, the 2006-2007 "dip" is a lie.

Here is another way to look at the same fundamental data – the ratio of national debt to GDP – spread over a much longer range showing how it was consensus policy across the Truman, Eisenhower, Kennedy and Johnson administrations (initials HST, DDE, JFK and LBJ) to ask the rich to help pay down debt left over from WWII. That pay-down continued even into the Vietnam quagmire. But this bipartisan consensus ended with the arrival of "Laffer Theory" – the basic juju underlying Supply Side incantations. Starting slowly under Nixon and Ford (RMN,

GRF), the cult incantation was "give the already-rich all the money, and they'll invest it wisely, stimulating an economy that's spectacular for all."

Of course that's being charitable. While there certainly were sincere lafferites, the core catechism became "give the already-rich all the money. Period.

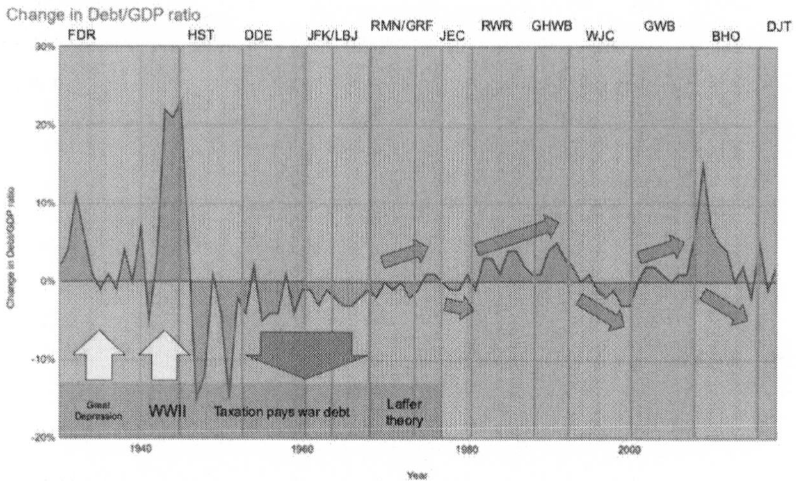

Take away their claim of 'economic pragmatism"

One concocted excuse for why we had budget surpluses under Bill Clinton is that "Congress controls the purse strings." Okay then, let's dissect it.

The GOP controlled Congress from 1995 to 2007. That's for six years *before* Bill Clinton left office and for 6 years *after* he departed. Notice that the 2nd Derivative of debt was *negative* during those first six, then swung sharply positive the *very instant* that a Republican president replaced him, when Clinton could no longer veto the annual Supply Side Voodoo Economics Bill, opening our arteries to the (non) "job-creator caste." Just one political factor changed, allowing the lightbulb switch from black to red ink. Oh no, credit for those surpluses does not go to the right.

As for Obama, he inherited the mess of Bush's 2007 economic calamity, so deficits started out huge, not only because of those Bush Supply Side tax cuts, but also as the feds rightfully stepped in with stimulation to prevent a depression. But notice the *second derivative...* the rate by which the rate of change of deficit changed... is negative. The center of curvature is way below the chart-line during Obama's terms. Even amid an inherited super-recession, with a GOP Congress refusing to tax the rich, the rate of bleeding was tipping downward again... until...

... till the 2016 election prompted a number of wagers over what would happen when a Republican was back in the White House with a GOP Congress, vowing grandly to get debt under control. Let's have a look:

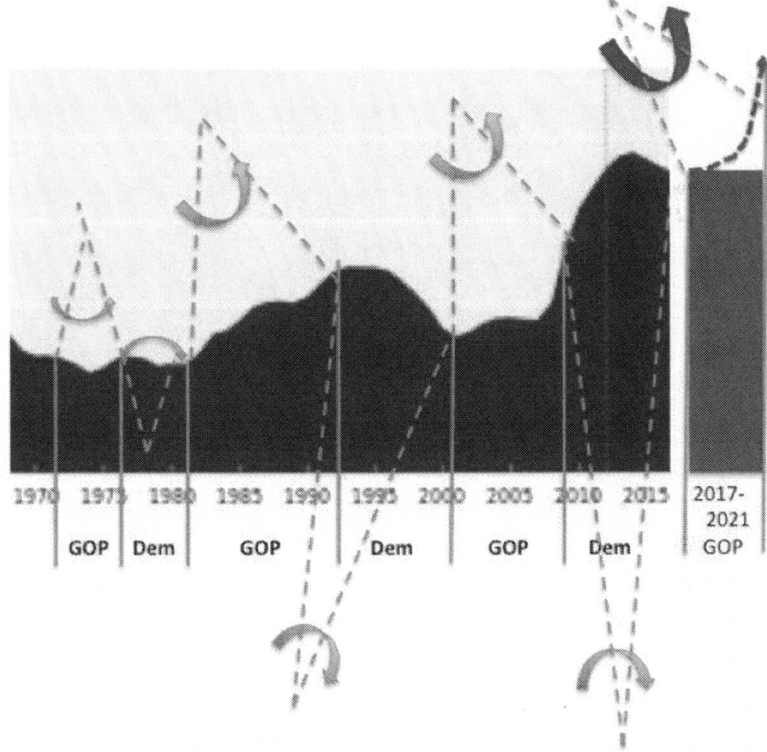

Indeed, deficits under Donald Trump skyrocketed past a *trillion* dollars per year. Naturally, GOP pundits rave that no fault should go to the *one major thing they changed,* post-Obama – the latest arterial gusher of largesse flowing to the top 0.001%, under the 2019 Tax Cuts. Supply Side voodoo that never made a single successful forecast. Even once, ever.

Again, the trend is absolute. Pure. A fact that you can set your watch by. We *always* see fiscal responsibility and debt deceleration across the span of Democratic administrations. There are *always* wastrel deficit skyrocketings across GOP presidential terms. Absolutely always.

You have been told a "truthy" lie all your lives – one that Democratic politicians and liberal/moderate pundits have *stupidly ceded.* Snap out of it!

And forget judo. Use this as a bludgeon.

And yes, more repetition! Still, this is where you should speak up. Suggestions welcome

Pause #11 for...

Things you can do. Yes, you.

The larger part of this tome is aimed upward, at elites of our own "Union" side in this phase of civil war – generals who have let us down, so far, with dullard failures of agility or imagination. But you've also found practical (or at least unusual) suggestions for average U.S. citizens. Ways they might individually make a difference. Here's a compact list:

– **Join several NGOs.** Arguably the 20th Century's greatest contribution to Enlightenment Democracy, member-based Non-Governmental Orgs are the western inventions that gall Vladimir Putin, Rupert Murdoch and their pals more than any other western enlightenment invention. The ACLU, Electronic Frontier Foundation, Sierra Club, Greenpeace... heck PETA or the NRA... you can mix and match to suit the exact set of ways that you want the world saved. As I describe elsewhere, those orgs will pool your membership with a million others, enabling them to hire analysts and attorneys on a par with any corrupt moguls or corporation. [262]

When it comes to the topic of this book... politics... you should spread it around, not limiting just to your favorite well-publicized candidate. Send dues or contributions to Lawrence Lessig's Equal Citizen, aiming to reform away cheating from our politics, or the Fair Fight campaign led by Stacy Abrams, that sends volunteers into the field, ensuring that marginalized citizens in battleground states can register and vote. [263] (The Abrams initiative could also use volunteers on the ground, emulating the Freedom Riders of old.)

– **Help shift power where it counts.** If you live in a state like Texas, where the legislature might get flipped, then your attention should be lo-

---

[262] "The Power of Proxy Activism." http://www.davidbrin.com/nonfiction/proxyactivism.html
[263] Stacy Abrams's initiative, Fair Fight 2020 https://fairfight.com/fair-fight-2020/

cal this election cycle, not national! [264] Seriously, that's where a vital shift might happen, so find the tightest state assembly or state senate race near you – or one of the counties that can swing your whole state – and help there. [265] (In fact, even if you live far away, you can "adopt" an assembly candidate in such a district, with various means of support.) There's no exaggerating how much more you might accomplish at that level with some volunteer hours and cash, with one added benefit. In these smaller races, the candidate you back to victory will at least become a nodding acquaintance, someone who even knows your name and will lend you an ear, now and then.

– **Stomp Splitterism and cynicism.** In the next Chapter (#12), I supply five rebuttals to those we all hear growling about "corporatist" Democratic politicians and/or "sellouts" or "Liberals in Name Only." Spreading memes that might come out of a Kremlin basement, splitterism can be noxiously contagious. Bernie Sanders in 2016 had choice words for such fair weather allies, as did Thomas Paine did in 1776. Tell them you'll listen, after everything on our "list of shared consensus goals" has passed.

– **Yes, go after RASRs and Ostriches.** I know it's hard. Our cousins and uncles and co-workers who are Residually Adult-Sane Republicans know their side and their party has gone insane! But they keep their heads buried, clutching Fox rationalizations that "every liberal is just like that screeching campus radical!!!" This book is filled with weapons and cudgels and moves to corner them, especially with challenges of wagers. They will writhe and squirm and evade and dodge! We know that...

... and yet, the effort is worthwhile. First because "Heaven rejoices at even a single sinner, saved." And each ostrich we pull out of a hole, blinking and deciding to become American again, will pay great dividends. But second, consider your image of the RASR I just described. It was a 'he,' wasn't it? Likely some grumpy, obstinate uncle, perhaps? Well, his wife may be listening, while you argue with him. And your aunt has a vote of her very own.

---

[264] The fight over Texas – https://www.salon.com/2019/08/17/blue-texas-at-last-maybe-but-the-real-fight-isnt-for-the-white-house/

[265] Ten Counties That Will Decide the Presidential Election https://www.electoral-vote.com/evp2019/Pres/Maps/Sep05.html#item-5

Finally, the ephemeral nature of victories in 1992 and 2008 shows that only fools will count on just mobilizing the base of seldom-voters. Remember 1994 and 2010. It's not enough.

– **Donate to national efforts.** Sure. Do that, too.

– **Adjust your official party membership tactically.** Just before Chapter 5 we had a Pause for a bizarre – but potentially useful – tactic. There I explained why you – a liberal or moderate "blue" American – might under certain conditions want to register Republican. You may feel revolted at the idea. But consider it if you live in a district that's been gerried by a cheater-party, so that only one election matters – the Primary of that district's dominant party. If that's the case where you live, and you feel you'll never get to vote for anyone who will represent you – in Congress or even state assembly – then you and local friends should consider registering (officially) as Republicans in that GOP-district! You might help tilt a primary fight from some Putin-puppet monster to an older-style conservative-but-decent Goldwater type who will negotiate like an adult. Remember, it was Tea Party agitation in Republican primaries that helped Dennis Hastert establish his never-negotiate "rule," and radicalize the GOP beyond all recognition. If enough "former" Democrats counter those fulminators, that's power worth having and using...

...especially since your GOP registration will also mess up their computer stats and resulting tactics! Sure, it's called "packing" and they've been doing it to us, for years. See it explained in more detail.[266] If enough people did this, it could both undermine the cheats and mess up the computers of every party machine. Yes, also Democratic party machines. Good. .

– Cajole a retired military officer to run as a Democrat – or heck as a moderate Republican if the district is deep red.

– **Look in a mirror,** every now and then, and remember that your Suspicion of Authority (SoA) and many other impudent/tolerant values were taught to you by generations of films and songs and legends and celebrity examples. That doesn't make any of it invalid! In fact, I totally approve of those messages. (I was raised by them, too.) Indeed, those values might help us make Star Trek. Still, watch out, any time you or a pal start talk-

---

[266] On electoral reform: http://davidbrin.blogspot.com/2013/11/the-simple-trick-allowing-citizens-to.html

ing as if you invented those traits, or have some exclusive ownership over them. Even many of our neighbor adversaries share a lot of them, deep down. They think THEY are the brave, insightful, elite-challenging heroes!

Use this to connect with them. And to control your fits of outrage. We need to be the sapient ones.

– **Consider all kinds of volunteerism.** Tutoring. Helping a school. Joining CERT – Community Emergency Response Teams – helping build our strength and resilience at the local level.

And finally, another valuable thing you might do for America...

..is spread the ideas from this book. Especially the notion of getting out of political trench warfare and taking advantage of the foe's weaknesses, pinning them till their fevered tantrum ebbs, by using polemical judo.

... or surely we will all hang separately...

Chapter 12

Unreliable Allies: Six Rebuttals To Use With Those Who Would "Split" Our Coalition.[267]

When I say we must stomp splitterism, I do *not* mean AOC and the sincere-liberal "left." Heck, my fave among the 20 Democratic Party candidates (as I write this) is Liz! The "squad" types are welcome to primary old-line dems in deep blue districts and create a big socialist caucus. Fine, earn it, fair n' square.

Only some dogmatic fools – plus Kremlin provocateurs – go much further. They aim to shatter our broad coalition against Putin-Fox-Trumpist treason. They denounce "corporatist Democrats" as "sockpuppets" for oligarchy, no different than Republicans. These splitters constitute the *one great hope* for Putin's putsch to avoid 2020 annihilation, or to make another huge comeback in 2022. All of you have friends teetering along that lunacy.

Here are five direct answers that might slap sense into them.

---

[267] Original postings: http://davidbrin.blogspot.com/2019/08/five-devastating-rebuttals-to-use-with.htmlAlso http://davidbrin.blogspot.com/2019/07/debate-special-shall-we-let-them-divide.html

FIRST REBUTTAL:
Those "sellout centrists" did a lot, when they had a rare opportunity.

Democrats had power to pass national legislation for just two years out of the last 25 – the 111th Congress 2009-2010, during which these "corporatist sellouts":

– passed the ACA, insuring 40 million more Americans,

– banned bias for pre-existing conditions (enraging the insurance companies who then donated heavily to Republicans in 2010),

– passed banking regulation (enraging that cabal, who donated heavily to Republicans in 2010, when many splitters didn't vote),

– created the Consumer Financial Protection Bureau whose destruction was Trump's top goal,

– vastly increased auto gas mileage standards, reducing carbon emissions and saving Americans billions at the pump,

– expanded support for sustainables, resulting in the solar+wind "takeoff,"

– did a sweeping overhaul of Wall Street rules (enraging that cabal, who donated heavily to Republicans in 2010),

– passed a $787 billion economic stimulus package,

– repealed "don't ask, don't tell," allowing gays to serve openly in the military, and much more...

President Obama called the 111th Congress the most productive in generations.[268] *"Measures that have almost become afterthoughts – like pay equity for women and the new power of the Food and Drug Administration to regulate tobacco – would have been signature achievements in other Congresses. And the Senate confirmed two of Mr. Obama's nominees to the Supreme Court – both women, one Hispanic."*

In fact, the 111th Congress is even more impressive in retrospect. For, in the face of Hastert Rule reflexive opposition, Democrats only had a filibuster-proof Democratic Senate for *72 days,*[269] after Al Franken was finally sworn in, till Edward Kennedy and Robert Byrd fell ill and were mostly absent. Then Scott Brown (R) won his election in Massachusetts,

---

[268] From The New York Times: https://www.nytimes.com/2010/12/23/us/politics/23cong.html

[269] https://sandiegofreepress.org/2012/09/the-myth-of-the-filibuster-proof-democratic-senate/

and Hastert's rule against Republican-negotiation fully kicked in. The window was effectively over. *A lot got done in just 72 days.*

Hey splitters, even having just read that list, could you describe those bills and their effects and why you think they were just meaningless gestures by "corporatist sellouts?" No? You won't even try, because knowledge can't replace that sanctimony high. Oh, and one more time – the GOP won back Congress in 2010 in large part because of Democratic stay-at-homes and splitters.

SECOND REBUTTAL:
Those "sellout centrists" do have power – in blue states! And are doing a lot.

Ask your splitter if he or she knows anything about the waves of legislation that have passed in *blue states,* where "corporatist sellout" Democrats had lots of power for *more* than just two out of 25 years. CA, OR, WA, CO, NY... these have been bulwarks against Trumpism. California infuriated Old Two Scoops by negotiating its own clean air and mileage deal with five auto giants, preserving gains made under Obama. New York has overcome many of the stonewall tactics used by Trumpists to conceal their depredations.

In a *single week* of October 2019, California's legislature banned private prisons, extended the statute of limitations for childhood sex abuse, passed new rules about guns in the hands of abusers and the mentally ill, augmented privacy regulations, restricted the power of oligarchs to make private beaches inaccessible to the public, followed scientific advice as the first state to let teens to start school later in the day, required choice options be made available to college women and much else.[270] A couple of weeks later, California passed a law requiring that all newly built homes have solar roofs. Face it, the list of legislative achievements under fine governors like Jerry Brown – and Washington State's Jay Inslee – is huge.

Oh, there are still gaps and disagreements among Democrats and some factional hissing. California governor Gavin Newsome's top job

---

270 https://news.google.com/articles/CAIiECCkd4rAs3ULCUCBmi5yC9EqFggEKg4IACoGCAowjKxcMOvhCzC5zg8?hl=en-US&gl=US&ceid=US%3Aen

– like Jerry Brown – was to negotiate practicality into some over-eager members of his own party. Still, dear splitter friends, these accomplishments are negotiated among women and men of goodwill who span the left to moderate spectrum, with input welcome from sincere conservatives. If you want to rave "corporatist sellouts!" how about you actually know something, first?

THIRD REBUTTAL: Consensus Goals

The fundamental Splitter premise is that there are vast policy chasms between a progressive left and so-called "corporatist-sellout centrist Republican-lite" old-school Democrats. The news media go along because conflict sells drama. Yet, I have never seen this divisive – perhaps crippling – assertion tested or proved. Not once a detailed list of ways that a majority of Democratic politicians have "sold out."

If you hurl accusations, shouldn't you back them up?

Yes, there are areas of difference! But those convey little meaning unless we also *have a look at what both groups have in common.* Shared objectives that would make alliance – even a temporary one – overwhelmingly worthwhile.

Here is my list of **31 consensus goals** that nearly all Democratic politicians, activists and candidates are for. Step up if you claim it's either minor stuff or that a majority doesn't want them.

- Electoral reform: end gerrymandering, rigged voting machines, voter suppression and other cheats,
- Election money transparency and steps toward reducing the political dominance of cash,
- Restore our alliances,
- Deter acts of war (cyber/electoral/trade etc.) against our nation/institutions,
- End "supply side" vampirism by the aristocracy we rebelled against in 1776,
- Infrastructure, paid for by ending supply side voodoo,
- DACA,
- Children out of cages, refugees given safe places to live and process,

• Whistleblower protections and rewards for those revealing corruption and blackmail; plus a ten-year limit on non-disclosure agreements,

• Attack international banking secrecy, shell company games, ownership& money laundering,

• A Marshall Plan for Central America. Hold their corrupt elites accountable,

• Medicare for all Children (a *start*, but one so popular the GOP can't dare filibuster or refuse),

• Climate action – vigorous first steps,

• Take major steps to incentivize efficiency and reduce the waste stream,

• Restore science, R&D and technological leadership as national strengths,

• Protect women's autonomy, credibility and command over their own bodies,

• Consumer protection, empower the Consumer Financial Protection Board.

• At least allow student debt refinancing. Analyze and start doing much more.

• Restore the postal savings bank for the un-banked,

• Basic, efficient, universal background checks,

• Basic-level Net Neutrality for consumers,

• A revised-throttled War Powers Act and limit presidential emergency powers,

• Civil Service protection,

• Reject racism, gender-phobia, Nazism, etc., as evils while calming all sanctimonies,

• Restored respect for things called *facts*. Support professions that use them,

• Restored rebuttal rules on "news" channels,

• Emoluments supervision. *Audit* the cheating, money-laundering oligarchy,

• Ease out of the damned drug war (at least don't impede states),

• Anti-trust breakup of monopoly/duopolies,

• Allow pharma renegotiation and stop the tricks that stymie generics,

• Restore some of the social contract set up by the FDR-loving "Greatest Generation" (GG).

...and finally number thirty-one...

• *Win.* Rip every branch and tool of power away from what has mutated into an international cabal of gangsters, carbon barons, casino moguls, slumlords, Wall Street parasites, petro-boyars, inheritance brats, drug kingpins, communist tyrants, "ex"-communist KGB agents and Nazis. Overwhelmingly and decisively defeat that confederacy of evil. Do it decisively.

Win.

Anyone on the right who shouts "socialism!" at *that* list is screaming at our parents, the Greatest Generationers who crushed Hitler, contained Stalinism, took us to the moon, loved science and built the world's greatest middle class.[271]

Anyone on the left who sneers that "blue dogs don't want those things" should be challenged to back up the slur. Or better yet, put money on a wager. In fact, almost all Democrats, most independents and a whole lot of RASRS want *all* of those things, and more! And if you think not, *show us the Democrats opposing any of those goals!* That "corporatist" malarkey comes right out of a Kremlin basement.

Are there disagreements over the *vigor* and/or ***degree* or the *order*** in which various Democrats would push these 31 desiderata? Sure! Plenty of demo pols would only travel along these roads *halfway* as far as *you* would go! Especially in the last six items. And "Medicare for everyone under age 26" won't satisfy you liberals... nor should it!

But "Medicare for everyone under age 26" could pass *within one week,* if we had a sane Congress and president. (Many Republican senators would not dare oppose it.) And then watch as the insurance companies rush to negotiate.

Want more? Like Medicare-for-All? That's when – yes – you'll get some stodgy DLC-types demanding to see the cash flow. Want to pay

---

[271] Other lists and other (actual) socialisms? Sure, complain and negotiate about lefty over-reaches beyond those 31. We'll listen... when you're a Goldwater, not a servant of oligarchy.

for it not *just* by retracting Supply Side, but targeting defense spending? There'll be fights, and the vets who won the House for the Democratic Party might go only partway.

So? Fight those battles *after* a wide, united coalition has achieved everything on that list. *Then* split! Gather your AOC/Bernie forces for further battle! At least you'll be fighting in a nation and world that again respects facts and justice and takes care of children and runs honest elections and loves the future. And doesn't lock toddlers in cages.

Which brings us to the tragedy. Not one pundit or politician, or liberal or moderate sage, has had the wit to offer up this list of positive, unifying goals. Imagine if – instead of repeating "my plan, my plan, my plan" – even one of them offered such a list of shared goals on a debate stage. She or he would electrify the nation.

FOURTH REBUTTAL:
The lethal allure of "third parties."

Ralph Nader and Jill Stein tipped the balance for Bush and Trump in 2000 and 2016, while raving what Sigmund Freud called "the narcissism of small differences." Oh sure, they had some ideas worth discussing. Still, don't try to holler[272] your way out of that.

Instead, let's *solve the problem* in a positive sum way. For example, third party folks' top priority ought to be campaigning for Ranked Choice Voting,[273] which would then open their path ahead without screwing us all. (See Chapter 4 and join the *Equal Citizens* movement to help make it happen!)

Meanwhile, every sincere Third Party person should campaign in deep-blue or deep-red states to build their donor base and recognition. But they must pledge to *stay out of #*$%*! Florida and key tipping states…* or we need to pounce with *fury.*

---

[272] Sanctimony addiction: http://tinyurl.com/wrathaddicts and: https://www.youtube.com/watch?v=i275AvgVvow

[273] https://equalcitizens.us/ranked-choice-voting/

FIFTH REBUTTAL:
"We'll win with radical purity!"

For ages we've heard this leftist mantra: "We can attract red-district, working class voters by offering them truly vigorous socialist solutions!"[274]

Alas, it's failed in every election. Every single one. In fact, 2018 was the final, blatant refutation to this insane nostrum. *Every* seat gained in the House – and the reason why Reps. Schiff and Nadler now have subpoena power – came where a crewcut (or hair-bun) military vet (or similar) who loves science and justice *invaded* a red or purple district and *took territory* away from some monstrous GOP (Giving Over to Putin) shill.[275]

Every… single… one of those crucial gains.

Again, the lefty-purity nostrum was tested and utterly failed one-hundred percent of the time. But we did learn what works. It's a wide tent. A broad coalition of the kind that was forged by Franklin Roosevelt. Moreover, so long as the candidate agrees to most or all of those 31 points, then our goal remains simple. *Win!*

SIXTH REBUTTAL:
Mobilize all the non-voters!

Okay, we've touched on this before, but it is one of the most catastrophic ways we have narrowed, rather than broadened. It's the nostrum: *Key to victory against the right will be mobilizing the vast trove of left and moderate voters who have opted not to vote, so many times in the past.*

In fact, this one is totally true!

As far as it goes.

I'll avow that none of my "judo weapons" in this book will matter as much – in November 2020 – as relentlessly boosting voter turnout.

---

[274] Offers commentator David Ivory: In Australia a Labor Party that espoused a leftist agenda scared the electorate (especially coal country Queensland) so much that a deeply unpopular right wing government was re-elected to the surprise of all. If the Labor Party had merely said "vote for us not the bozos in office now and we'll make sure the economy stays the course" then they would have roared in. https://www.theguardian.com/australia-news/2019/may/19/labor-unloseable-election-morrison-australia-plan

[275] Or next to a military base!

And yes, maybe Liz will inspire that better than Joe Biden. I'm listening. By all means help register the lazy! And cattle prod them to the polls. We've seen that's how to win a single election.[276]

Only we've also seen why Rupert and Putin laugh at that prospect! They *know* they'll lose their grip on America, for brief intervals. It happened in 1992, and in 2008, when blue turnout tsunamis overwhelmed all their cheats. Only then what followed? Many of those democratic wave-voters slumped back into indolence. Or worse cynicism. "See, I got off the couch and voted and nothing much changed!"

A smug, self-indulgent lie… that let the red-tide sweep back, in 1994 and 2010.

Yes, by all means mobilize infrequent voters! They *can* overwhelm the cheating confederacy, briefly. And the oligarchs plan to wait it out, counting on their base to surge back, just enough *to freeze U.S. politics and accomplish no meaningful change.* For that central goal of the right, you don't need a consistent majority! A powerful, fervent minority – plus a lot of cheating – will suffice.

Can you see that is why Donald Trump and Fox are making no efforts at outreach or to expand their confederate base? But they pull out the stops – with endless rallies and fevered propaganda – to prop up that core and keep it fervent?[277] *That* is why methods of polemical judo are so vital! Because, in order to end this wretched cycle of civil war, the confederate base must shatter! And in Chapter 15 I'll show you how.

This is not zero-sum.

It's not either-or.

In the near term, yes, turn out a fire hose of blue voters enraged by Trump!

But history shows how insane it will be, to leave things there.

Don't just win an election, here and there. Take and hold territory. Take back America. All of it.

---

[276] David Ivory notes that in Australia voting is compulsory! "Failure to vote should be regarded as un-American. Much of the rest of the West is stunned by the apathy of citizens by the self-proclaimed most powerful democracy in the world. America on current numbers is not. India votes at a rate of 67% with 900 million registered voters, Indonesia votes at a rate of 80% with 154 million registered voters – the same as the United States but from a smaller population of 271 million. Meanwhile only 55% of Americans of voting age voted."

[277] Perhaps even fervent enough to spew a bitter fever of new Timothy McVeighs, an option if the enlightenment comes roaring back.

To do that, we must lure millions of our neighbors back from madness.

The bonus reason to oppose splitterism?

Because Vladimir Putin.

Because Putin has already spent tens of millions and will devote vast resources to *encourage* Splitterism. Splitter memes are already pouring in a tsunami from those Kremlin basement trolls. The Confederacy and Fox can only win against a divided Union. In fact, *here is what the AOC social democrats should do!*

Want to primary-oust some old "moderate" from your deep blue district? Knock yerself out! Create a big socialist caucus? I already said fine.

But each of you should *also* adopt and raise funds for some crewcut (or hair-bun) vet who loves science and justice and progress, helping her (or him) invade and take back some red or purple district. *Because our only chance to oust Moscow Mitch McConnell is named Amy McGrath.* (Look her up.[278]) And that's more important than any pompous-purist-preening sanctimony high.

By doing so, AOC and her pals would say: "We can argue later over how much socialism to do beyond the basics, or how much of the FDR social contract to build upon. But right now, let's focus *on* those huge basic steps we all want and the oligarchs are desperate to prevent. We are united in saving the USA and our revolution."

=====

"The best lack all conviction, while the worst are full of passionate intensity."
From Yeats, "The Second Coming"

---

[278] Amy McGrath https://www.vox.com/2019/7/9/20687411/amy-mcgrath-announces-senate-race-mitch-mcconnell

Beloved figures, often horribly misquoted.

Pause #12 for...

Not just Adam Smith. Steal back from them Goldwater, Hayek and Heinlein!

*** Mister we could use conservatives like this again.**

Much is made of a quotation from Barry Goldwater, whose version of conservatism - while sometimes wrong - at least uttered cogent criticisms. And it wasn't completely mad. Or treason.

"Mark my word, if and when these preachers get control of the [Republican] party, and they're sure trying to do so, it's going to be a terrible damn problem. Frankly, these people frighten me. Politics and governing demand compromise. But these Christians believe they are acting in the name of God, so they can't and won't compromise. I know, I've tried to deal with them."

And yes, I sometimes wonder if that joke I made up: "Do you know Arizona draws a quarter of its electricity from the spinning in Barry Goldwater's grave?"

... is truly a joke, after all.

*** A rightist icon who wasn't all that right... and a "leftist" who wasn't, either.**

One of the most popular of the most enjoyable of the popular, online "Rap Battles From History" was this amusing tiff[279] between John Maynard Keynes and Friedrich Hayek, two Nobel winning economists who are often misquoted by political factions of left and right.

Recall how I defined a "decent conservative" as someone whose suspicion-of-authority (SoA) worries more about government bureaucrats, while

---

[279] Rap Battle: Hayek vs. Keynes. https://www.youtube.com/watch?v=GTQnarzmTOc

a "decent liberal" frets about Big Brother aspirations by aristocrats and corporations? Well, yes, Hayek spoke far more often – and at length – about how markets might cloy or lose their agility, when the state intervenes or meddles overmuch. He bought into some of the "Tytler" style notions of cyclical decadence. And sure, all of that made him a person of the right.

Yet, Hayek's biggest point[280] was that no band of self-selected elites can ever have complete knowledge of the factors that roil through a complex economy. Moreover, any such clique will suffer – whatever their moralizing justifications – from group-think and our human tendency toward delusion. When pressed, even though he railed against allocating bureaucrats, Hayek admitted that this fault was endemic in all previous oligarchies, kingdoms, theocracies… and will recur in any cabal of capitalist lords. His core assertion was that markets can do investment, employment and allocation wisely, if those mass composite decisions result from the actions and choices of the maximum number of highly knowledgeable and empowered participants. Moreover, anything that limited the empowerment of diverse talent was a betrayal of market wisdom.

This means that Hayek could be called a modern "liberal" because the core catechism of liberalism, ever since Adam Smith, can be distilled down to "stop wasting talent!" Prejudice, poverty, oppression, and information deprivation all limit the market's access to highly knowledgeable and empowered participants. Hence all are betrayals of market wisdom.

As for Keynes? Well, his praise for government intervention to smooth out up-and-down business cycles was more limited than many folks believe. His aim was to save capitalism from the crises of the 1930s. And I'll leave for others[281] the argument that he was no true person of the Left.

The lesson? Watch out for the ways you might betray your own cultural/political icons. They may rise from the grave and smack you one.

---

[280] From Evonomics: http://evonomics.com/friedrich-hayek-intellectual-hero-ideologue/

[281] https://evonomics.com/keynes-was-really-a-conservative/ "Keynes popularized the idea of using budget deficits to stimulate growth in his 1936 book, *The General Theory of Employment, Interest and Money*. For this reason, Keynes, even more so than Karl Marx, is the principal bête noire of free market economists. But Keynes understood that democratic societies cannot long tolerate high levels of unemployment. At some point, people will jettison capitalism for some sort of socialism, which would threaten democracy as well. As Keynes himself explained, "the class war will find me on the side of the educated bourgeoisie." He expressed contempt for the British Labor Party, calling its members, "sectaries of an outworn creed mumbling moss-grown demi-semi Fabian Marxism." He also termed it an "immense destructive force" that responded to "anti-communist rubbish with anti-capitalist rubbish."

Papa Heinlein would want you to use him right now, against fascists and traitors

Throughout this book I keep returning to Adam Smith, the intellectual founder of modern liberalism, who (I claim) would today be a vigorous – even furious – Democrat. But for sheer cognitive dissonance – revealing a top mind who kept refusing to be pigeonholed – let me offer a Grand Master of my own guild... one of the mighty figures of science fiction, Robert Heinlein.

Once again, we see liberals allowing their opponents to clutch and appropriate both symbols and august figures they don't deserve. In the case of Heinlein, who ran for office as a Roosevelt Democrat, the matter is complex – he was an ornery and contrary fellow who would toss grenades just to see who ducked. And yes, his final decades somewhat resembled the curmudgeonly libertarian of his stereotype. Still, this is the author of Revolt in 2100, who portrayed with dread the rise of a fundamentalist preacher who stole elections, then the White House, and finally all our freedoms, when he wrote:[282]

> *"As for ... the idea that we could lose our freedom by succumbing to a wave of religious hysteria, I am sorry to say that I consider it possible. I hope that it is not probable. But there is a latent deep strain of religious fanaticism in this, our culture; it is rooted in our history and it has broken out many times in the past.*
>
> *"It is with us now; there has been a sharp rise in strongly evangelical sects in this country in recent years, some of which hold beliefs theocratic in the extreme, anti-intellectual, anti-scientific, and anti-libertarian."*

---

[282] Looking back at Heinlein's Future History – coming true before our eyes. http://davidbrin.blogspot.com/2017/03/looking-back-at-heinleins-future.html

Heinlein tore into the potential for an alliance of oligarchs and pulpit pounders taking over America... a cabal that would –

> *"–promise a material heaven here on earth, add a dash of anti-Semitism, anti-Catholicism, anti-Negroism, and a good large dose of anti-'furriners' in general and anti-intellectuals here at home, and the result might be something quite frightening – particularly when one recalls that our voting system is such that a minority distributed as pluralities in enough states can constitute a working majority in Washington."*

Wow.

While much has already been made of the racism and other nasty trends Heinlein foresaw all too well, that first phrase about promising a material heaven here on Earth was even more incredibly prescient about today's cult of "Dominionism," which promises deep-red fundamentalists that they will soon get the material possessions of all the immoral smarty-pants types. Oh, and you Catholics? Don't imagine you'll be exempt. Not when it hits the fan. Or Methodists or Mormons or Israelis, either.

Here's another Heinleinism that resonates with The Transparent Society:

> *"I began to sense that secrecy is the keystone of all tyranny. Not force, but secrecy ... censorship. When any government, or any church for that matter, undertakes to say to its subjects, 'This you may not read, this you must not see, this you are forbidden to know,' the end result is tyranny and oppression, no matter how holy the motives. Mighty little force is needed to control a man whose mind has been hoodwinked; contrariwise, no amount of force can control a free man, a man whose mind is free. No, not the rack, not*

fission bombs, not anything – you can't conquer a free man; the most you can do is kill him." [283]

Oh, I've only scratched the surface. Heinlein also predicted America would pass through "The Crazy Years." And look up a character named "Nehemia Scudder."

All right, many of you have never heard of the man. I get that. Your loss. But science fiction - humanity's R&D department for horizon-probing ideas - would not have been the same without him. Moreover, he would have fought for America, I believe, in this hour of our need. Here's one more quotation:

"You can sway a thousand men by ap-
pealing to their prejudices
quicker than you can convince one man by logic."

— Robert Heinlein, *Revolt in 2100/*
Methuselah's Children

You think me and Papa are exaggerating?

These fears are well-founded. More than half of the Republicans surveyed in a 2019 Pew poll said colleges and universities are hurting the country,[284] a drastic shift from how the same group viewed such institutions two years ago. There's a lot to this new Know Nothing movement, of course, and I explore the disease in Chapter 5, as well as this article: "Declining trust in our expert castes: what are underlying causes?"[285] This Orwellian hate fest toward fact-people undermines the very ones standing in the way of a re-imposition of feudalism. Of course nearly all fact-folks were influenced by colleges and universities.

Now comes an exposé in Foreign Policy[286] revealing how alt-righters are savagely attacking the very idea of a career civil service, a campaign ac-

---

[283] From Heinlein's "If This Goes On" – Chapter 6.
[284] http://www.huffingtonpost.com/entry/republicans-college-poll_us_59639fe2e4b0d5b458ec4481?ncid=inblnkushpmg00000009
[285] http://davidbrin.blogspot.com/2017/04/declining-trust-in-rising-fear-of-our.html
[286] http://foreignpolicy.com/2017/07/10/trumps-trolls-are-waging-war-on-americas-civil-servants/?utm_content=bufferdb673&utm_medium=social&utm_source=twitter.com&utm_campaign=buffer

celerating in the era of Trump. *"Career civil servants often endure stressful working conditions, but in the Trump White House, some of them face online trolling from alt-right bloggers who seek to portray them as clandestine partisans plotting to sabotage the president's agenda. The online attacks often cite information that appears to be provided by unnamed White House officials or Trump loyalists."*

Now, I have a libertarian corner of me that is willing to discuss how bureaucracies are ever in need of being refreshed, to prevent cloying meddlesomeness or capture. Still, there are reasons that we have nations with rules and compromises that we agreed to by sovereign political processes. And while politics has been (temporarily) destroyed by the Murdochian-confederates, we still have a civilization to maintain, and civil servants are there to keep a complex society spinning. A steep burden of proof falls on those who declare "Now let's revert to the whims of autarchy!"

Of course we are talking about the failure mode that the great historian Arnold Toynbee called the destroyer of nations... the demolition of *trust and investment in our creative or knowledge castes.*

Now who would possibly benefit from that?

What we could accomplish, if the way ahead opened…

Chapter 13

Can We Make A Deal? "What would adults do?"

Our main focus[287] has been to explore overlooked meme weapons that might help us break past political trench warfare, like the overlooked power of *wagers* (Chapter 15). And examples of adversary brilliance, e.g. Newt Gingrich's brilliant/deceitful polemical judo twist, the 'Contract With America.' Only here let's consider what to *do* with political victory, if we achieve it.

What positive things should we offer the American people?

What will we actually do, if and when we win!

It won't surprise you that I'm critical of the approach chosen by the 20 Democratic candidates for president (as of August 2019). In apparent contempt for voters' limited attention span, each tended to *narrow things down,* concentrating on a couple of issues that appear to poll best. Moreover, they fall for the media's need for fireworks, emphasizing differences between specific "plans."

What if a candidate said this:

"Look at all the talent you've seen on these debate stages! Less than two years from now, most of us here will be seated at a Cabinet table, along with other highly-qualified, mature and dedicated public servants, comparing ambitious reforms aimed at getting America moving again. If we're wise, those gatherings will include representatives from all major interests, including the very finest men and women from mature and patriotic U.S. conservatism.

---

[287] Other than my own unqualified ruminations on philosophy, history and economics. Other than those.

"And yes, one of us standing here will be president, skillfully drawing out great ideas that the best of us have to contribute. I think that president... the one presiding at that ongoing working group... should be me. In fact the traits you should be looking for are maturity, balance, and the likelihood that I will – that any of us will –get the most out of that vigorous and diverse team of rivals... so refreshingly different from anything we've seen, during this or any Republican administration.

"So let's start down that road, reminding voters that this isn't so much about left or right, or details of Medicare for All. It's about replacing Rule-By-Cranky-Rich-Toddlers, bringing maturity and grownup process back to the government we all own and share."

A prioritized list of things to get done... ...immediately, ASAP and in due time.

Oh, sure we must make plans and prioritize. But I propose that priority order should be based on *time*. First, what clear, urgent and obvious reforms can be accomplished almost *immediately*, fixing potential lethalities while paving the way for more progress? These things can be done *while* committees start their hearings and legislative markups for the sort of changes that require a year or more of hard legislative work.

Bear in mind the price we all paid in 1993-4, when Hillary Clinton concentrated only on the latter, shooting for a comprehensive health care system all in one swell foop... and wound up accomplishing nothing. Remember that enemies of the Republic are canny and backed by infinite resources. Even if America wins victories in 2020, *the Confederacy may come roaring back, as we saw in 1994 and 2010.*

In the preceding chapter on "Splitterism," I offered **31 flavors** – or action items – that have broad Democratic support, that can and should get action in the new Congress's first 90 days, some of them even the first week! And yes, many would be "incremental" down payments. But just expanding Medicare *to include all children and youths up to age 25* might pass almost instantly, because every parent in America would punish any obstructors![288]

So let's start this chapter on *things to do* by looking again at a swarm of quick bills that each contain incentives for the opposition to negotiate.

We'll also look at reforms we never knew to be necessary, till a weirdly unbalanced, narcissist chief executive made us ponder them.

Then come reforms *that will surprise the foe!* And the public! Judo moves in keeping with the title of this book.

Finally – because I'm also a science fiction author – we'll throw in some "crackpot" proposals that seem... well... so crazy that some of them just might work.

Prioritize these immediately.

Again, your time in power may be brief! So Democrats and Americans who want reform – and even any wakened/woke conservatives – ought to *jump* at these ... *even just as down payments for more.*

1. Those 31 basic consensus goals shared by almost all Democratic Party candidates, representatives and pundits, are repeated here from Chapter 12:

- Electoral reform: end gerrymandering, rigged voting machines, voter suppression and other cheats,
- Election money transparency and steps toward reducing the political dominance of cash,
- Restore our alliances and fair trade,
- Deter acts of war (cyber/electoral/trade etc.) against our nation/ institutions,
- End "supply side" vampirism by the aristocracy we rebelled against in 1776,
- Infrastructure, paid for by ending supply side voodoo,
- DACA,
- Children out of cages, refugees given safe places to live and process,

[288] Want to ensure further increments? Just include an escalator clause ramping *up* that youth cut-off yearly, to 26, then 27... and bringing the Senior Citizen end downward from 65. With those clocks ticking, just watch as the insurance companies rush to negotiate!

- Whistleblower protections and rewards for those revealing corruption and blackmail; plus a ten year limit on non-disclosure agreements,
- Attack international banking secrecy, shell company games, hidden ownership, money laundering,
- A Marshall Plan for Central America. Hold their corrupt elites accountable,
- Medicare for all children (a *start*, so popular the GOP can't dare refuse),
- Climate action – vigorous first steps,
- Restore science, R&D and technological leadership as national strengths,
- Protect women's autonomy, credibility and command over their own bodies,
- Consumer protection, empower the Consumer Financial Protection Board.
- At least allow student debt refinancing. Analyze and start doing much more.
- Restore the postal savings bank for the un-banked,
- Basic, efficient, universal background checks,
- Basic-level Net Neutrality for consumers,
- A revised-throttled War Powers Act and limit presidential emergency powers,
- Civil Service protection,
- Reject racism, gender-phobia, Nazism etc. as evils while calming all sanctimonies,
- Restore respect for things called *facts*. Support professions that use them,
- Restore rebuttal rules on "news" channels,
- Emoluments supervision. *Audit* the cheating, money-laundering oligarchy,
- Ease out of the damned drug war (at least don't impede states),
- Anti-trust breakup of monopoly/duopolies,
- Allow pharma renegotiation and stop the tricks that stymie generics,

• Restore some of the social contract set up by the FDR-loving "Greatest Generation" (GG).

...and finally number thirty-one...

• *Win.* Rip every branch and tool of power away from what has mutated into an international cabal of gangsters, carbon kings, casino moguls, slumlords, Wall Street parasites, petro-boyars, inheritance brats, drug kingpins, communist tyrants, "ex"-communist KGB agents and Nazis. Overwhelmingly and decisively defeat that monstrous consortium and save civilization.

2. Double emphasis on quickly enacting these specifics. (Admittedly my own top priorities.)

• Whistleblower protection and forgiveness as a lure to end blackmail or corruption of public servants.[289]

• Under the 13th Amendment, require all states with voter ID laws to devote enough *compliance assistance* to cut the number of citizens with ID problems in half, each year.

• Limit non-disclosure agreements with amnesty for exposing those revealing crimes.

• A national Election Day (or perhaps even better a half-day) holiday, for those who actually vote.

• In every "red" state where the GOP grasp on power (legislature and governor) loosens even for just one term, quickly institute a *referendum process* allowing citizens to bypass the legislature by petitioning ballot measures, as proved effective already in half of the states. Let the GOP try to rescind that power later, if they get back in. Let them just try.

• A world ownership treaty. Okay, I'll leave that one mysterious, for later. But Liz's wealth tax idea will be futile without it.

3. Weaknesses in our system that were exposed by Donald Trump, that must be corrected. Congress needs to remedy a number of potentially calamitous holes in current law, or even the Constitution, exposed by this raving phenomenon. And if Courts say we can't constrain him, then constrain his resources. Several of these are already included in the

---

[289] Written *long* before the Whistleblower Affair of October 2019.

list of 31 consensus goals. But Trump has made them urgent. Explanations here are brief, but with some links.

- No foreign meetings without multiple trustworthy U.S. witnesses. (Needs no explanation.)
- War powers. Adjustments, long needed, are especially urgent in time of Trump. This must be done *carefully,* so as not to play into adversary hands. But it must be done. Along with revised rules for when the chief executive may declare an "emergency."
- *Carefully* revive the special prosecutor law. Democrats were tricked into letting it go, in exhaustion after the insanely absurd and fruitless "Clinton investigations." There must be a way to sunset witch hunts – say if they fail to get grand jury indictments during any three month period – while *empowering* those that do.)
- Strengthen the 25th amendment. It was originally intended to deal with non-hostile transfers of power due to incapacity. A president with a fanatically loyal cabinet and/or VP is immune. One incremental step: establish the amendment's "other body" out of the nation's most august retired judges, scientists and presidents. (See Chapter 16 or "Exit strategies: Surprising aspects of the 25th Amendment."[290])
- Establish by law a role for professional organizations (e.g. the Bar Association) in the vetting of presidential appointment nominees.
- Make physical and mental examination by external experts annually routine for all senior office holders including President, Vice President, and leaders of Congress.
- Enact limitations on "acting" officials. Cabinet offices left empty past a certain interval get assigned to senior civil servants.
- Charge the new Inspector General of the United States (IGUS – see below) to investigate and report on emoluments and other constitutional matters.
- Can't indict a sitting president? We *must* overcome by law that vague "guidance letter" issued by the Justice Department's Office of Legal Council (OLC), preventing that monstrous assertion from becoming established precedent! … One alternative is *slow indictment.*

---

[290] "Exit strategies Part II: Surprising aspects of the 25th Amendment." http://davidbrin.blogspot.com/2017/08/exit-strategies-part-ii-surprising.html Extensively updated to be part of Chapter 16 in this volume.

"A president cannot be burdened with more than ten hours a week spent on all personal legal defenses." Yes, that would still allow the Oval Office to slow things down. It might frustrate us all. But *slowing* accountability is not the same thing as *murdering* it, which Trump's lawyers seek to dojustice could at least be seen grinding forward, without conceding an insane principle that *presidents are above the law.*

- Does a President have the power to *declassify* anything? Everything? Fix this, while strengthening time limits on classification.
- Compulsory briefings – for example, the Science Adviser shall have uninterrupted access to the President for at least two one-hour sessions per month. (See below in this chapter: "honoring the losing side.")
- Severely tighten whim and vacation expenses reimbursement rules.
- By law establish a civil service position of *White House Manager, whose function is to supervise all non-political functions and staff.* This would include building maintenance for the Executive Mansion and the Eisenhower Executive Office Building, but also the switchboard, the Travel Office and … the Secret Service protection detail, since there are no justifications for the President of political staff to have any command authority over such apolitical employees.
- Assign to the Government Accountability Office a new task – a bureau that will answer any Congressional member's request to score on fact versus lies. Taking into account many kinds of ambiguity, we still need *something* to replace today's chaos of "Sez you!" Until we get the FACT Act.[291]

4. True Judo. Do the unexpected.

All right, those lists concentrated on measures that might be taken *right away,* even as committees and conferences begin pondering more complex issues, like long-term health care. *Prominent Democrats should offer such lists,* reminding splitters how briefly they held real power, in 1993 and 2009.

---

[291] Newt Gingrich's 2018 assault on the Congressional Budget Office as "partisan" is nothing new. In 95, Newt led in demolishing the Office of Technology Assessment or OTA, science & tech advisors who had been hired by earlier (mostly Republican) Congresses to render neutral advice on what's pragmatic under physical law. This advice proved irksome to dogmatists. Instead of correcting any "bias" by adding some conservative techies to OTA, they burned out the bureau, letting GOP reps declare anything they liked to be "true" without quibbles from boffins.

Now I want to do something that keeps faith with the title of this book. In section 4, below, we'll offer *judo moves* that would make Newt Gingrich – at his most agile – seem a clunking doofus. We're about to propose…

– 4.1 How the majority can both establish new precedents and gain huge public cred, by doing the unexpected… by honoring losing side.[292]

– 4.2 A sudden and unexpected judo move: give every House member *one subpoena per term*. Plus modest suggestions about floor votes and filibusters!

– 4.3 We'll know we're emerging from this childish era – that Robert Heinlein predicted as the "crazy years" – when candidates agree to stipulation![293]

– 4.4 Here's a choice one that'll stick in their craws. Judo enact the 'good parts" of Newt Gingrich's "Contract With America!" This would convey a sense of maturity and willingness to take ideas from all directions. Plus it pokes the GOP, revealing that all pretense at reform was just another lie. But we'll make it good.

– 4.5 And I'll say more about one reform I think could make the most difference. Establishing the office and independent agency of the *Inspector General of the United States.*

Let's begin with one of my older (lightly updated) political posts. And yes, it seems naïve in an era I now call civil war. But gestures like the following could help lure millions of citizens back to civilized argument.

4.1 Honoring tens of millions of American "losers." [294]

As we launch into another Presidential campaign, get ready for the same tiresome metaphors relating politics to sports, to war and even to revenge. The front-runner will fight to maintain his or her *lead* over the *underdog* in key *battleground* states where crucial clumps of electors are awarded by winner-takes-all. Those on the *victorious* side will gather every marble, leaving citizens on the *losing side* bitterly muttering about getting even next time.

---

[292] Honoring the losing side. http://www.davidbrin.com/nonfiction/losingmajority.html

[293] Candidates might show their maturity through… stipulation! http://www.davidbrin.com/nonfiction/candidatestipulation.html

[294] Originally posted: http://www.davidbrin.com/nonfiction/losingmajority.html

Are we really on opposing armies, bent on total victory over our neighbors? Yes, elections and majority rule constitute a vast improvement over coercive aristocracies of the past. Still, majority rule isn't perfect. A nation that treats the losing minority with contempt is asking for trouble. (And yes, this includes those lonely "flyover states who feel so neglected – whether it's true or not.)

In fact, majority rule is already tempered in American political life. Congress seldom passes a law supported by just 51% of the people, while vigorously opposed by nearly half. Minority objections are eased by negotiation and tradeoffs. Small but intensely passionate lobbies may effectively veto measures that are desired only tepidly by much greater majorities. This dance of factions can be frustrating when popular measures get sidetracked by vigorous advocacy groups like, say, the National Rifle Association. And yes, that is still a far cry from *consensus* – especially in recent years.

Things are different in the Executive Branch. Consider Ronald Reagan's "landslide" victory over Walter Mondale in 1984, or Lyndon Johnson's over Barry Goldwater in 1964. If your candidate wins by a 60/40 vote margin, you can legitimately call it a ringing victory, but it still means four in ten voting citizens did *not* want your guy in office. To that forty percent, the word «mandate» translates as – *drop dead!* All the more so after a close election, or – as we all saw in 2000 (and 2016) – when odd-suspicious electoral quirks put in office the man with fewer popular votes. Even if Al Gore had come out ahead in the Florida recounts – or Hillary visited Wisconsin – eking Electoral College victory to accompany their popular vote win, would that razor-thin endorsement entitle them to claim a clear cut mantle of history?

Can 50.1 percent legitimately ignore the wishes of 49.9 percent who disagreed?

The European model of coalition parliamentary government offers little to America. We've seen benefits to letting a president appoint loyal officers, governing without undue interference from within. Still, George Washington understood the temptations of human nature, which can transform well-meaning leaders into lonely monarchs, broody, isolated, and paranoid. It is disturbing to witness our top elected official insulate himself (as has happened often in living memory) with all access to the inner sanctum barred by an ideologically driven staff, justified by a sense of entitlement, cultural mandate and narrow-minded mission. [295]

An inquiring press can help to moderate this trend, as do Constitutional checks and balances. Yet, more is needed, like some way to honor the millions of Americans who lose each election – whether by squeaker or landslide –ensuring that their concerns will at least be heard.

There is precedent. Originally, the Constitution awarded a prize for second place – the *Vice Presidency.* After near-disaster in 1804 the system was amended, making the VP more a deputy, chosen by the winning party. Still, it's clear the Founders intended for the losing side to get *something.*[296]

So, might there be some way to acknowledge the losing minority – or even a losing majority – without grinding their face in humiliation, making them determined to do likewise, when their turn comes around? First, here›s an idea that may seem a bit silly. Imagine how it might have mollified millions of Democrats, and created a more collegial atmosphere after the bitter election of 2000, if just *one* of George W. Bush›s electors had switched sides when it came to the vote for Vice President. By helping install a Democrat as VP, they could have made a gesture toward government by negotiation, consensus and respect, while still handing the reins of actual power to their chosen man. All right, that suggestion is far-fetched (if thought provoking.)

But here's another one that's plausible, requiring no miracles or kludges, no meddling in the Constitution or legitimate powers of the chief executive. Yet, it's so reasonable that only a churl could possibly refuse. Imagine a candidate or new President-Elect making the following pledge:

"If I win, I promise to ask my honorable opponent to pick a panel of Americans who will have *control over my appointment calendar one afternoon per month.* And I expect my opponent to serve on that panel. On that afternoon, I shall meet with – and listen to – any individuals or delegations that panel may choose. Millions of Americans will then

---

[295] Yes, I wrote this long before Donald Trump got installed by elements wishing us harm.

[296] President Lincoln famously appointed former Whigs and Democrats to his Republican Cabinet. The Team of Rivals. https://www.amazon.com/Team-Rivals-Political-Abraham-Lincoln

know that I do not live in a tower of ideological isolation. I will answer questions and hear dissenting points of view."

Such a pledge would cost a candidate and president little to make or to fulfill. There is no obligation to act on what the delegations say, only to be accessible, listening occasionally to more than one ideology. More than one brain trust of cloned advisors. Indeed, the legitimacy of any administration will be enhanced if we see the president receive articulate, passionate emissaries, representing diverse opinions and walks of life.

During the first era of our republic, private citizens used to knock on the door of the White House and ask to see their nation's leader. As recently as the time of Harry Truman, there was a slim chance of seeing the president somewhere in public, buying socks for real, not as a publicity stunt. There is genuine peril in losing this connection between power and everyday life. So, if today's president cannot safely venture among us, representatives of sundry outlooks should have a route to him or her. Not just public figures, but individuals from the ranks of the poor and dispossessed might win a chance to plead their case before the highest official in the land. Even if such meetings don't benefit multitudes, at least a few worthy petitioners might get hearings, and possibly some justice.

Moreover, this would give those tens of millions who lost the election *something*. A token – or perhaps more. A vow to *listen*. If a nominee's goal is to live as a potentate, insulated from his or her countrymen, this is one pledge to avoid. But if the aim is to be president of *all* Americans, then what harm could such a promise do?

4.2 The Subpoena Individuation

This idea's simple. Spread the *power of subpoena* – and include the minority party!

Why should Speaker Nancy Pelosi and her committee chairs do this, when that minority party is Republican? Seriously Congressional Democrats; remember, a day will come when you'll be back on the outs. (The lesson of 1994 and 2010!) *Now is the time to set permanent precedents* that ensure you'll still have a little power to poke after truth. Establish processes *now* so that even a congressional minority can hold some future Bush-like or Trump-like administration somewhat accountable!

One way: give today's GOP minority what they never had the maturity to give you – the general power to summon witnesses and demand some answers, even when their party is out of power.

Better yet, give *every individual member of the House one subpoena per term,* that can compel testimony from any person before one of that member's sub-committees for three hours. Or if that's too much, allow any *three* representatives to jointly issue one subpoena per year beyond those voted by committees – and provide a venue with some staff support. That should cause some backroom wrangling! One for every three members – that's 140 member-chosen testimonies... maybe sixty a year – or per term – from the minority party. A large enough number to make sure that pokes-at-truth will keep going on, even during eras when a single party machine dominates every branch of government. And yet, it's small enough not to disrupt House business overmuch.

Think about it. Pelosi and Schumer can afford that. It wouldn't block legislation. Would some mad-rightists use their subpoenas to annoy? BFD! Just imagine how valuable that would have been for minority Democrats, during the first two years of the Trump Era.

There's another aspect to this. Many Republicans would feel motivated to break party discipline and *hoard* their subpoenas for use in some way that impresses the home district. And thus, it could help shatter their caucus cohesion, encouraging individual autonomy![297]

The public relations benefits are clear, demolishing forever any accusations that "Democrats run roughshod over minority party rights." And if Republicans later reneged? That would also be a black eye before the American public.

When I first offered this proposal it was 2007 and Democrats in the House seemed to be riding high. I added: "There is no way that Speaker Pelosi and the leadership will want to do this, now that the GOP is reduced to an irksome nuisance. Still, please think about it. Just giving them the right to grill a few people won't let them do much mischief to an open and honest and competent Obama Administration. Meanwhile,

---

[297] Again, if gopper reps used theirs, while in minority, then it could establish a firm precedent for when – not if – Democrats slump back into exile! Think how valuable that would have been, during the 22 out of 26 years the GOP owned the House. Especially 2017-2019, when that rule could have peeled away at Trumpian travesties.

such a precedent could guarantee we'll never again have an era as dark as the Bush years, without the other side getting to light some candles."

Was I naïve? Or would we have been better off *right now*, if this precedent had been set back then?

Here are a couple more judo procedural moves that could maybe dilute leader power, a little, but inspire citizens to know which party's on their side:

– In both House and Senate, let any 45% minority bring up to five votes per month to the chamber floor.

– First replace the idiotic *tacit* filibuster (60 votes needed to advance a bill) with the old-style *talk*-filibuster. But even more effective a partial reform – try treating filibusters like *sports timeouts.* Your party starts each session with a fixed number. When they're gone, they're gone.

4.3 Why Candidates Should Stipulate

The previous two proposals for cross-party outreach don't require that *both* sides be mature. They show how the winners of an election might gain favor with voters by both appearing – and truly being – the better and more grownup party, establishing precedents that could serve us all well.

The next one truly does require that *both* sides be capable of rising above the fray, with some sincerity and wisdom. [298] Yeah, yeah, I'm a scifi-fantasy author. But as Garth said in *Wayne's World,* "Hey, it could happen!"

Let's start with a flawed example that stands out, instructive even in its failure. In 2008, Nancy Pelosi – then Speaker of the U.S. House of Representatives – sat with former Speaker Newt Gingrich on a small couch in front of the Capitol, to film a brief joint statement.[299] They began with a charming – some might say artless – admission that they had few areas of agreement. But the pair then went on to urge action on the pressing matter of climate change. No specific methods came up, whether government or incentives for industry. Both did avow faith

---

[298] http://www.davidbrin.com/nonfiction/candidatestipulation.html

[299] Pelosi-Gingrich "couch commercial" jointly urging climate action. https://www.youtube.com/watch?v=qi6n_-wB154

in our ability to develop clean, efficient energy systems, if we make it a priority.

Alas, what followed was emblematic of this (so far) benighted century. Fox and the GOP establishment raged at Gingrich, eviscerating his betrayal of the Hastert Rule against seeking common ground with the enemy. [300] So volcanic was the response, especially from Republican donors, that Newt unctuously swerved back into line.[301] And yes, I'm beginning this section on "stipulation" with an abject failure – but a colorful one, that's still a bit inspiring.

It's been said that a politician gets to be perfectly honest just once in a long career – at its end. Refreshing candor sometimes pours after an old pol has faced the last campaign. No more fund raisers, or need to flatter voters. One final chance, before the cameras, to tell the truth.

Not all retiring officials spill their hearts, but when they do it can be colorful. Take the day in 1991 when both Republican Senator Warren Rudman and Democrat Paul Tsongas withdrew from public life. They made headlines by jointly suggesting that everyone was at fault for the country's condition at the time, from then-President Bush to the then Democrat-controlled Congress, all the way to the American people. The pair castigated politicians of all parties for not telling citizens that burgeoning budget deficits threatened our economic well-being. Responsible economists agreed. A few even credit Rudman and Tsongas for spurring reforms that helped lead to the Clinton era surpluses.

A more recent example of post-retirement candor came with ex-Treasury Secretary Paul O'Neill's revelations about the second Bush Administration. It resulted in a fire storm of attacks from his own party. O'Neill's explanation for this candor? That he was "old and rich" and unafraid to speak his mind.

---

[300] https://www.foxnews.com/politics/gingrich-feels-the-heat-for-appearing-in-global-warming-ad-with-pelosi

[301] So furious was the reaction from the right that Gingrich made abject pilgrimages of abasement before the Koch Brothers and other GOP powers, banishing forever-more his science-loving-statesman side and doubling down on the 'loyal-gladiator.' His reward for vociferously supporting Donald Trump was to be the only major GOP leader between Reagan and Ryan honored – or even mentioned – at the 2016 Republican National Convention. Pelosi, too, took some flack from her left – which she easily shrugged off, as a large majority of Democrats approved. The lesson? Courage and enlightenment ain't easy. https://www.foxnews.com/politics/gingrich-feels-the-heat-for-appearing-in-global-warming-ad-with-pelosi

However one feels about those specific examples, we can all agree they are rare. One of the chief flaws of our electoral system is that real candor is punished. Both sides may rail against each other, but they›ll never aim bad news at *us*. Even if both nominees believe in their hearts that the public needs to face some hard truth, neither will dare be first to say it, lest the other side take advantage. Think about it. Throughout the coming election we will learn how the candidates *disagree* on a myriad issues, plus platitudes that voters want to hear. But logically, there's a third category – areas where these well-informed professionals *agree with each other, but are afraid to speak out.* We'll never hear whatever topics or beliefs occupy that logical box, because neither candidate will dare speak first.

Now consider: *there's no political cost to telling voters what you really believe... if your opponent says the same thing.*[302]

Yeah, that statement sounds absurdly simpleminded. The metaphor for an election "give 'em hell" combat. But wait. What's wrong with two leaders finding a patch of consensus amid a sea of discord? We cheer when heads of state overcome differences between nations, finding common ground. Why not between candidates?

It's called *stipulation...* as when the attorneys representing opposite sides in a trial *agree to agree* about a set of points, helping move the trial forward by focusing thereafter on areas where they disagree. So will you bear with me for a "what-if" thought experiment? A weird, but possible scenario? [303]

Suppose, amidst the 2008 campaign, Republican candidate John McCain and his Democratic opponent Barack Obama were to suspend mutual attacks to *meet for an afternoon.* First, they and their staffs would cover issues such as scheduling debates, and how to prevent spirals of mudslinging. *The people would applaud any agreement on fair campaigning principles.* Heck, just seeing them talk to each other like adults might be refreshing. Think how the image might affect the rancorous mood we see in politics today, independent of policy disagreements.

---

[302] But... but Newt on the couch! Okay, I wrote this in a slightly more hopeful time. But such times may come again.

[303] Again, *this book is a* mélange of edited and update essays, articles and postings I've written over the years. That explains much of the irksome repetition! And also some of these time travel artifacts that I've decided to leave in place.

So far, so good. Only then suppose the two nominees do something unprecedented. They go for a walk, unpressured by cameras and media flacks, seeking just a few points of consensus.

Don't dismiss this too readily! For all his faults, McCain did this sort of thing before. So have Democrats like Bill or Hillary Clinton and Obama. Oh, neither candidate will change the other's mind concerning major divisions. But here we have two knowledgeable public persons, concerned about America's future. Surely there would be *some areas of overlap?* Things that both of them feel we, as a nation, should do.

Now imagine that this overlap results in a joint statement. Though reiterating a myriad points of disagreement, they go on to make public, simultaneously, their shared belief that America should, for its own good, pass law "X", or repeal restriction "Y" or reform a particular flaw. Further, they agree that neither will attack the other for taking this stand.

No longer pandered to, a lot of folks might say – "Gosh, if both of them agree that the country needs this strong medicine, let's give it some thought."

This would *not* free candidates from the stifling effects of mass-politics. But it could let them display something we›ve seen rarely... leadership. Even statesmanship. Setting aside self-interest in favor of hard truth, telling the people what they need to hear, whether they like it or not.

Unprecedented? Well, actually, *it happened before,* during the Presidential campaign of 1940. When Franklin Roosevelt was running for a third term, he approached the Republican candidate, Wendell Wilkie, to negotiate just such a stipulated agreement in the area of foreign policy. Britain badly needed escort vessels for the North Atlantic and the U.S. had over-age destroyers to spare. But Roosevelt feared political repercussions during a campaign in which he was already under attack for breaking neutrality. Wilkie agreed to FDR's request, and declared that lend-lease would be his policy too, if he were elected.

Everyone benefited – Wilkie rose in stature. FDR got his policy implemented, and the world was better off because political advantage got briefly put aside for the common good. On other issues, Roosevelt and

Wilkie battled as fiercely as ever. Yet, that historical act of stipulation shines as in memory.

How might today's politics differ if two adults – each the standard bearer of a major party – agreed to let it be known how, in a few ways, they agree? Might they take on some of our most politically impossible subjects? Perhaps a cow as sacred as the Social Security retirement age, a compromise on gun control, some campaign finance reform, or perhaps shifting strategy in the endless, brain-dead War on Drugs? That would still leave plenty for us to fight over, don't worry.

Is this quixotic proposal too much to ask of today's opportunistic brand of politician?[304] Perhaps. Still, American politics can evolve. Only during the most recent generation has the tradition of *Presidential debates* become so entrenched that no front-runner can now duck them. Ancient hurdles of age, race, and gender are falling. So why not barriers against candor?

Might the Candidates' Post-Convention Stipulation Summit become traditional, like doldrums in July and mudslinging in October? Someday, the whole nation may look forward to the occasion, once every four years, with a sort of delicious, nervous anticipation – awaiting the one day when two eminent politicians will say not what is politically wise, but what is simply wise.

Now let's put that dreamy fantasy aside, and get back to metaphors of war.

4.4 Judo enact the 'good parts" of Newt Gingrich's "Contract With America!"

All right, I am beating this drum pretty hard. But the best way to learn judo is by defeating it! Remember, too, that the "good parts"[305] truly did attract millions to believe (*cough*) that Gingrich's party wanted reform:

Among the better "contract" ideas that were betrayed:

– requiring all laws that apply to the rest of the country also apply equally to the Congress;

---

[304] Reminder, except for some light updating, this essay is from mid 2008. And yes, I know how absurd it looks, slipping Donald Trump or Mike Pence into this scenario. But, times can and must change.

[305] "Should Democrats Issue Their Own 'Contract with America'?" http://www.davidbrin.com/nonfiction/contract.html

– arranging for regular comprehensive audits of Congress for waste, fraud or abuse;

– limiting the terms of all committee chairs and party leadership posts;

– banning the casting of proxy votes in committee and law-writing by lobbyists;

– requiring committee meetings to be open to the public;

– guaranteeing an honest accounting of our Federal Budget.

Elsewhere I point to ways that this good promise – and subsequent hypocritical betrayal – could launch into genuine Congressional reforms, starting with restoring independent advisory agencies for science, technology other areas of skilled analysis, to counsel Congress without bias or dogma-driven pressure. [306] This might ensure that technical reports may not be re-written by politicians, changing their meaning at the last minute.

As I've said repeatedly it would convey a sense of maturity, plus really dig at the GOP, saying clearly that they had been liars. And yet still, we'll cull the bad and enact the stuff the people really wanted, turning lies into truth.

4.5 Create the office of Inspector General of the United States...[307]

...or IGUS, who will head a uniformed agency akin to the Public Health Service, charged with protecting the ethical health of government. It's something I've long pushed – (it's in the FACT Act) – that could make more of a difference than any other proposal.

And yes, I saved this one – likely the most important suggestion of all – till the very end of the chapter.

Currently, the inspectors – or IGs – in all government agencies experience some conflict of interest, having to investigate people who appointed them and to whom they are beholden. That will change when IGs are appointed out of a dedicated and disciplined service, reporting directly to IGUS.

---

[306] http://www.davidbrin.com/nonfiction/advisoryagencies.html
[307] http://www.davidbrin.com/nonfiction/inspectorgeneral.html

The Inspector General of the United States will advise the President and Congress concerning potential breaches of the law and will have authority, independent of the Justice Department, to summon grand juries. IGUS will create a corps of trusted observers, cleared to go anywhere and assure the American people that the government is still theirs, to own and control.[308]

[308] IGUS will be appointed by a commission consisting of all past presidents and retired justices of the US Supreme Court, with advice and consent of Congress. Note a historical item. When Sun Yatsen crafted the 1911 constitution of the Republic of China, he established the Inspectorate as a separate branch of government, independent of the Executive and even the Judiciary.

They want us given wedgies....

Pause #13 for:

Obama Derangement and Trump's "Mandate of Heaven."

Elsewhere I mention "WODI" or "What if Obama Did It?"... one of numerous verbal or polemical tactics that are used far too seldom. In Pause #15 we'll take a hard, statistical look at the day-vs.-night differences in skill, honesty and integrity between the Obama and Clinton Administrations, on the one hand, and the turpitude-drenched and proved-criminal Bush and Trump regimes.

But for now... more generally and briefly... let's go to New York Times commentator Charles Blow, who in October 2019 said: [309]

"Conservatives scoured every facet of his [Obama's] life looking for a scandal and found none. They picked at every imaginary faux pas – wearing a tan suit, putting his feet on the desk, putting mustard on his burger – and yet they not only defend Trump's truly vulgar behaviors, they cheer them.

"Sarah Palin made a whole campaign out of saying that Obama "pals around with terrorists," while Trump quite literally cozies up to murderous dictators and brags about the love letters he exchanges with one. Republicans see nothing wrong here. Trump is a rich white man defending white supremacy and white nationalism. For him, the rules are different."

Mr. Blow continues, zeroing in on the way Trump may have pushed even his own rabid followers too far.

"Pat Robertson, upset over Trump's unconscionable abandoning of the Kurds in northern Syria, said: 'The president of the United States is in danger of losing the mandate of heaven if he permits this to happen.'"

---

[309] From The New York Times: https://www.nytimes.com/2019/10/13/opinion/trump-republicans.html

Say what? You've seen me many times reiterate that it takes some truly muscular mental forcefulness for our fundie neighbors to proclaim the most opposite-to-Jesus person as the elect champion of righteousness, akin to the Persian King Cyrus who – while a pagan – was God's instrument to liberate the Israelites from Babylon. Likewise Trump is liberating the red demographics from suffering indignities at the hands of those they most despise... smartypants professions and fact people. Liberating them from modernity and change.

Let me reiterate: it's a mistake to claim that right-wing putschism is solely... or even mostly... about racism. Yes, the *victims* who hurt the most have been minorities, non-binaries, immigrants, children and so on. But only a fool ignores the clades who are truly most-hated by this madness, the professions who deal in facts and who stand in the way of an oligarchic takeover, around the world. (Chapter 5.)

This is not zero sum. The confederates have plenty of hate to spread around. I simply assert that they reviled Barack Obama as much for his nerdiness as for the color of his skin.

CIVIL WAR

Different dreams...

Chapter 14

Our 250 year Family Feud – Phase 8 of the Civil War?

"Either the United States will destroy ignorance or ignorance will destroy the United States."
-W.E.B. Du Bois

In my novel *The Postman,*[310] I portrayed the aftermath of a terrible struggle that ripped apart America and the world, not just between nations and ideologies, or religions, but over the very notion of our Enlightenment Experiment.[311] I'm not the only one seeing scary harbingers for the American Union. I've called this era we're in Phase Eight of the U.S. Civil War, a recurring curse and mental illness dating back at least to 1778.

Without meaning to depress anyone, I want to emphasize how deeply embedded this "culture war" must be, afflicting the American psyche. It helps explain the vociferous loathing that some of our neighbors now express toward things we all should take for granted.[312] Moreover, this streak of madness shows that, even if Enlightenment America wins overwhelmingly at the ballot box (and I hope tactics in this book prove helpful), millions of neighbors *will* deny us any mandate to govern, refusing even to negotiate.[313]

---

[310] Filmed in 1997, loosely though colorfully and with some heart, by Kevin Costner.

[311] Other recent works to vividly and disturbingly portray a future 'hot civil war' include Sean Smith's novel *Tears of Abraham* and Craig DiLouie's *Our War,* which portray how many millions might die, if things get hot, as our enemies – foreign and domestic – clearly intend.

[312] Recall Chapter 1: "Below the surface – themes and beliefs we share."

[313] Of course, if he is not deemed by Putin/Murdoch to be more useful as a martyr, Donald Trump will certainly contest any electoral results as "faked" in a grand conspiracy, summoning rallies to rile up a new generation of Timothy McVeighs.

As I collected and prepared these older postings for book publication (late 2019), abruptly the "civil war" phrasing has rocketed in mass media. Heather Cox Richardson, a history professor at Boston College, drew eerie parallels[314] between our era and the antebellum period, when the plantation aristocracy persuaded a million poor whites to fight and die for their neo-feudal privileges. "Mob-rule" rationalizations for suppression of citizen-sovereignty are now voiced openly by oligarchs to justify cheat methods like gerrymandering.[315] Donald Trump tweet-promoted far-right threats of violent civil war, were any impeachment process to move forward. [316]

I'm not without hope! We survived earlier phases of this periodic fever. Lincoln preached how to behave in victory (with "malice toward none"). M. L. King taught us to treat every defeat as a temporary setback. And so, here are two historical perspectives about a sickness that cyclically tries to rip us apart, but we can overcome.

THE 1860S AMERICAN CIVIL WAR – ROOTED IN ROMANTICISM[317]

In 2013 we watched the Ken Burns *Civil War* documentary with our then 16 year old – a terrific work of high-class, dramatic, enriching media. Still, it seemed light on the underlying causes of that national trauma. Oh, sure, slavery was central. Those who try to minimize that, or make excuses, should read the secession declarations of South Carolina

---

[314] "Historian warns today's America looks 'eerily similar' to period before the civil war, compares movement conservatives to slaveholder elite." https://www.newsweek.com/historian-trump-civil-war-impeachment-movement-conservatives-slaveholders-1462240

[315] Mudsill theory is a sociological term indicating the proposition that there must be a lower class for the upper classes to rest upon. The analogy to a mudsill, the lowest threshold that supports the foundation for a building, was posed by South Carolina Senator/Governor James Henry Hammond, a plantation owner, in1858, to justify what he saw as the willingness of the lower classes and non-whites to perform menial work which enabled the higher classes to move civilization forward. "In all social systems there must be a class to do the menial duties, to perform the drudgery of life. ... It constitutes the very mudsill of society." Northern soldiers fighting in the Western Theater of the Civil War turned this derogatory term into one of self pride, as in "Western Mudsill". https://en.wikipedia.org/wiki/James_Henry_Hammond

[316] "Trump's 'civil war' quote tweet is actually grounds for impeachment, says Harvard law professor."https://www.newsweek.com/trump-civil-war-tweet-grounds-impeachment-1462044

[317] From "Past keeping faith with future... and day with night" (2013) http://davidbrin.blogspot.com/2013/02/past-keeping-faith-with-future-and-day.html

and other rebel states, which proudly used that very word – "slavery" – dozens of times.

Those declarations presented "grievances" which pretty much consisted of hating northern folks for *not* shutting down abolitionist newspapers! I kid you not. Almost every secession declaration distilled down to: "All you Yankees allow freedom of the press, letting people say mean things about us. And now you had the nerve to win an election! Okay then, we spurn all the sacred oaths we swore. Goodbye."

As we'll see, the South had pretty much owned and operated the U.S. Federal Government for thirty years, till Lincoln's election ended that long run, so "States' Rights" were scarcely mentioned.

It began earlier than we're taught.

Blatantly, the Civil War did not start with the firing on Fort Sumter, but in 1852 with passage – and brutal enforcement – of the Fugitive Slave Act, supported by a Supreme Court led by the infamous John Taney. What followed could only be called an invasion, as northern states from Michigan to Massachusetts suffered raids by squadrons of *irregular southern cavalry,* committing outrages and depredations, kidnapping people off the street, smashing into homes, terrorizing neighbors and dragging off friends you knew since childhood. When decent citizens objected, these raiding parties were supported by federal authority, first southern-appointed U.S. Marshals and later – when locals began resisting – by *troops* ordered in by South-sympathetic presidents. These purported "slave-catcher" incursions were among many provocations that radicalized northerners into re-starting their dormant state militias. It's what drove many of them to support Lincoln in the 1860 election, something unthinkable just eight years before. Nothing like it happened to the south until Sherman.[318]

But slavery is gone, you say. So why are we still palpably fighting the same Civil War 150 years later, across pretty similar geographical and cultural divides? Can it be something deeper, even psychological? An enduring flux that churns through our national veins? One hint can be

---

[318] Those accusing Sherman of burning Georgia plantations in 1864, while liberating tens of thousands of enslaved human beings, should look into what Confederate armies did in 1862, in Kentucky and Ohio, burning everything in sight and dragging off human war booty, before lecturing us about who set the first example.

found in Ted Turner's excellent 1993 film, *Gettysburg*, based upon a 1974 novel, The Killer Angels by Michael Shaara.[319] In one scene a British military observer, sympathetic to the Confederate cause, comments to General Longstreet that both sides spoke the same language, sang the same songs... but had *different dreams.*

This resonates with something that Mark Twain said – blaming the ill-fated rebellion on Sir Walter Scott's addictive quasi-fantasy novels and a streak of *romanticism* that wove through Southern sensibilities. Indeed, Sam Houston is quoted in the Ken Burns documentary, predicting that hot southern blood would be overcome by northern coolness, concentration and ponderous momentum of resolve.

A Side-Riff on Romanticism

I can't help diving into this matter of romanticism, since it's more important than almost anyone realizes. A hundred years ago, folks like Spengler, Spencer, Wells and Stapledon took *regional character* seriously – contrasting the 'pragmatic cynicism' of the French and British vs. German and Russian romanticism. And yes, Nazism was the most thoroughly romantic movement ever conceived.[320]

Sired by generations of poets, I have a romantic soul… that's been tempered by discipline in science. I know what both are good for. Romance blossoms in the evening, when daytime's work of contributing to civilization is done. When the drudgery of adult endeavors – cooperation, competition, accountability and all that – gets put aside. The stars come out. A chill breeze… then the snapping of a twig can send shivers up your spine!

Romance renounces accountability and so-called objective reality, in favor of the subjectively vivid. That's fine, when watching a good movie. But almost every culture took it much farther, declaring: "our worldview is perfect and the enemy is subhuman!" Today, this prejudicial passion resurges in the Riefenstahlian machinations of Rupert Murdoch and in

---

[319] Don't bother with its putrid film prequel "Gods and Generals."

[320] Just listen to the music of Wagner, or read about the Horbigger cult, spend 5 minutes imbued in SS symbolism-obsession, or watch Leni Riefenstahl's film *The Triumph of the Will.* It is one reason why I'm chilled by Tolkien, though I respect him. And it is why I find so deeply disturbing the ultra-romantic, enlightenment-hating visions of George Lucas. (See "The Dark Side: Star Wars, Mythology and Ingratitude." http://www.davidbrin.com/nonfiction/starwars1.html)

Rush Limbaugh's red-faced incantations. Or Vladimir Putin's pomp. Al Qaeda's puritanism. Or residual torches of recidivist leftism and post-modernist incantation that keep trying to warp the liberal mindset.

When romanticism ruled our daylight hours, ten thousand years of living nightmare ensued. Till enlightenment taught us – painfully, gradually – to utter the great catechism of both science and decency: "I suppose I might be wrong. Let's find out."

It's how civilization built those daylight arts – negotiation, compromise, fact-checking and the gradual banishment of rage. Justice, science and saving the world – these pursuits can't afford delusion, no matter how vivid and tantalizing.

But that doesn't require purging romance from our hearts.

Our "confederate" neighbors may feel that's the aim of our sterile fact-trips. But we don't aim to rip away that love, nor even some of your beloved symbols, so long as they don't oppress others.

Just don't treat enlightenment as your enemy. Daytime is when we craft justice and progress. And you're welcome to join us out here, under the light.

———————

A year or two later, stages of the sequence grew more clear…

PHASES OF THE AMERICAN CIVIL WAR[321]

Cyclically, we find ourselves mired in dogma instead of pragmatism, intransigent hatred instead of negotiation, nostalgia and romanticism instead of belief that we can craft a better tomorrow. I've come to see our current era of American politics as the latest phase of the U.S. Civil War, in part because the political maps so blatantly copy a pattern that goes back almost 200 years.

Others see this same breakdown. *New York Magazine's* Jonathan Chait – in "A Southern GOP Can't Be the Party of Lincoln" – decrypts how there seem always to have been two Americas. The Nixonian "Southern Strategy" flip-swapped the banners of the two sides, and Blue-vs.-Gray

---

[321] "Phases Of The American Civil War." (2014) http://davidbrin.blogspot.com/2014/09/phases-of-american-civil-war.html… *modified for this book with adjustments and insertions.*

has become Blue-vs.-Red. But while overall correct, this article misses how long the social movement called the "confederacy" has been at this.[322]

Phase one of the American Civil War arguably took place during the 1770s Revolution, when General Henry Clinton and Lord Cornwallis took an army South, where the British expected – and found – their strongest support among Loyalist/Tory militias in Georgia and the Carolinas. There it was Scots-Irish hill settlers, fighting for Daniel Morgan, who tipped the balance in favor of what would become the American Experiment. But it wasn't over.[323]

Phase two featured a period when southern politicians grew ever stronger in control of the U.S. federal government. True, Andrew Jackson clamped down on John C. Calhoun›s 1830s secessionism and kept the nation together. But Mr. Chait is correct that Jackson's overall sentiments were what we'd call "confederate." Indeed, southern control over levers of power only grew until, by 1860, five of nine Supreme Court justices owned slaves.

This extended through the **next phase**, starting in 1852, when the Fugitive Slave Act unleashed what were – in effect – small units of southern irregular cavalry, who commenced rampaging across northern states, seizing anyone they deemed an "escaped slave" and often family members, even friends. [324] (As mentioned above) these raider squadrons had the support of U.S. Marshals and later federal troops.

Hence, *the "confederate" social movement is not always anti-central-government!* They only oppose federal authority when *they* don't control those levers of power. Witness the tepidness of anti-government proclamations during the tenure of GW Bush (or when wreaked later, by Donald Trump clamping down against vigorous popular governance in states like California). Indeed, it is a wrathful unwillingness to let the electoral winners have their legitimate turn that was behind the hysterical reaction to Lincoln's election and – one might argue – Obama's.

---

322 http://nymag.com/daily/intelligencer/2014/09/southern-gop-cant-be-the-party-of-lincoln.html

323 British friends point out that it likely goes back farther, to the English Civil War of the 1600s, when romantics in lace fought for the king while "roundhead" puritans rallied for Parliament.
324 http://davidbrin.blogspot.com/2013/02/past-keeping-faith-with-future-and-day.html

By the way, those bands of rampaging southern raiders were self-defeating. They *radicalized* northerners to arm themselves, revive their dormant militias and (eventually) vote for the abolitionist Lincoln. An effect one can see happening across Blue America, today.[325]

Up to this point, what we might call Confederacy Society (CS) had lost phase one (allowing the establishment of a true federal republic), played for a draw in the Calhoun-Jackson era, and won phase three – in that its agendas controlled the national government and processes.

But finally, Blue America got fed up. And what ensued was **Phase Four** – the one we normally think of as "The Civil War." Unable to stomach their opponents ever having brief tenancy in even one branch of government, CS did not bother sending delegations to negotiate with president-elect Lincoln, and thus they forsook all rights to justify oath-breaking treason by referring to the U.S. Declaration of Independence. (Jefferson's treatise that secession *can* be supportable, but only after great exertions at redress and negotiation are exhausted.)

We all know Phase Four well. Hence, I'll bypass it and speed through the rest.

Phase Five came in the 1870s when the South bargained to cede the White House to Republican Rutherford Hayes in exchange for what they really wanted, an early end of Reconstruction. The "confederacy" won this phase, big time, by dickering an end of Civil Rights protections and a surge of Jim Crow laws that ripped from freed slaves the right to vote. The real losers, though? Not just minorities, but in every pragmatic sense the *entire South,* which thereupon slumped into a backwater of economic retardation and romantic, old-timey hatred of progress.

(You'd deny this? Then explain how China went from poverty to economic superpower in just 30 years... while many swathes of the U.S. South had 150 years of lavish help, but still blame backwardness on Sherman.)

Phase 6. Bryan populism and the rise of the Klan… this phase is not entirely associated with "confederate society" though it was core to that era's Democratic Party. It featured William Jennings Bryan's white-

---

[325] This is why Gun Control is such a pathetically illogical hot button on the right. Yes, blue American demand reforms. But what's ignored is that, under Bush (and later Trump), many liberals started quietly arming themselves.

Christian populism, 'Free Silver,' and a rebuke to the steamroller effects of consolidated northern corporations. States of the Great Plains began edging toward alliance with the Olde South. It can be argued that Northern oligarchs won phase six… though two new things emerged.

First, the Progressive Movement, manifesting all over America was taken up by Theodore Roosevelt, whose family specialized in repeatedly saving America's wealthy from the price of limitless greed.[326] Alas, a different wing spun off from Bryan's populism into a horrific peak of activity by the Ku Klux Klan. Chalk that up as a victory for Confederacy.

Phase 7 – The 1940s through 1970s … the civil rights movement gained huge momentum from Harry Truman's bold desegregation of the U.S. military, then Dwight Eisenhower's firm support of school desegregation rulings. The essential and too-long delayed resumption of Reconstruction included Lyndon Johnson's effort to re-industrialize and re-invigorate the South. But above all, the arrival of TV and other modern media meant that protestors like Martin Luther King could be heard – and seen facing oppression with noble courage – by millions. This phase was clearly won by Blue America (though the South benefited prodigiously, economically and in every other way.) Only we achieved all that at a steep political cost – which came as….

Phase 8 – …the Nixonian, southern-strategy "flip" led ultimately to today's waves of romantic anti-professionalism, troglodyte racism and searing culture war, that have weakened America profoundly and that were lately exacerbated by foreign and domestic manipulators of mass media. Gradual in building, it's become nothing less than a full scale New Confederacy effort to finally destroy the United States of America. Not by force of arms, but by ending the effectiveness of *politics* as a pragmatic, open-minded process by which un-dogmatic citizens negotiate a mix of public-private experiments and find out what works – the methodology behind all of our successes. Replacing all of that with *dogma* more intense than communism ever was. A conviction of moral superiority that cannot be shaken by facts.

---

[326] If only today's oligarchs understood that their greatest need, right now, is another Roosevelt! Without gentle, moderate reforms, our current momentum can only lead to tumbrels and guillotines. Watch Ken Burns's wonderful PBS series "The Roosevelts."

Those facts are devastating. Run through a long list of social ills:[327] rates of teenage sexual activity, teen pregnancies, STDs, domestic violence, divorce rates, gambling and addiction and alcoholism, bankruptcy and debt default rates, education levels, economic productivity, net dependency on federal government… even obesity rates. Mountains of evidence refute every hoary claim that salt-of-the-earth types are better at life or raising kids than "decadent" university-city-folk. Indeed, by all of those measures... and countless more[328]... they get spectacularly worse outcomes.

So? Then spurn statistics. Truthiness is all that matters.

Want something even worse? How about the insipid inability of blue "generals" to respond to any of it with agile tactics, or to even conceive the notion of *maneuver.*

Does all of this truly have anything to do with that metaphor – the hoary, stupid so-called "left right political axis" – that has lobotomized political discourse for a century? Our civil war seems far more emotional and cultural – *a clash of two immiscible strains of American utopianism* that is both ancient and culturally deeply rooted.[329] Recall again Ted Turner's wonderful *Gettysburg*, wherein one character opines that blue and gray America sang the same songs... but *dreamed different dreams.* Mark Twain concurred that the confederacy's recurring rage reflects a deeply nostalgic, past-obsessed romanticism.[330]

---

[327] Statistical proof of many of these turpitude indexes: http://www.hhs.gov/ash/oah/adolescent-health-topics/reproductive-health/teen-pregnancy/trends.html

http://www.foxnews.com/health/2014/05/07/state-by-state-where-its-easiest-to-catch-or-avoid-stds/

http://www.vpc.org/press/1309wmmw.htm

http://www.ranker.com/list/highest-u-s-divorce-rates-by-state/taylor-ratcliff

http://www.statemaster.com/graph/eco_ban_fil_percap-economy-bankruptcy-filings-per-capita

http://multivu.prnewswire.com/mnr/corelogic/50016/

http://dashboard.ed.gov/statecomparison.aspx?i=e&id=5&wt=0

http://www.washingtonpost.com/blogs/wonkblog/wp/2014/09/04/the-states-where-americans-are-the-most-and-least-obese/

[328] I will concede that blue folk seem inferior when it comes to formal courtesy and gracious verbal cues.

[329] I admit and avow that urban/university American has done one terrible thing to rural/bedrock America, repeatedly, every autumn for more than a hundred years. It was a "good" thing! But also something poignantly tragic and devastating on a deeply psychic level. And I'll reveal it later on.

[330] "Conservatives say we've abandoned reason and civility. The Old South said that, too," said Eve Fairbanks 2019 in the Washington Post. https://www.washingtonpost.com/outlook/2019/08/29/conservatives-say-weve-abandoned-reason-civility-old-south-said-that-too/

Where is it all heading? Recall in Pause #6 where I asked you to re-read Abraham Lincoln's Gettysburg Address, as if it were written exactly for you. Specifically about right now.

Today's neo-confederacy doesn't aim to secede. This time, it found the massive foreign support that it lacked in 1862. That coalition achieved what Jeff Davis never could, taking Washington, while slashing all hateful things, especially science, which is the #1 enemy of nostalgia. But also any chance of American pragmatism prevailing in the kind of experiment-by-politics that has always been our national genius.

And yes, they may yet ensure that "government of the people, by the people, for the people" *shall* perish from the Earth.

"If destruction be our lot, we must ourselves be its author and finisher. As a nation of freemen, we must live through all time, or die by suicide. I hope I am over wary; but if I am not, there is, even now, something of ill-omen, amongst us. I mean the increasing disregard for law which pervades the country; the growing disposition to substitute the wild and furious passions, in lieu of the sober judgment of Courts; and the worse than savage mobs, for the executive ministers of justice. ..."

Abraham Lincoln's Lyceum Address[331]

---

331 Abraham Lincoln's Lyceum Address. http://www.abrahamlincolnonline.org/lincoln/speeches/lyceum.htm

A matter of dimensionality...

Pause #14 for...

Traps we keep falling for.

LETTING THE ENEMIES OF MARKETS CLAIM TO BE DEFENDERS

"Capitalism" is used as a whipping boy term that loses all meaning. And yes, even more foolishly/ignorantly on the left than on the right.

In fact – I'll repeat it yet again – flat-fair-competitive-accountable market enterprise has been the cornucopia goose that's laid our golden eggs, creating the vast wealth that could then be taxed, enabling us to build universities and water systems, schools and courts and research labs. Wealth that gave us confidence to go after ancient crimes like racism and sexism.

Moreover, flat-fair-competitive-accountable market enterprise has had one main enemy across 4000 years and it wasn't "socialism." It was oligarchy. It was cheating by owner-lords and monopolists of the sort the American Revolution was truly about. And yes, flat-fair-competitive-accountable market enterprise does better... far better, as a matter of measurable outcomes ... across the span of Democratic administrations than GOP ones.

Yes, there are many problems with capitalism.

As Marx showed, there are inherent contradictions that can... unless countered by enlightened rules and referees... lead to the collapse of flat-fair-creative competition.

Those on the right who scream hate at the word "regulation" are either fools or tools or oligarchs. But equally unwise is the left's reflex to despise "competition," which is almost as deeply human as cooperation or love.

Regulated Competition is what works! Look at any sports league and tell me what would happen if you removed either word, for even a single weekend. Those who would have us focus only on a one-dimensional "left-right" simplistic axis overlap with those who'd have us fail.

It truly does shatter their core delusion.
Too bad no one gives this weapon a try...

Chapter 15

Hammer Their Macho With Wagers! And The Name-an-Exception Challenge

During a televised debate in late 2011, while seeking his party's presidential nomination, Mitt Romney challenged Texas Gov. Rick Perry to put some money-where-his-mouth-is. "Rick, I'll tell you what," Romney said, extending his hand. "Ten thousand bucks? Ten thousand dollar bet?"

Perry declined, snarling, "I'm not in the betting business."

Now, many ironies abound here. First off, Perry *was* part of the Republican wave who enabled and empowered the vast expansion of *gambling* in America, till casino moguls now rival even Rupert Murdoch, or the Mercers or Saudis, or even Vladimir Putin in party influence. So yes, he *was in the betting business.*

Also ironic; Perry would have trivially *won* a wager over whether Romney had supported Obamacare-style individual mandates.[332] Of course Romney – with a $200+ million fortune, came off as a bullying rich man. Here's what one pundit railed,[333] at the time:

"Twitter lit up with jokes about what $10,000 could buy for non-millionaires, and ... that Iowa's per capita income is about $38,000. Before the debate was over, Jon Huntsman's campaign bought the domain

---

332 He had. Obamacare was based largely on "RomneyCare" in Massachusetts, which was cloned from the GOP approved Heritage plan, as described elsewhere in this book. And the individual mandate was a centerpiece, the pride and joy of its authors... till Obama gave it cooties.

333 Romney's 'bet' https://theweek.com/articles/479518/mitt-romneys-touch-10000-bet

10kbet.com, and other GOP rivals were quick to pounce, too. How badly will this off-the-cuff wager hurt Romney?"[334]

Um, not at all? *Perry* faded after that evening. Romney, undamaged by the "*Wager*gate Gaffe," handily won the sought-for nomination, though he later lost the general election to President Barack Obama. Note that Romney's notoriously ham-handed $10k bet stunt *raised* his cred across the Republican base, but more broadly discredited an entire general approach to dealing with lies and liars... almost as if that had been his intent. It also – if considered closely – helped point to possible solutions.

Stop relying on what doesn't work.

We are *not* handling well the right's war on facts; it's proved every day. Those who are spurring the all-out campaign against evidence-based reason laugh at all our efforts to fight back with nerd-stuff...

... like long *lists of Trumpian lies*[335]... or *"fact-checking services"*[336]... or *reports* signed by all top experts in a field... or condemnations by scores of past eminent statespersons against lunatic behaviors at the top... or exposés by top journalists. Yes, those are grownup methods – and there are ways (discussed in Chapter 5) to improve them greatly. But alas, our elites of politics, law, journalism, punditry and science seem obstinately incapable of lifting their gaze: to realize *their "sumo" methods aren't working.*

Fact-checking services range from Snopes to FactCheck.org to *The Washington Post* – and none of them even nibble along the edges of Republican base support. They fail before a convenient Fox counter-narrative:

"These so-called fact-checkers are just more fake-news. They reveal their bias when they point out far more falsehoods by Republicans than Democrats!"

Do you find that "logic" infuriating? Well, your impotent frustration is their food. How often must you slam your head against the same wall, before admitting the power of *"Sez you"?* Again, from Chapter 5: if you offer a cogent, fact-filled link as evidence, your "red" cousin will flood

[334] Romney's 'Out of Touch' $10,000 Bet." https://theweek.com/articles/479518/mitt-romneys-touch-10000-bet

[335] 12,000 Trump lies as of August 2019. https://www.washingtonpost.com/politics/2019/08/12/president-trump-has-made-false-or-misleading-claims-over-days/

[336] From The Washington Post: https://www.washingtonpost.com/news/fact-checker/

you with counter-links! And who are *you* to claim yours are better? If you cite experts, you're a slave of conformist authority (Chapter 2.)

There *are* endeavors that might bring rationality back to discourse – like competitive Disputation Arenas[337] and the Fact Act – but none will work quickly enough, across a near-term electoral time scale. Meanwhile, we need rapid and effective ways to pound through the obstinacy of *Sez you!* So let me put this in both boldface and italics:

There is one area where your "red" uncle, cousin, colleague or neighbor still admits the primacy of fact. A wager. One that's fair, well-parsed and tightly framed with clear stakes and an accepted, neutral judge.

The most clear-cut example is a *sports bet.* And for the sake of this one point, in this one paragraph, let's drop any pretense of gender neutrality, shall we? We're talking Neanderthal-hormonal preening, here. A *real man* has the guts to slap cash on the bar to back up his bluster-claims. It's how to separate a fellah with *cojones* from a blowhard, or a coward.

Sure, when you expand from sports into areas like science or politics – and get less explicitly sexist – things become complicated. There are ways for wager-challenges to stumble, like the Romney Stunt of trying to bully with deep pockets. Or agreeing over who holds the stakes.[338] Or zeroing in on exactly what facts to bet upon. (See the next section.)

Yes, for politicians and public figures, this is a bit of a minefield.[339] It helps to make the wager's beneficiary "my chosen charity versus yours." That can work if it's an amiable encounter, like when late night host Jimmy Kimmel took on Texas Sen. Ted Cruz in one-on-one basketball. No one formula will work in all situations, so here's a *general way* to pose it:

"I've tried getting you to commit to a position (say on climate change) and you keep slipping aside. So will you *negotiate* some way to make this a fact-based wager? Is there *any* stake we might all deem

---

[337] For a rather intense look at how "truth" is determined in science, democracy, courts and markets, see the lead article in the American Bar Association's Journal on Dispute Resolution (Ohio State University), v.15, N.3, pp 597-618, Aug. 2000, "Disputation Arenas: Harnessing Conflict and Competition." http://www.amazon.com/Disputation-Arenas-ebook/dp/B005AK2R74/?_encoding=UTF8&tag=contbrin-20

[338] I often demand that the red-capped fellah escrow funds with a reputable lawyer, before I'll waste my time working out proofs.

[339] Which is why this might best be implemented by some liberal/moderate millionaire, making it her 'thing' to hammer wager challenges relentlessly, perhaps at some oligarch peer, spending what it takes to pin him down.

fair? *Any* august sage you'd accept as arbiter? *Any* way you'd let this narrow down to something clear-cut, we all can judge, yes-or-no?"

It's the core challenge to throw down before a fact-evading cult: "Is there *any way* you'll stop squirming, so we can nail this down, one verified fact at a time?"

(Earlier I offered a version having to do with fact-checking that I'd love to see an eminent personage like Paul Krugman, Robert Reich, or George F. Will hurl at Sean Hannity.[340])

Want examples? Let's start with very simple bets that offer your con-fed no wriggle room, because they *do* boil down to clearly verifiable fact.

– Are the oceans getting more *acidic,* to a potentially deadly degree? And is it because of human generated greenhouse gas?

– Would you put money on a randomly chosen Trump accusation of "fake news?" From the past or some random day in the near future? Or randomly chosen items from WaPo's list of 12,000 lies? [341]

– Have any Republican "supply side" tax cuts for the rich ever resulted in the promised vast increases in capital investment, millions of high-paying jobs, sustained GDP growth and plummeting deficits? Ever?

– The Caspian and Black Seas are almost dead. The Mediterranean and Caribbean appear to be dying. Is preventable pollution to blame? Put down a wager, or else shall we save them?

– Who crafted nearly all the key provisions for what came to be called Obamacare, Democrats or Republicans?

– Which political party generally leaves U.S. defenses, alliances and resilience in better shape than how they found them? Which party nearly always leaves the American military worse off than before they took over?

– Are glaciers retreating or "setting records"?[342] Or I bet you can't prove any allegations of busloads of fake voters swarming the polls.

[340] "Will you pick half a dozen widely respected conservative eminences to serve on a panel to advise which fact-checking services are partisan? I'll pick as many respected-moderate liberals. They can together choose some libertarians. Not a 'Ministry of Truth,' but a panel of sages who might help us struggle out of this mess. Or are you afraid they'll conclude *you* are the fake news?"

[341] Pick – even randomly – any five of the 12,000+ outright Trumpian falsehoods listed by the Washington Post's "Fact-Checker" Glenn Kessler. https://www.washingtonpost.com/news/fact-checker/

[342] Glaciers. https://www.reuters.com/article/us-climatechange-trump/trumps-view-that-ice-caps-setting-records-baffles-scientists-idUSKBN1FI1WK

Or the "biggest inauguration, ever," or hours spent on golf. Or Those 'birther' claims. Or....

– Have any *five* other presidents (combined) been "betrayed" by as many appointees as Trump? Officials and aides whom he earlier called "great guys?" And what does this say of Donald Trump as a judge of character?

Those challenges offer examples of the needed traits for an aggressive wager-challenge. They are clear and simple, selected for low "squirm factor" – or ability to weasel... say by demanding *"define acidic!"* They come from a very long list sampled in other sections.

Don't try to tell me "We've already challenged Republicans on all those things!" No. You have not. I repeat; you have not. You have *whined* about them. You've done it in ways they can simply shrug off, while relishing your frustration.

Okay, now comes the kicker, again in both boldface/italic:

Almost never will they accept any kind of wager! Efforts to pin them down will fail.

They'll writhe and prevaricate, squirm and ramble and "whatabout"-distract.[343]

They will not agree to actual stakes over a clearly defined matter of evidence, with impartial arbiters.

Um. So. Brin. Did you just admit this entire "wager" thing won't work?

No, I did not admit that.

What I said is they'll refuse to bet!

And if you've learned anything at all about polemical judo, you'll see what an opportunity that opens.

Dig it. The research of cognitive linguist George Lakoff proved that roughly half of Americans prefer a "strong father" over the liberals' "nurturing parent." Fundamentalists idolize a man who is opposite-to-Jesus in every way, because he galls the same people they hate. Every GOP convention and rally is now a festival of macho puffery. Even a third of

---

[343] How many times have you seen a Republican legislator evade questions of climate change with "I'm not a scientist" and Trump with "windmills cause cancer!" The Fact Act would nail all that, but this method works, too.

U.S. Hispanic males revere Trump's caudillo bluster, despite all the offensive racism.

It seems an impervious castle that no gambit by enlightenment forces can penetrate,[344] because any appeal to fact or reason makes *us* seem the weakling whiners! A strong father doesn't need to be right, only strong! Objective refutation won't undermine him, though *compromise* might. So he'll never compromise.

Above all, any sign of weakness is lethal. So his one aim will be to avoid showing any.

Did you think I was talking about Donald Trump, just now? If so, you miss the point. Macho bully-bluster is the core foundation of today's entire rightist populism. It has always been the soul of the confederacy.

Which is where wagers come in. Because the substance of the bet is less significant than their *refusal* to ante-up. It opens our real opportunity – to hammer with ridicule, undermining that delusional *image of virile strength.* Of manliness. They base their brand upon it. So that's where to aim savage kicks, and repeat over and over.

The refrain is *"coward!"*

It can work. It already has.

How many of you have followed the lawsuit in which Alex Jones, the infamous conspiracy-spewer and purveyor of perverted paranoias, was finally chased down by victims of his insanely vicious Sandy Hook attacks? *Dig it, the Sandy Hook parents' lawsuit was essentially a forced wager!* Oh, how Jones backpedaled from his rants that the mourning parents were all actors, grieving over nonexistent lost children. He swerved, first claiming he was innocently mistaken, then that his slanderous lies had simply been a 'stage performance.' Finally, he's been pleading insanity! All to no avail.

Yes, it's time for a great many more such lawsuits and forced wagers. But that misses the point of this chapter. Because it is the very act of cornering them, and seeing them *refuse* to bet, that gives this method power.

My favorite is *ocean acidification – O.A.* – because it has every trait we need. O.A. sidesteps all the narratives of distraction over climate change.

---

[344] Indeed, they generally assail the wrong fort, even the wrong mountain!

In fact, Fox et. al. avoid ever mentioning it, since the cause is inarguable, the symptoms are easily measured by non-experts, and the deadly effects are indisputable. Start with a glass of water and a straw and two swimming pool test strips. Just blowing bubbles from your CO2-rich lungs will turn the water acidic. Then offer to go down to the shore with a pH meter… or visit the chemistry teacher at a community college… or…

Choose carefully. Learn to pick a challenge that has no ambiguity, no room to squirm. Share tips and videos with each other. When they try to dodge, dare them to help pick arbiters and stake-holders who – even if "conservative" – are reputably adult and judicious. And if they demur, then chide: "Oh, your cult can't supply any?"

When they waver and hedge and quibble and try to claim they never bet, remember to taunt: "Of course you *bet!* You're so sure of this Foxite crap that you're willing to bet the lives of our planet and nation and children, but not a hundred bucks?" Slap a sawbuck on the table and demand "If you're so sure, come and *take my money!*"

At which point we reach our final boldface/italic riff:

Your effort to pin them down – offering real stakes – shows YOUR confident strength, by THEIR standards. When they refuse to bet, it will result in either backpedaling or else frantic flight. Either way, you win something for all fact people. A small victory for this civilization.

If they backpedal from one climate-denial position to a slightly less-insane one, then you may be dealing with a RASR… a Residually Adult-Sane Republican… who could be worth the effort of pursuit, chopping away rationalizations, one by one, aiming toward the greatest possible reward. Redemption of a useful fellow citizen, who might then influence others.

And if he flees?

Then you have turned the macho tables. Chase his quivering manly heinie with *"coward!"*

I mean that, and nothing less. Enjoy the immaturity, because it's their language! And your immature enjoyment is something that playground bullies deeply understand. *They* made this a variant of war.[345]

---

345 Sherman did not invent slash-burn during the Civil War. The Confederacy did, though Sherman finished it. Likewise, they think we cannot learn; but some of us (those with the requisite

NOEC: The Name One Exception Challenge [346]

Here's a related approach that's more sophisticated, but it can be effective with a different kind of person – generally someone who makes a show of seeming logical. You may have to think about this one carefully, but it applies well beyond politics.

Consider. If I make a **specific accusation** – say that you committed a particular crime – then the burden of proof is on me. Fair enough. But what happens when I make a **universal assertion?**

Say: "The daylight sky is always blue!"

...or: "The ocean is always wet!"

...or: "Snails never deliver Hamlet soliloquies."

Do I bear a burden of proof then? Well, that depends on "always" and "never."

When I challenge you to disprove a Universal Assertion, it should be easy! Just find *one exception.* If you cite even one, then the statement might still be *frequently or generally* true, but it's not a *universal.* For example, anyone can point to days when the sky's another color. Blue sky is a general truth that's proved *not* to be *universal.* It's the "always" part that's disproved by a single counter-example.

The wet-ocean generality *is* universal, unless the argument dissolves into definition quibbles. But when it comes to Shakespearean gastropods, well the *burden of proof* falls on anyone who claims the universal "never" ain't so. Your failure to find even one slimy-shelled melancholy Dane proves me right![347]

Not in a court of law. Indeed, if your opponent *can* name exceptions, then the argument falls back under rules of preponderance of evidence. "Never" just becomes "hardly ever."

Applying This To Politics. Any member of the Climate Denialist Cult can cite weather examples that seem to violate global warming, hence it cannot be proved by Name an Exception, but by tediously showing the factual basis for why 99% of scientists agree that global warming

---

predatory knack, underneath our civilized values) are able to adapt. Our goal remains "with malice toward none and with charity for all." But in order to get there – to save America – we'll fight.

[346] Earlier version of "Name an Exception." http://davidbrin.blogspot.com/2015/06/the-name-one-exception-challenge.html

[347] At least until slimy aliens arrive, or the gene labs get very busy, or the Society of Secretly Speedy Shakespearian Sea Slugs gets angry at this tome, and finally finds the guts to step up.

endangers all our children. This Name An Exception riff isn't applicable to that hard fight.

But when a general accusation is very broad, and your opponent *cannot* name even *one* counter-example, it has profoundly effective import. At that point the generality enters territory like "the sun always rises at dawn," or "a rock that you throw in the air will always come down." One counter-example – even one – will destroy the word "always." But failure to cite *any* counter-example makes "always" powerful!

Especially when the assertion is in history or politics. Jiminy, almost *everything* in those fields has exceptions! If you can't find even one, then it means you are wrong, wrong, incredibly wrong.

For the following general assertions, a burden of proof falls on your conservative friend to show how the accusations have *any* exceptions, any at all! And if your RASR fails to find even one, *then they are true.*

Moreover, if *any* of these Name One Exception Challenges (NOEC) – even one of them – cannot be refuted with a single counter-example, then your opponent's movement is not a political party. It is a dangerously insane and incompetent cult.

(At this point in the book, you're already familiar with these dares and challenges. I make no apologies, as the chapters of this tome are compiled from many articles. In any event, perhaps by you now see the value of repetition.)

1 – NAME ONE fact-centered profession of high knowledge and skill that's not under attack by Fox/Trump and cohorts. Teachers, medical doctors, journalists, civil servants, law professionals, economists, skilled labor, professors… oh, yes and science.[348] Thirty years ago, 40% of U.S. scientists called themselves Republican. Now it's 2% and plummeting. They are voting with their feet, the smartest, wisest, most logical and by far the most competitive humans our species ever produced.

Now? As I've repeated many times (and so should you) the Republican enemies list includes the FBI and law professionals, the vast variety of civil servants, plus the U.S. military and intelligence officer corps. All are dismissed as "deep state" foes conspiring against goodness and free-

---

[348] From New Yorker: http://www.newyorker.com/news/news-desk/the-mistrust-of-science?linkId=25842187

dom. Oh no, this is not your mommy's or daddy's conservatism. Name one exception.[349]

2 – NAME ONE *major GOP leader between Reagan and Ryan who was even mentioned* at the 2016 Republican Convention. Except for Newt Gingrich, all were brushed under the rug, including both Bushes, Cheney, Rumsfeld, Dennis Hastert, Tom (convicted felon) DeLay, Boehner. In fact, name a republican top leader between *Eisenhower* and Ryan who was even mentioned by the party at the 2016 RNC, other than Reagan and Newt! This shows how writhing ashamed Republicans are, of their record at governance. And if you disavow those past Republican administrations as incompetent, Russia-hating, enterprise-destroying, warmongering liars, then where is your party's credibility?

3 – NAME ONE of the *dark fantasies about Obama,* from black UN helicopters to taking away all our guns, that provably and verifiably happened, or was even tepidly tried. Heck, let's throw in the Kenyan birth and Sharia Law stuff. Indeed, after 25 years and half a billion dollars of Clinton-Obama investigations… well… see #5.

4 – NAME ONE *time when supply side (voodoo) "economics" made a successful prediction?* Ever? One time when slashing taxes on the rich led to reduced deficits, to vastly stimulated economic activity, or even much investment in "supply" capital? Or increased money velocity or middle class health? Once when the outcomes weren't diametrically opposite to all promises. One time when this cult religion actually delivered? (Chapter 11.)

A related riff we saw in Chapter 3 might also be used as a NOEC: *When was "America Great"?* While we're sending probes past Pluto, and rovers across Mars, discovering thousands of planets across the galaxy, curing diseases, raising billions of children out of poverty around the

---

[349] Although I led the list with this one, having wracked my brains for years and exposed this challenge to a community of fierce minds, let me admit that there might be a couple of exceptions here. Knowledge/skill/fact professions not under assault by Fox & co. Only, I won't reveal them here! Even if your RASR comes up with one, the fact that he/she had to really think about it hard proves the point. Their "side" has gone insane.

world and so on. But sure, tell us when you think it was all better! *The 1950s?* Run by the Greatest Generation who adored FDR? They knew the dangers of oligarchy and passed many rules to control it. Rules like forbidding companies to waste money on stock buybacks, where nearly all of the recent Trump Tax Cut was frittered away, without tangible investment in R&D or factories. In fact, *every major move away from the Rooseveltian social contract resulted in lower growth, wider wealth disparity, shorter commercial ROI horizons, declines in R&D and increasing dominance by a crazy MBA caste.* Name an exception!

5 – NAME ONE time in American – or human – history, *when an administration spanning eight years had zero – or close to zero – scandals or indictments* concerning proved malfeasance in the performance of official duties. It happened twice in American – or human – history. The administrations of Bill Clinton and Barack Obama. Name another! There *was* one *four*-year U.S. administration that had no malfeasance-of-office scandals… that of Jimmy Carter. (Yes, there were a few scandals outside that description, "malfeasance in the performance of official duties," though fewer overall than any month or week of a Trump or Bush administration.)

Let's be clear. The Reagan, Bush and Bush administrations looked *hard* for evidence, some smoking-gun, to pin on Carter, Clinton and Obama. They sifted like crazy when they owned every federal department and ran dozens of investigatory committees, wasting hundreds of millions looking for something – anything. "W" ordered federal agents transferred from counter terror duties to join this hunt before 9/11… arguably costing thousands of American lives. And they found, what? A husband fibbed about infidelity… then a wife made the same email mistake as both Bushes, Colin Powell, Condi Rice and Jared Kushner.

In contrast, GOP administrations – all of them – were rife with indictments, convictions and pardons. We'll elaborate on this one in the next "pause" section.

But for now… name an exception.

6 – NAME ONE counter-example to *Republicans damaging every strength that won the Cold War.* Almost every thing that bolstered us during that struggle is being systematically dismantled, from our alliances to science, from dedicated intelligence and law agencies to the moral high ground and the rule of law and the respect of the world. There may be exceptions, though I know of none.

The next one has become iffy amid the "great Trump economy!" But I choose (in September 2019) to include it here because it was generally true ever since Reagan, and by the time you get to these words, it (sadly) may be true again.

7 – NAME ONE *major metric of U.S. national health* that did better across the entire spans of any completed GOP administration, than across the spans of the Clinton and Obama terms. Nearly all such metrics declined – many plummeting – across both Bush regimes. (See Chapters 10 & 11.) Nearly all of them – from scientific accomplishment to world reputation – rose, many of them by a lot, across both terms of the last two Democratic Administrations. That includes every sane *conservative* desideratum like rate of change of deficits (Chapter 11) and even *military readiness!* The condition of our alliances. Small business startups. Entrepreneurship.

Here's hoping this last one breaks the pattern, with America doing well all the way to Trump's finish. But I'm sadly sure we'll get to cite this one too, and demand that our Residually Adult-Sane Republican friends *name one exception.*

Okay, Part 2 of this chapter was a whole lot more complicated than the macho-targeting missile of Part 1. The *Name One Exception Challenge* is more for use with your logical (or at least pretending to be) RASR cousin.

Sure, they are still koolaid-slurpers. They'll shout "squirrel!" and point offstage at some assertion or distraction, concocting scenarios and excuses to explain why they cannot answer any of those NOEC challenges.

And yet, on rare occasion I meet the real McCoy – a genuinely sincere conservative "ostrich" willing to lift his or her head, when tugged by these dares. I have seen them budge.

Please understand the value of that. *Because sanity, like insanity, can be infectious.*

It can spread.

Ian Fleming knew what to make of this.

All right, this chapter was about something that most blue Americans have given up as hopeless, breaking through the seemingly impenetrable walls that Fox and Putin and Trump have built to protect their red-confederate base. *You* may call it futile and useless. But you have only to look at how much treasure and effort *they* are pouring into shoring up those walls, to realize how any breach terrifies them!

As I've repeated. They know they'll lose an occasional election, like 1992 and 2008. But history shows they can come roaring back (1994 and 2010) so long as the base is secure. Moreover, even if that base diminishes, but stays *riled enough*, our enemies can still harm America by unleashing floods of lava hot Timothy McVeighs.

Yes, the methods in this chapter are worth trying. *Someone must.* The obstinate refusal of our blue 'generals' – pundits, politicians etc. – to ever try anything except what never worked has to be overcome, the way Lincoln sought, and finally found, warriors who could fight.

We must recall the wisdom found in good fiction:

Fool us once? Shame on you.

Fool us a million times? Then fire all our pundits!

Better yet, let's go to the font of wisdom, when it comes to dealing with skullduggerous plots and schemes.

Goldfinger's Rule: [350]

"Once, Mr. Bond, may be happenstance.

"Twice could be coincidence.

"Three times is enemy action."

[350] Goldfinger's Rule: https://www.goodreads.com/quotes/418466-once-is-happenstance-twice-is-coincidence-three-times-is-enemy

A derangement that gave them delusions to rally around. Smash it…

Pause #15 for…

Clinton-Obama Obsession

As we saw earlier, nothing presses confederate buttons harder than Clinton-Obama Derangement Syndrome – tan suits and "mom pants" and bowing too low to an Arab king. Black UN helicopters and imminent gun-seizures. Murdered aides and Kenyan births. But what galls especially is the failure of all the conspiracy theories to amount to more than mist and vague-vapor.

What follows is a bit of a rant! So skip it if you came for the pragmatic stuff...

....

Still here? Okay then, I've repeated it several times throughout these blogs and this book, and I'll continue till I hear some prominent politician or pundit hammer the point: roughly half a billion dollars of mostly our money was spent – across 25 years – investigating the Clintons and Obamas, the most thoroughly probed humans in the history of our species. Every document scrutinized, every file dissected, every junior assistant grilled and nothing withheld.

Somewhere like half of all subpoenas issued by the last five indolent, do-nothing GOP Congresses were part of that futile, desperate search, in one repetitious, pompously posing hearing after another. Yet, Clinton/Obama never stonewalled or demanded that the investigations stop, the way today's scaredy-cat toddler does, daily. Below, see comparison of indictments and convictions after just the first two years of the Trump Administration, whose numbers have since then gone through the stratosphere. (I am seeking later versions, for update.) Also it does not include outside officials like lobbyists, or KGB agents like Maria Butina, or the 2016 Republican Party Presidential Campaign Manager Paul Manafort.

EXECUTIVE BRANCH CRIMINAL ACTIVITIES BY PARTY SINCE 1968

ADMINISTRATION	TOTAL YEARS IN OFFICE	CRIMINAL INDICTMENTS	CRIMINAL CONVICTIONS	PRISON SENTENCES
DEMOCRATIC	20	3	1	1
REPUBLICAN	28	120	89	34

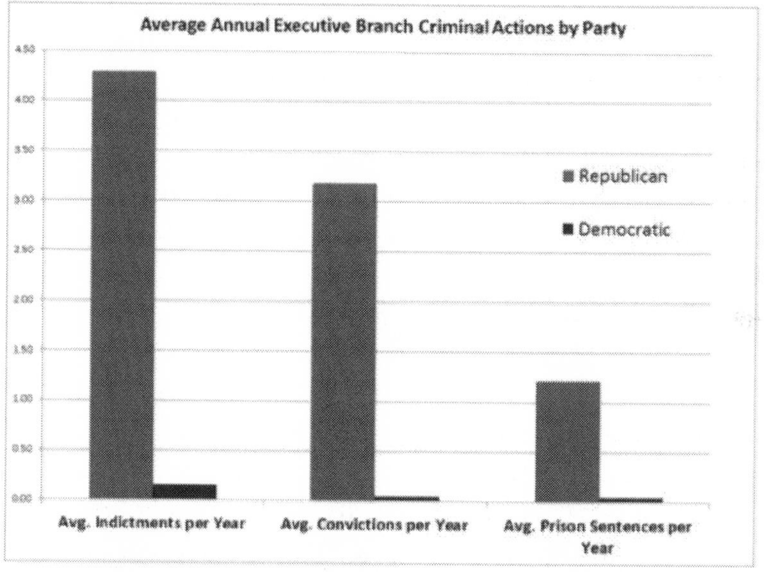

Average annual executive branch criminal actions by party dating back to 1969.

It gets worse. The Kochs and Mercers etc. offered "protection" plus immense whistleblower rewards for any Clinton-connected person to reveal a smoking gun, ratting out alleged "secret Democrat deals and travesties." Not $130,000, but millions. And oh, they did get nibbles from folks in the Clinton orbit, eagerly offering "dirt," but never anything of use. Fox, too, offered lucrative commentator posts… and got only hot air. Never the sort of indictable evidence that the Mueller probe, then grand juries, and then Pelosi-era House hearings got daily on Republicans of the pre-Trump and current eras, revelations ranging from child molesters to money launderers to Kremlin stooges.

Indeed, this goes way back. George W. Bush allegedly diverted federal investigators from anti-terror duties, before the 9/11 attacks. (It should have been a scandal.) Before that, came the railings of Newt Gingrich and Dennis Hastert, and the Clinton impeachment trial, prosecuted hypocritically by a dozen, largely divorced GOP House members. A quarter century of 'investigations" to prove... a shame-faced husband fibbed about some third base adult-consensual infidelity... and the wife was caught using exactly the same sort of somewhat improper email system as Colin Powell, Dick Cheney, John McCain, Mike Pence, George Bush and Jared Kushner.

Clinton Derangement Syndrome can be turned around and weaponized! Beyond just listing all of those prodigious efforts and expenses spent in the hunt for a smoking gun, follow with:

— May you someday be hounded with made-up rumors and accusations, never able to quell them with demands for proof.

But no, that's immature, even in the context of this rant. Don't use it. Instead, I'll offer two other answers, below.

Breaking news as we're about to post: On October 18, 2019, the U.S. State Department, headed by Trump appointees, announced that their 3 year probe into Hillary Clinton's emails found no deliberate mishandling of classified information - a final outcome identical to the results of every heated Clinton Investigation by the Republican controlled "Benghazi" and other breathless House committees that eventually petered-out and slunk away. Well don't feel too bad, you did put in the hours and effort... and lots of our money.[351]

Not Just by Degree, but Different Species.

Compare all that to more than a hundred charges filed against almost three score individuals in the Trump Administration (as of September 2019), along with confessions and convictions already piling up - not to mention firings and resignations and "great guys" who get re-classified as "rats." Daily we see secret meetings with hostile dictators, ongoing acts-of-war against our elections and infrastructure, along with pedophiles, playmate-bribers, and casino-mafiosi. Just the contents of David Pecker's

351 https://www.washingtonpost.com/national-security/state-department-probe-of-clinton-emails-finds-no-deliberate-mishandling-of-classified-information/2019/10/18/83339446-f1dc-11e9-8693-f487e46784aa_story.html

National Enquirer safe ought to fill any American with flaming, nonpartisan curiosity, along with the scores of Non Disclosure Agreements (NDA) that Donald Trump openly brags about.

Sure, both sides get caught in scandals, now and then. Democrats Anthony Weiner and Eliot Spitzer were caught in sexual embarrassments that were arguably adult-consensual... like the "Tallahasee Trail" imbroglio of Republican Gov. Mark Sanford. In that range, Sanford and Spitzer and Al Franken are testing the "algebra of forgiveness," with some success. But show us liberal parallels to Republicans Larry Craig and Dennis Hastert and Roy Moore, blatant child abusers or predatory perverts.

Perhaps someone might do a study of the *divorce* rates among Republican office holders, vs. Democrats. (Reagan, Gingrich, McConnell, Hastert and Trump had twelve wives among them.)

Back to a Deep State Cabal

Frustration over that 25 year failure to nail the Clintons for tangible crimes led to a face-saving rationalization that threatens the very core of our state, blaming interference and protection by the Deep State. Is there a shred of evidence that more than 250,000 professionals in the FBI, Intelligence Agencies and US military officer corps are violating their oaths en masse, with secrecy and competence never shown by any other government endeavor except the moon landings? [352]

Cited evidence for a Deep State cabal: those who investigated the Clintons include some FBI/Justice/prosecutor/investigators who are now toppling Trumpians. Hence Mueller, Comey, Sessions, Rosenstein etc. – all of them Republican appointees, like nearly all the judges who signed war-

[352] Most right wing conspiracy theories are not meant to prove anything, but rather to leave an impression. Ponder the Seth Rich tizzy. Supposedly, he was murdered because he – and not Moscow agents – had spilled those Democratic Party files to Wikileaks. Tasty, since it lets Sean Hannity proclaim "It wasn't Russians, after all!" Sure, whatever you say, Ivan. Only let's apply question number 3. Were those files worth killing anybody over? In fact, almost nothing revealed about Clinton or the DNC was intrinsically all that harmful, just briefly embarrassing. Only the timing, at a perfect moment in the campaign, did Clinton any real harm. (There was no fire, but well-timed smoke did help to kill her.) So, seriously, you'll commit a capital felony – murder – over files that contain nothing toxic? Below, we'll see how this "conspiracy" fails every other simple test. Anyway, after the earlier (and equally credible) Vince Foster stories made the rounds ... wouldn't anyone intending to squeal on the deadly, mass-murdering Clintons know to take basic precautions? Like a post-death reveal cache?

rants – were 'biased'. As an incantation-spell it might suffice for today's confederate. But two other theories better satisfy Occam's Razor, requiring no super-conspiracy by a quarter of a million sworn civil servants.

First, might Obama and the Clintons be... mostly... innocent, while today's GOP is suborned and corrupt? The Bill Clinton Administration was the first 8 year regime in human – not just American – history not to have a single major official even indicted for malfeasance of office. The second – in human history – was the Obama Administration. [353] (Jimmy Carter's blemish-free term was only four years.) Oh no, we can't have that.

Okay, okay. There's another way to explain this failure. Maybe the Clintons and Obamas evaded all proof of their countless nefarious schemes because... they're geniuses! Movie-perfect evil masterminds, too clever to get caught! Smarter than all other conspirators across time.

Well, then? If so, dems are vastly competent – while republicans can't light a match from a lit candle and are left with several parsecs of futile conspiracy yarn. In which case why would you ever tie your allegiance and destiny to a party so ineffectual?

As for those Democrat masterminds, if you can't beat such competence, is there any plausible reason not to join them?

Nah. I pick innocent, because boy were the dems drooling incompetent in the 2016 election, to leave us in this mess, allowing the risen-treasonous Confederacy and their Kremlin allies to take Washington. In fact, the political incompetence of well-meaning Democrats is what this book's all about.

With that, let's turn off rant-mode
and consider various pragmatic means
to get out of this mess.

[353] https://www.reddit.com/r/greatawakening/comments/98yduw/connnecting_some_dots/

Okay so how to get rid of the infection?

Chapter 16

Exit Strategies – Impeachment, Indictment, the 25th Amendment and all that[354]

You desperately want to envision a quick way out of this torment. Okay then, without any preamble or delay – and from the fast-changing perspective of October 2019 – let's ponder four general scenarios:

Impeachment

Sorry, but as of October 2019, despite the frenzied urgings of sumo-fighters, Speaker Nancy Pelosi is right about investigating first and impeaching later. Even if the House indicts[355] Donald Trump, Senate conviction requires cooperation from *eighteen* GOP Senators. That is extremely unlikely till conditions are right.

Those conditions may occur! Trump revelations may pass a certain (as yet unknown) threshold, especially if disclosures from Deutsche Bank[356] bear any resemblance to rumors, or in the event of a truly major

[354] Sources: Exit strategies – 25th Amendment https://ieet.org/index.php/IEET2/more/Brin20170903http://davidbrin.blogspot.com/2017/08/gloom-and-doom-scenarios.html and https://ieet.org/index.php/IEET2/more/Brin20170903

[355] Impeachment is like grand jury indictment. GOP complaints about not getting to "confront witnesses" who have whistleblower confidentiality would have bearing during the *trial* phase – in the Senate – which is somewhat analogous to a courtroom. But even then, this is constitutional, not judicial. In fact, since life and property are not at stake, the proper analogy is more like a board of directors deciding whether to fire a corrupt employee. As of late October 2019, none of the GOP plaints have any validity. Though future ones might.

[356] Rumored revelations from Deutsche Bank. https://www.reuters.com/article/us-usa-trump-banks/trump-urges-u-s-court-to-shield-deutsche-bank-records-from-house-democrats-

national crisis. When President Trump becomes a terminal liability to his masters... if they perceive him dragging down their investment in a worldwide oligarchic putsch... they may seek a *new formula* to salvage a win-win.

How? By letting the Democrats clean up the GOP's mess? By extorting or bribing just enough Republican Senator 'defectors' to help remove Donald Trump despite fury from the base, compensating those "defectors" with enough cash (or blackmailing them) to compensate for the end of their political careers. (And perhaps not even that, if the volunteers have four years till their own re-election campaigns.)

There is a rub to this scenario, and we'll get to it. Till then, you'll never get the 18 Republican Senate votes needed for conviction and removal. And that's why we don't hurry, but rather look at this tactically, in phases.

Phases. I am not an expert politician like Pelosi and Schiff, but here are my guesses at how they view timing, during the months ahead.

a) *Before the 2020 primary season,* there are risks at both the high and low end.

Low end. Assume further revelations just keep perking along, piling ever-higher at a rate similar to the last 3 years, then RASRs and ostriches and professionals will keep leaking away from the Republican Party, but the Trump-rally core of Red America will be like the proverbial frog in a saucepan, never confronting a break-point they can't rationalize. *Especially if none of the polemical methods in this book are used to corner them.*

Mountains of turpitudes will be shrugged off as 'witch hunt' stuff. Any premature House impeachment vote will be seen as just a sterile, partisan gesture – a tit-for-tat against Bill Clinton's impeachment in the nineties. [357] That's how they'll spin it, as comparable events, despite one being a zit and the other a basketball-sized tumor. The Senate will vote "no," and that will be that.

At the high end, even supposing revelations accelerate to some breaking point (which they might as I am typing this, canceling out much of my book!), think about the consequences if impeachment and Senate

---

idUSKCN1VD0Y2

[357] For fibbing about some 3rd base marital infidelity, which both his wife and a majority of female voters forgave? Do you want the tsunami of Trumpist horrors dismissed as equivalent?

removal come too soon. Republicans might just go ahead and replace Trump, then campaign for Paul Ryan (or Romney, or worst-case Pence), without breaking stride, pretending it all never happened! Remember, they did *exactly that* recently, when the 2016 GOP Convention omitted mention of every party leader between Reagan and Ryan, even two Republican presidents.[358]

And they got away with it. Because Democrats let that happen without mention or comment.

Either way, McConnell wants a rapid pace! The eagerness of liberals for a Thanksgiving season vote is dumb and plays into his hands. Rushing in is not judo.

b) *Impeach during primary season.* Time it right and continuing revelations might help challengers like William Weld to become noticeable irritants. Not enough, probably, to deny Trump the nomination, but sufficient to drive him into ever greater hysteria. Again this depends on the magnitude of revelations. But short of that putative video of him shooting someone on Fifth Avenue, actual impeachment during this phase would be risky – Dems will be accused of doing it as an election ploy. Still, it's a better time than before or after. A sweet spot? Cornered by revelations and outrages, but terrified of home voters, GOP Senators don't dare convict Trump – but they do collaborate on *emergency bills limiting his powers.*[359] He is lethally wounded for November. Republicans cry *sauve qui peut!* and scurry to the lifeboats, trying to save themselves while Romney (or some Russian front-man) tries to form a third party.

c) *Impeach during the general election season.* Oy, what a mess. Howls of "Let the voters decide!" While voting machines go haywire.

d) *Final revenge.* A deliciously awful opportunity might come after a major victory for America in November 2020 – during a brief window between the seating of a new, Dem-majority Senate and Inauguration Day, 2021.[360] With a little help from off-year GOP Senators, Trump might be removed from office, dragged out of the White House, and kept off the inaugural stage — an indignity that would be mostly about

---

[358] Except Newt Gingrich.

[359] Limit presidential powers? At surface, they'll cooperate to constrain a loose cannon Trump, but with an eye to weakening the coming Dem president. Do this carefully!

[360] Of course, that would be about revenge.

vengeance. I mention it because, frankly, I expect revelations to mount that high. All told, it's a minefield. And liberals who play armchair general shouldn't just assume they know what's best. The way *I'm* behaving, for example.

Chess Moves

Now for a rub. The fact that must keep Vlad and Rupert up at night. Suppose Trump becomes an unbearable liability, dragging down everything they've built, but he refuses to go quietly? No buy-out offer or threat works and he sees the Republican Party trying to rally around a new, "fresh" standard bearer. Well, this would finally give Donald Trump *the reality show role he was born for* –

– as furious, livid-living *martyr.* Liberated from the prison of the White House. Free to stage rally after rally, howling about schemes and injustices 24/7, while riling the confed base to volcanic fury. And he turns it all against the GOP.

There are two ways out for Rupert and Vlad.

(i) make democrats do all the work and armtwist just enough Republican Senators to go along, drawing Trump's wrath *mostly* upon Democrats. (See variants, below.) Or else…

(ii) real martyrdom. The biggest win-win for Fox and Moscow. Eliminate their irritant the same way that cynical executives got rid of their liability, Howard Beale, in *Network.* Blame those cityfolk and liberals! Or an ethnic patsy. And it's likely we'd tumble into hot civil war. Putin's win-win.

Ponder these chess moves in advance and don't fall for them. If it comes to (i) then I'd ask a dozen *Democratic Senators* to *play sick,* so the GOP must pony up an *equal* number of their own, to reach two-thirds and removal.

And if it ever comes down to possibility (ii) then *it is vital that Democrats not pour into the streets, celebrating! Rather, react with rage at the blatant culprits — an oligarchy that cruelly used-up and then disposed of a sick, addled old man, as soon as they were done with him.*

Pity.

It works, at so many levels.[361]

Does all of this sound like fantasy?

No, what is *stupid* is not to work out possible chess moves, in advance.

The Secret Santa Variant

Let's dig further down the rabbit hole of Mitch McConnell's possible ploys. All right, so imagine that he and his masters have deemed Donald Trump a liability. Mike Pence has agreed to follow orders. Ideally, Trump would resign or take a leave of absence and head off to have fun riling his base against Democrats... but he refuses, or he can't be trusted not to blab the deal.

Moreover, thanks to the skill and professionalism of the Secret Service, any "Howard Beale" martyrdom option is off the table.

Well, there's impeachment and removal, under the Constitution. But were McConnell to go along by providing 18 Republican votes for Senate conviction, Trump would go off the assigned rails, turning volcanic rage — and his base — *against the Republican Party* and possibly even the oligarchy that controls it!

Are there ways that Mitch (with likely nods from John Roberts) might arrange this to happen without incurring Trumpian fury on the GOP?

Well, for starters, there is nothing preventing either the House or the Senate from holding a *secret vote* (with the tally put under seal until past the next election cycle). This would free people to vote their conscience. In fact, this is already being discussed re: the House impeachment decision, perhaps giving some protection to Democrats who represent reddish districts. (It won't work, but it does help give Speaker Pelosi an excuse to follow her own tactical timetable.)

In the Senate, secret voting would almost certainly result in conviction, as at least two dozen Republicans eagerly cast folded ballots into a box to rid the nation of their party's greatest embarrassment. There are two problems with this option though:

1. It would raise a fire storm in public and press, especially when *every* Republican Senator claims to have voted *"nay."*.

---

[361] At last! On October 16, 2019, Speaker Nancy Pelosi spoke of praying for the mental health of a clearly sick Donald Trump. It played out as I predicted, rousing effective responses in all directions.

2. It would not mollify Trump's reflex to lash out at the GOP leaders who 'betrayed' him.

The Go-Limp Option

There is a sneaky – if barely plausible – way out of this trap. Who says the number of Republican defectors has to be 18? That's only required if every Senator attends the trial. Only now look at the Constitution:

> **Art. I, Sec. 3, Cl. 6 & 7:** *The Senate shall have the sole Power to try all Impeachments. When sitting for that Purpose, they shall be on oath or affirmation. When the President of the United States is tried, the Chief Justice shall preside: and no Person shall be convicted without Concurrence of two-thirds of the Members present.*[362]

"Two thirds of the Members present." A quorum of at least 51 Senators is required, in order to be in session, hence it might theoretically take just 34 to convict and remove a sitting president! And if those voting 'yea' are 100% Democrats, then a deposed and enraged Trump wouldn't go after the GOP, would he?

Let's assume all 47 Democrats (and partners) vote to convict. That will amount to the required two-thirds if no more than 70 Senators are present, 23 of them Republicans. That can happen if *thirty GOP Senators somehow don't show up*. Perhaps they call in sick. Or they declare a "boycott" of a "kangaroo proceeding," or claim "terrorists threatened my family." (Or, if you are writing a cheap thriller novel, you'd portray thirty of them blown up at a conference, blame Democrats and the "deep state," and trigger a truly hot war, leaving Putin on top of the world.[363]) However Mitch arranges such a mass absence, Democrats could then remove Trump all by themselves, on a party line vote, 47 to 23.[364]

Would they be so stupid? So propelled by reflex hate that they fall into such a trap?

---

[362] "An Overview of the Impeachment Process" Congressional Research Service. https://www.senate.gov/reference/resources/pdf/98-806.pdf

[363] A good reason for Republican Senators to avoid caucus meetings outside the Capitol?

[364] Or make it less obvious by letting a few RINOS vote to convict. Few enough not to trigger Trump against the whole party. – Oh, while I have you here – How about another weird scenario. Say the Senate is held by an impeached president's opposition, but they have much fewer votes than needed to convict. They go into recess before holding the trial "to consult with voters"... then the majority party senators all sneak back, form a quorum and vote to convict needing less than 67... as little as 34. Yipe.

Not if they reply "He's *your* problem, Mitch. Deal with it." And especially not if they look at the alternative.

Trump's impeachment insurance.

Sure premature impeachment might be a trap that a hundred million liberals will eagerly charge into. But that's not my biggest reason for siding with Pelosi's go-slow approach. My worry is… *the alternative.* While Donald Trump is a dangerous/loony foreign agent, at least his Murdoch/Moscow masters don't want the world to end.

It is absolutely verified that Mike Pence does. We're talking *literally.* So let me lay it out.

With only one exception, GOP presidents always appoint someone utterly unqualified as their Vice Presidents. (Reagan did choose a *qualified* VP… who became the worst president of the 20th Century.) Whether or not this is done as *impeachment insurance,* we need to consider all potential outcomes.

Right now, Trump's White House leaks like a sieve. The civil service and intel/military officers are wary and careful. Cauterized, he can do limited harm. In contrast, Mike Pence would fill the Executive Mansion with dedicated and utterly disciplined Dominionists who would strive – tight-lipped – toward the same goal. Each and every one prays daily for events described in the *Book of Revelation* to all come true. They are open about it, as is the president-in-waiting.

An end to all human ambition, democracy or science. An end to all generations of children. An end to the United States of America. And brutal endless torment for 90%+ of Americans.

President Pence will croon smoothly about ending our "national nightmare." Hundreds of thousands of officers etc. will moan with relief and hurry to serve. Pence might even pull his name from consideration as a candidate. All that will mean is that the clock is ticking a rapid countdown.

The 25th Amendment

I talk about this Constitutional quirk in detail, below. And I see little chance it will work, unless the Republican masters forsake Don as a liability. And if that happens, they'll prefer *martyrdom* over making VP Mike Pence the fall guy, which would happen under the 25th.

Let's suppose Pence corralled a majority of cabinet officers (do "acting" secretaries count?) into invoking the 25th. Trump and Pence would then send "letters" back and forth at an ever-accelerating rate until the email servers melt. Congressional Republicans will dither, covering their ears to the blatant psychological meltdown of the man-with-nukes. Till the Supreme Court has to step in with some kind of non-Constitutional arbiter. Insane amounts of damage. Which of course will make some parties giggle with glee.

Yes, Congress could appoint that "other body" I described elsewhere, to bypass the Cabinet… a commission of sages that could have real power for good, under the 25th. I also comment on this, below. If the right people were on it, our nation could ease out of civil war. And the chances that McConnell would go along, or that a Trump veto could be overridden, are nil.

Donald Trump is pressured to resign

Um right. That would require something on the order of the Pee Tape. Nothing less and probably much more. You got hopes.

A hybrid seems possible. DT takes a "stress break." A vacation with no electronics of any kind. Or maybe blame his recent worsening hysteria on a brain tumor. (Ideally one induced by Democratic windmills.) Dems should insist on independent examinations and that they get to see him, daily.

Status quo

The circus goes on and on. We depend utterly on the sane adults of the civil service, intel community, law professionals and the U.S. military officer corps to keep us safe (though alas not the Kurds), while Donald Trump adds fuel to phase 8 of the Civil War, destroying the Republican brand and riling up the Union to truly take up the fight.... ending ideally with America – not the confederacy – winning overwhelming victory at the ballot box. (Though that will also require dems wising up on tactics.)[365]

---

[365] http://davidbrin.blogspot.com/2017/06/a-time-for-colonels-part-two-working.html

Status Quo doesn't mean passivity! Congress must rescind the 2001 War Powers Act now! And set up a commission of sages that can (if unanimous) allow the military to pause a presidential command. That commission could be explicitly granted 25th Amendment "other body" powers giving it real muscle. (If it is partisan, then we're entering Venezuela territory. So start with all the ex-presidents, ex-Vice Presidents and ex Supreme Court Justices. Throw in every U.S. Nobel laureate?)

The unspeakable

Any "fifth option" I can think of is too horrific for words – though one of them starts with "M" and I've used it several times here in this chapter. A way for Trump's masters to both eliminate a liability and rile up the base to hot-war violence. I denounce it, in advance. In fact I am on record asking that Trump be careful what he eats, especially with his foreign "friends." And God bless the U.S. Secret Service.

My advice, especially to Democratic politicians, remains not to fall for traps. Calm down.

We're supposed to be smart people, it's what Putin/Murdoch fear about us, right? We have all of the fact-user professions. Use that. Think.

And now, from a separate, edited essay –
– expect overlaps and repetitions, but also value…

DETAILS: THE 25TH AMENDMENT

Above I posed "four options." Among those exit strategies, I urged that we take on impeachment with the skill and savvy and patience of judo masters. Indeed, as the clinical symptoms displayed by President Trump grow ever more extravagantly unhinged, folks have started to stare longingly at the 25th amendment to the U.S. Constitution. Most articles discussing this option are extremely shallow and missing key points we'll reveal here. But for starters, do give it a careful read, because things could get critical very fast. The pertinent stuff starts here:

Section 4. Whenever the Vice President and a majority of either the principal officers of the executive departments or of such other body as Congress may by law provide, transmit to the President pro tempore of the Senate and the Speaker of the House of Representatives their written declaration that the President is unable to discharge the powers and duties of his office, the Vice President shall immediately assume the powers and duties of the office as Acting President.

Note this line in particular: "...or of such *other body* as Congress may by law provide..." Has anyone, especially in Congress, actually thought through the implications? Even assuming that Pence were to try invoking the 25th – the group that he might normally go to – the Cabinet– is filled with Trumpists, "acting" appointees and some bona fide crazies. They will at best be slow to act on any Vice Presidential request to declare POTUS incapacitated... and hence the VP may hesitate to ask, even at some critically dangerous moment.

But consider that *other body* the 25th talks about. Note: there is no prescribed time sequence, so an alternative commission could be *created in advance,* and thenceforth serve as a warning to the President to remain calm. In order to be established "by law," over-riding a presidential veto, the 'other body' would have to be bipartisan.

This commission of sages would be able to act – in concert with the VP – almost instantly, should POTUS issue bizarre or especially dangerous orders, offering a way for sane grownups to cancel some crazy action or command. The mere existence of such a commission might ease the pangs of our Officer Corps, knowing they would have a place to turn, if some spasmodic-insane order came down. I know of nowhere else that they could turn.

Without such a Congressionally established commission in existence, the VP would have to assemble the Cabinet behind the President's back and persuade a majority to betray the man who hand-picked them and to whom they owe everything. Which path do you think is more likely to act as a brake on sudden, spasm-lunacy?

The 25th Amendment continues: *Thereafter, when the President transmits to the President pro tempore of the Senate and the Speaker of the House of Representatives his written declaration that no inability exists, he shall resume the powers and duties of his office unless the Vice President and a majority of either the principal officers of the executive department or of such other body as Congress may by law provide, transmit within four days to the President pro tempore of the Senate and the Speaker of the House of Representatives their written declaration that the President is unable to discharge the powers and duties of his office.*

There it is again. The "other body" or Congressionally-appointed commission – in conjunction with the VP – may then reject the President's demand to be reinstated... sending the matter for decision by Congress. A 2/3 vote is then required in both houses to keep POTUS suspended.

Thus we have an answer to anyone who claims this step would bypass the popular will, or create undue burdens on the presidency. There are several places where 2/3 majorities are required from both houses, plus cooperation from the Vice President... a far steeper set of obstacles, by the way, than is required for impeachment.

"Thereupon Congress shall decide the issue, assembling within forty-eight hours for that purpose if not in session. If the Congress, within twenty-one days after receipt of the latter written declaration, or, if Congress is not in session, within twenty-one days after Congress is required to assemble, determines by two-thirds vote of both Houses that the President is unable to discharge the powers and duties of his office, the Vice President shall continue to discharge the same as Acting President; otherwise, the President shall resume the powers and duties of his office."

It is infuriatingly unclear what happens during the two days that Congress has to assemble and the 21 days it has to deliberate. I would assert that during those twenty-five days the VP is in charge. The Supreme Court would almost certainly have to decide.

What is clear is that there's a way for Congress to lay groundwork in advance, to protect the Republic from an unstable president. A commission can be established... right now... that waits, ready to bypass the Cabinet in this one matter, but still requires both consent and courageous leadership from the Vice President.

As a way to firm-up its trust and moral authority – especially since establishing it requires a law and hence likely an over-ridden veto – any such commission should be nonpartisan. I'd envision it starting with all the former presidents, vice presidents and retired Supreme Court Justices, plus an array of mighty American notables. (I'd add all U.S. winners of the Nobel Prize.) And recall, that commission would be backed by the Constitution itself and empowered to cancel or postpone any rash presidential order, by exercising its right to hand reins over to the VP for a limited time.

The circuit breaker for a mentally ill president is already provided for... if Congress chooses to use it. Note also that Senators and Representatives who might balk at a rush to impeach and remove might go along with simply creating a commission that could elevate the veep for a few days.

Even if such an action has only brief effect and POTUS is reinstated – recall it takes 2/3 of both houses to prevent that – the effect will still be to assure a pause for calm and reflection, during which any rash orders may be put on hold.

Believe me, I see flaws in this as well! Given that Mike Pence is a member of an end-the-world-as-soon-as-possible cult, and has expressed utter devotion to Donald Trump, I'm not greatly eased. Still, I have to wonder. Do you think Congressional leaders are even aware of all this? Has anyone worked it out down to this level? That the U.S. Constitution itself would support establishing a commission of sages in advance? One that would thereupon be able to act swiftly to protect us?

Addendum: Someone Has, Indeed, Thought Of It...

Since posting this, I stumbled across proof that others noticed the same thing. Alas, though, it's a Democrat. And his well-meant efforts may have harmed, rather than helped promote such a commission.[366] "Rep. Jamie Raskin's (D-Md.) bill seeks to create the Oversight Commission on Presidential Capacity to fill a role outlined by the Constitution's 25th Amendment, which sets up presidential removal procedures."

There's real overlap with my approach, but with emphasis on the commission being much more medical in nature: "Raskin wants to provide a specific 'body' comprised of 10 physicians, psychiatrists and retired former leaders – like presidents and vice presidents – chosen by House and Senate leaders of both parties."

---

[366] "House Dem seeks to create commission on 'presidential capacity'." https://thehill.com/homenews/house/333193-house-dem-seeks-to-create-commission-on-presidential-capacity

This could be a basis for negotiation about the actual bill, which would have to pass both houses... likely by 2/3 to override a Trump veto. But I think Rep Raskin misses the point that even if Congress creates it, this "other body" cannot do a thing without the Vice President's cooperation and consent. The VP is central. Moreover, this will be dismissed as partisan posturing, unless it is promulgated above-all by Mitch McConnell and Rupert Murdoch. And they won't make any such move until it's almost too late.

So here's my clever political recommendation. Staffers for Pelosi and McConnell must discreetly approach a dozen important retired generals and admirals and ask them:

"Do you believe that establishing such a commission in advance, so that the Vice President can act swiftly in a crisis, would enhance the security and safety of the United States?"

That's it. If the response is yes, then it should happen. And history may remember those who prevented the simple measure.

Another Use

Okay, let me share a Doonesbury-level summer daydream. Such a commission – established for one constitutional purpose – could serve us in other ways. For example, by informally using the members' high-renown to help set up or endorse reputable fact-checking services that are beyond partisan reproach.

Imagine past Presidents and Vice Presidents joining Sandra Day O'Conner and a dozen other luminaries who have already agreed to serve on the "other body" taking on an added and more important task that I have pleaded for several times, across this tome. As I described in Chapter 5, such a conclave of American sages could save us all just by saying "*facts exist and here are several groups we trust to debunk many of the lies going around.*"

Nothing would help us more than some process by which Americans could declare "our greatest sages and best minds say that's false. So let's put at least that lie behind us."

DETAILS AT PRESS TIME: REPUBLICANS WRITHE

Developments pummel forth as I complete this project for publication. The latest Fox/GOP line is to stonewall the impeachment hearings because House committee chairs won't let them have access to the whistleblowers.[367] Senate majority leader Mitch McConnell decried House Democrats for allegedly failing to give the president full benefit of due process appropriate to a court trial. House Republican leader Kevin McCarthy went further, asserting (October 29, 2019) that every piece of evidence against Donald Trump, no matter how explicit and damning, should be tossed because of lethal flaws in the earliest phases of investigation. "If you were in the legal term," says McCarthy "it'd be the fruit from the poisonous tree."

Ironies are rich. McCarthy and Republicans are now invoking a doctrine they always hated – when it applied to safeguarding the rights of Joe and Jane on the street. The "poison" McCarthy refers to is possible bias by FBI counter-intelligence chief Peter Strzok – who chased KGB spies on our behalf for 30 years – and the *second* layer of "Steele Dossier" investigations. (The first layer was commissioned by "biased" Republicans.) Both of those were supposedly tainted by an agenda to find malfeasance or criminal behavior by Donald Trump and his associates.

Yes, bias can be poisonous in certain ways during the *trial* process. But impeachment is an *indictment,* not the trial phase. By nature, impeachment hearings are like those of a Grand Jury, where secret testimony and even hearsay are absolutely normal, and where protection of fearful witnesses (e.g. the 'Whistleblower') plays an absolutely vital role. Moreover, Mitch McConnell and his allies know this, since they declared exactly that, during the Clinton impeachment process.

Sure, after any indictment all must eventually come out in the *trial phase* and defenders are free to argue "bias" to the judge and jury. But

---

367 From The Washington Post: https://www.washingtonpost.com/powerpost/gop-players-in-benghazi-probe-drop-strong-defense-of-congressional-oversight/2019/10/09/9dc2a99e-eaa4-11e9-9c6d-436a0df4f31d_story.html

it almost never applies to the initial phases of investigation, when the police have committed no outright crime.

"The fruit of the poisonous tree doctrine only applies when someone's constitutional rights have been violated," says former deputy Watergate special prosecutor Nick Akerman, "That's like saying every indictment issued by a grand jury has to be dismissed because the defendant didn't have a chance to be in the grand jury room to defend himself. I mean, that is just off the wall, it comes from outer space."[368]

Worse, demanding to expose the Whistleblower's identity prematurely amounts to no less than attempted intimidation, in violation of whistleblower laws – especially when his/her assertions have all been subsequently verified by blatant and open facts, as well as dozens of testimonies and the Ukraine related transcripts.

It's the Senate, where impeachment (indictment) would be tried, that is presently biased – in Donald Trump's favor. Which is why McConnell is the one trying to speed things up, and why (as of October 2019) Nancy Pelosi is taking her time. (My prediction: Ukraine will be a barely-remembered side-show, when the Deutsche Bank dike fails amid a tsunami of new revelations and we all get to see the full Russia-Trump story.)

Anyway, even a Grand Jury analogy is too rigid for impeachment, which is not juridical but constitutional. The proper parallel is a company board of directors deciding to fire a corrupt CEO. This is an *employment matter* as America's stock plummets all around the world and deficits skyrocket and our most-skilled employees courageously lodge complaints, or else abandon ship.

Finally, let me reiterate for the umpteenth time… 25 years and half a billion dollars of Clinton-Obama investigations sifted every record from two Democratic administrations, grilled every appointee and civil servant and were never stonewalled. Now GOP House members who were strong proponents of iron-fisted oversight of Democratic administrations, including repeated, futile 2-year Benghazi probes, have dropped

---

[368] McCarthy's "fruit of a poison tree" assertion: https://www.independent.co.uk/voices/alexander-vindman-trump-impeachment-republicans-testimony-ukraine-scandal-a9176791.html

their former, stout defense of congressional prerogatives, endorsing instead Trump's campaign of massive resistance.

I refer you back to our first "pause" section, after Chapter One, that list of zingers, challenges and wagers where we got to the heart of this matter. About the core catechism of the American right, which is: *"Don't look! We mustn't know! If there's anything going on, under all that smoke, I don't want to find out! Look away. Look away."*

There is one word that undermines all of this, incinerating the kernel out of their one tenacious premise – and Donald Trump's – the premise of macho bluster.

That searing word is *Cowards!*

They don't expect to hear it from nerds and libs. And so, for all of its playground immaturity, that word will be more effective than any weight of facts. It will serve well as polemical judo. Use it to good effect.

And may we all survive interesting times.

Oh, there are other exit strategies…
but all of it supposes we can summon leaders
with the patience and sagacity to play chess,
instead of falling into trap after trap.

Conclusion Of POLEMICAL JUDO: Volume I

Here we must take a break, finishing off volume one so that something can get out there, a year before the 2020 election.

Are there other topics? Riffs on immigration and guns? Putin and the world mafia? Climate and racism? Defense and war? See the table of contents (tentative) for volume two, below, along with links to where early drafts were posted on Contrary Brin. I'll modernize and expand those sections in preparing Part II… if there's time.

But for now… a rare moment of perspective and honesty. Arrogant as I am, I know these yammered suggestions will be ignored – almost entirely – by anyone out there with the power or position to use them. Futility – alas – seems certain.

And so, let me close now with the wisdom I am so often sent, by readers and fans.

"Why don't you stick to what you're good at, Brin? Be a sensible sci fi author and do a little astronomy. Be a citizen and help get out the vote. Civilization will thrive or fail with ponderous momentum and history will unroll… with you or without you."

To hell with that!

I intend to go down fighting. So should you.

POLEMICAL JUDO:
Planned VOLUME TWO
Table of Contents

---

[369] Flag pins vs PC category bragging… and ship name fetishes – http://davidbrin.blogspot.com/2015/04/the-politics-of-naming-aircraft.html and https://ieet.org/index.php/IEET2/more/Bri20171101

[370] The "Jefferson Rifle" proposal vs. the *Slippery Slope syndrome* preventing decent gun owners from listening to compromise. http://www.tinyurl.com/jrifle

APPENDICES

1. The Minimal Overlap solution to gerrymandering

2. Very crackpotty ideas.

Appendix 1 Gerrymandering Redux: The Minimal Overlap Solution

In Chapter 4 ("End the Cheating First), we covered a wide range of ways that the Oligarchic Putsch has corrupted our institutions and electoral practices, in order to overcome and repress "the mob" and its democratic will. The worst of these cheats is gerrymandering. So now – after many detours – let's get down to my own proposal for how to solve this mess.

And yes, as promised, it will address every excuse offered by Supreme Court wafflers. And it fits in *three sentences.*

EXCUSES, EXCUSES AND HOW TO GET AROUND THEM

Ideally, solutions should come from negotiated legislation. When power abuse is generated by legislatures themselves, courts must step in. Indeed, it seemed on several occasions as if even the conservative-biased U.S. Supreme Court would actually do something. But twice since the turn of the century it has copped out.

First, about a decade ago, Justice Anthony Kennedy[371] provided the deciding "it's a bad thing but we can't see a way around it" vote. How was that rationalized? Even in the face of blatant injustice, judges like to have two things:

1) A simple, unambiguous metric that proves actionable harm.

2) At least one clean and simple remedy they can point to as an example.[372]

---

[371] Justice Kennedy was widely seen as the swing vote on gerrymandering in a court divided between liberals, who see the practice as unconstitutional, and conservatives, who regard it as a political problem, not a legal one. Indeed, he single-handedly preserved it as a judicial question, in a 2004 case involving Pennsylvania's Legislature, when he declined to join four other justices who declared that it is impossible to determine when a political map becomes unacceptably partisan. "That no such standard has emerged in this case," he wrote then, "should not be taken to prove that none will emerge in the future." Hence he dangled hope before us… before suddenly "retiring" just as we needed that hope fulfilled, as the 'standard' he wanted arrived. Why did he do that? Well…. Ponder chapters 7 & 8; that's all I will say.https://www.nytimes.com/2018/06/30/us/kennedy-scotus-gerrymandering.html

[372] Simple remedy: http://www.campaignlegalcenter.org/case/gill-v-whitford

The first requirement has since been provided by an elegant standard of "voter efficiency," by which it's overwhelmingly proved that citizens are being cheated for partisan gain. This New Yorker article dissects the problem, describing some new insights from logic and mathematics that should have helped the Court better to understand a foul practice that has warped American democracy.[373]

But for the Court to articulate a workable *baseline remedy* – Kennedy's second objection – what's needed is a fallback solution that is inarguably better than the present state of affairs, one that can be ordered if a state proves unable to devise a fair and impartial redistricting process on its own. Here, the blatant success of states like California's citizen redistricting commissions at achieving better voter efficiency has chipped away the "no clear remedy" objection. And my own "Minimal Overlap" proposal, outlined below, does it even more clearly, by requiring no independent commissions at all! Just three sentences.

With those first two excuses satisfied, conservative think tanks had to come up with another, fast! And they did, just in time for a second wave of gerrymandering cases. Providing a deciding vote in mid-2019, the Chief Justice of the United States of America issued what ought to from now on be known as the "Roberts Doctrine" – for which I believe history will remember him in infamy alongside the likes of John Taney.[374] But putting aside my angry interpretation, we can distill the Roberts Doctrine to this essence:

3) Courts should be ever mindful of respecting – and avoid interfering with – the separated power of legislatures. [375] Hence, the matter is "non-justiciable."[376]

---

[373] On the mathematics of gerrymandering, from The New Yorker: http://www.newyorker.com/tech/elements/a-summer-school-for-mathematicians-fed-up-with-gerrymandering

[374] Justice Kagan issued a blistering dissent of the Roberts Doctrine, laying down harshly effective reasoning that *state courts* have been applying, such as in North Carolina, to begin taking on this travesty.

[375] This doctrine – in which courts rule themselves powerless to interpose to settle subpoena disputes between the executive (Trump) and the legislative branches, has (as of October 2019) appeared to be a blatant support of executive stonewalling of Congressional oversight powers. But I describe elsewhere describe how this "non-justiciable" doctrine is one Democrats can use to advantage, as a perfect way to enforce Congressional subpoenas.

[376] In Gill v. Whitford, a group of Wisconsin residents challenged a 2011 state assembly redistricting plan as an unconstitutional partisan gerrymander. On January 23, 2019, the court granted in part the State Assembly's motion to stay the case, postponing trial until the U.S. Supreme Court ruled on partisan gerrymandering appeals from North Carolina and Maryland on June 27, 2019. The Supreme Court's opinion in those cases held that partisan gerrymandering claims are

This new and virtually unprecedented doctrine forbids federal courts from even considering gerrymandering cases, for the reason that *the judicial branch has no business interfering in the internal affairs of another branch.* Not even when majorities in those legislatures institute cheats that guarantee they'll never be ejected by the state's citizen-voters, who are the ones truly vested in sovereignty.

And so we appear to have been stymied. Thieves relish a golden excuse to keep thieving. Except that I propose *a solution to all three objections,* and one so simple it can be expressed in three sentences.

THE MINIMAL OVERLAP PLAN

Here are those three sentences:

1. With allowances for contorted state borders, like Maryland's panhandle, the districts that are drawn for State Assembly, State Senate and Congress shall meet a basic compactness standard, not falling below a reasonably generous area-to-perimeter ratio limit set by the court.
2. On advice from a non-partisan and unbiased commission, the State Legislature may thereupon assign boundaries to the districts of the State Assembly however they see fit.
3. Once those State Assembly boundaries are set, the drawing of boundaries for State Senate and Congressional districts will be computer-generated, with the core provision that they must have MINIMAL OVERLAP with each other and with the State Assembly districts, sharing as few voters as practically possible.

There you have it. Three sentences. I've offered this suggestion for a decade and I promise that (alas) you'll find it nowhere else.[377] It means that the State Legislature may, if they choose, ignore the neutral commission and connive, jigger or gerrymander districts for *one house* – the

---

non-justiciable. On July 2, 2019, the court dismissed the case. https://www.brennancenter.org/our-work/court-cases/gill-v-whitford

[377] As it happens, Congress has the power, established for 150+ years, to forbid gerrymandering and it often did, when re-assigning representation according to census data, until the Apportionment Act of 1929 set the mathematical formula for districting in stone – and the size of the House at 435.

State Assembly – limited only by some basic rule of compactness. This should satisfy the 'legislative sovereignty' objection!

But provision #3 ensures that the *districts for State Senate and Congress* will be utterly different. The more carefully the legislature's majority partisans gerry-rig one house, the less effective will be their efforts in the other two.

The chief aim of gerrymander-cheating – to achieve government dominance by the most rabid of hyper-partisans – will be devastated and then grow weaker, over time.

ILLUSTRATING MINIMAL OVERLAP

For some reason, the notion of minimal overlap seems obvious to a lot of people, while others find it difficult to grasp. So let's try using illustrations. Sentence/provision #1 takes care of the worst, egregious cases, illustrated in our first figure.

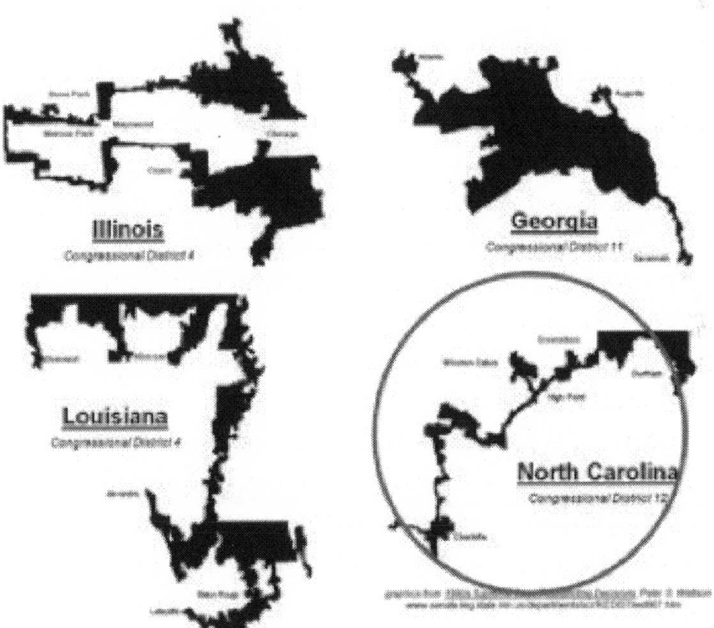

As Figure 1 shows, a large fraction of gerrymander travesties would be eliminated by a compactness rule, setting upper limits to perimeter-area ratios. This limit can be fairly generous, since the rest of the solution happens through minimal overlap.

In Figure 2 we present a strawman set of six State Assembly districts that are (for the sake of simplicity) highly compact.

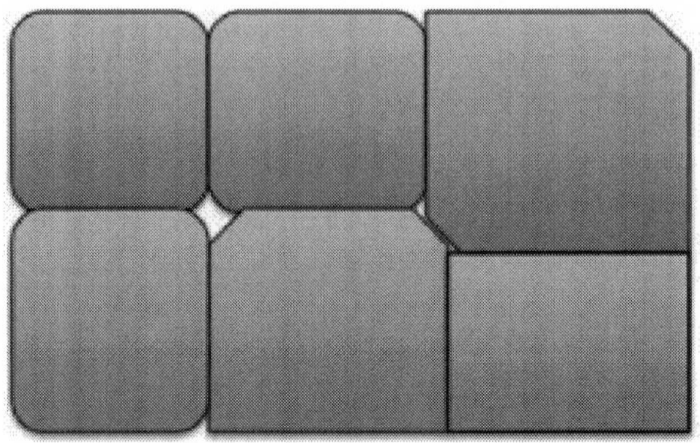

Fig2: Simplified boundaries of a State Assembly, under compactness rule, but somewhat gerrymandered

Let's assume that the state legislature has, under rule #2, but limited by the compactness rule #1, arranged these assembly districts to maximize gerrymander benefits for the majority party.

Now, in our third illustration, let's overlay districts for State Senate. These are required – under the court-ordered remedy of Minimal Overlap to be computer-optimized so that each senate district shares as little territory and as few voters as possible with any one assembly district. [378]

Assuming the compactness rule is enforced, and that Senate districts are truly drawn according to provision #3, then Minimal Overlap – also called "anti-nesting" – means that the political character of the Senate will not be warped by gerrymandering. Citizens who were disenfranchised before will likely get attention and an effective vote, in at least one chamber.

---

[378] A cheat method called "rotating spokes" would have to be dealt with, as many red states have Blue Islands surrounding their urban hubs and universities, that are gerried with pie slice districts. Minimal overlap might be stymied if districts for a second house (say the State Senate) were simply *rotated* pie slices. That might require a fourth sentence.

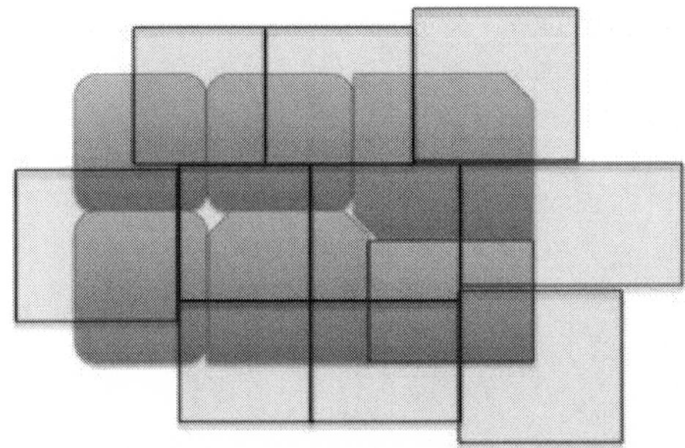

Fig3: State Senate districts (in beige) overlain upon Assembly Districts according to Minimal Overlap, ensuring that any gerry-rigging of the Assembly will be disrupted in the Senate.

Congressional districts – generally larger – would also be computer-optimized not just for compactness, but minimal overlap with the gerried Assembly districts.

The districts for Congress, presumably larger, will nevertheless be kept off-kilter from the gerried State Assembly districts. The party in power will thus only get to have one chamber warped by self-serving, partisan political cheating.

Moreover, even if this method has flaws, it is a well-defined limiting case that deprives the courts of any "we see no clear remedy" excuse. For all its faults, Minimal Overlap is palliative, equitable and enforceable. It also gives a nod to state sovereignty, separation of powers and legislature privilege, by allowing the legislature to continue discretionary control over one chamber, while the other two are set by a neutral computer reacting to their assembly boundaries.

ARGUMENTS AGAINST MINIMAL OVERLAP

One objection that opponents to such a solution will assert is that voters should be represented by "communities of interest." For example, one of the commonly used excuses for gerrymandering is that contorted arrangements are necessary in order to ensure that minority populations get some representatives who are of their ethnic persuasion.

There are two decisive answers:

(a) The "communities of interest" argument is served by having *one* of three chambers divided that way. So long as those communities of interest are firmly ensconced and represented in one chamber, there is no inherent need for duplication. This is an original merit of bicameral legislatures.

In fact, there are strong arguments in favor of voters facing *different coalition needs,* and different communities of interest, in different houses. Why should their Assembly, State Senate and Congressional delegates be clones of each other? Apportioned one way – say in the Assembly – the community of interest might map onto national political parties, or else be optimized for ethnic representation. But mapped orthogonally in another house, entirely different matters of community interest – based on geography, markets, or some other basis – might come to the fore. State Senators will discuss different priorities at their town hall meetings than Assembly members, to the benefit of political problem-solving.

Anyway, a state senator who must negotiate among multiple constituencies and interests will be a busier one, and possibly one who achieves a lot more to break down our divisions.

(b) This method is a fallback, intended to persuade courts – possibly even the Supreme Court – that gerrymandering can be solved intrinsically, in a simple fashion that is inherently more fair than the present, biased-partisan cheating. And what could be simpler than three sentences?

Under the Minimal Overlap method, voters who now feel completely disenfranchised in all ways and in all chambers will thereupon very likely see their position improved. They will gain a chance that at least one of their three representatives will be someone who heeds their concerns. That is an improvement and a palliation of harm, and one that is far from arbitrary.

Voters thus would be guaranteed some relief from a conspiratorial injustice, in a fashion that is simple to execute. States may opt for some other method to eliminate the injustice. Many already have. But this method provides a backstop ensuring that the worst, most pervasive effects of gerrymandering will end.

IMPLICATIONS OF MINIMAL OVERLAP

Notice one "judo" aspect of this approach – that it allows hyper-partisans to have their way, somewhat, for a while, in one house. This might lessen resistance to reform by the most fundamentally powerful entities in American political life, state assembly members. It also splits away the self-interest of State Senators, reducing their motivation for hyper-partisanship – which is a desirable outcome in its own right. Why should Assembly members and Senators connive together? Vive la difference! Moreover, as State Senate and Congressional delegations become more moderate and less partisan, they will then tend to pressure the State Assembly to damp down its own cheating and partisanship.

The Court should also be made aware of the effect that impartial redistricting has had in many blue states and a few purples. While California remains dominated by the Democratic Party, impartial redistricting and other reforms (e.g. non-party primaries) have resulted in less bitterness between parties, not more. Less acrimony. Even in districts that wind up heavily Democratic or Republican, voters who are members of the minority party now feel more listened-to than before.

Earlier I mentioned that Illinois and Maryland and few other Democrat-dominated holdouts still outrageously gerrymander. Former President Barack Obama and former U.S. Attorney General Eric Holder have specifically targeted these states, arm-twisting state legislators to end the foul practice. When those Democratic Party holdouts comply, this horrifically blatant cheat and crime will be seen as an odious offense perpetrated primarily by just one party against the citizens of this great nation.

Appendix 2 – Even More Crackpot Ideas!

Back in Chapter 13 we covered a wide range of unusual and usual political ideas for things we might do if a sensible majority could legislate, and even – getting into fantasy territory – if the opposition decided to sensibly negotiate, too.

The IGUS concept and the Subpoena Gambit are among the most potentially transformative of my earlier "political suggestions," going back to 2006 and earlier.[379] If you care to visit those earlier postings… they do include *some agenda items that never made it into this book.*

Okay, then. I held off for a little bit, exercising some self – control! But now, well, it's time.

Minor but significant stuff.

First a few items that'd be worthwhile, even if not huge or sexy.

– At some point when gas prices are low, take an advantage of an opportunity to switch from a cents-per-gallon tax to a percentage tax.

– Every other major country has *replaced its currency* by now, with important positive effects for honest taxpayers. The rationalizations offered by opponents – who claim the greenback is forever special, different, and sacred – are getting ridiculous and awfully long in the tooth. Just think of all the drug lords and Mafiosi who would be discomfited. And the American greenback is easily counterfeited and *filthy.*[380]

– Tell all Americans to update their computer security packages, because a bill is about to refine data tort law, making responsibility similar to public health codes. If you neglect hygiene and your device becomes a

---

[379] Political suggestions from 2006 and earlier. http://www.davidbrin.com/nonfiction/suggestions4congress.html

[380] The 2019 "Ig Nobel" Economics Prize was awarded for testing which country's paper money was "best at transmitting dangerous bacteria" (the Romanian Leu won, but the US Dollar was a finalist).

hijacked 'botnet" source of harm to others, then you'll share in the civil damages that result.

Crackpot suggestions.

All right, we're about to tip into notions that are more than just "unusual" or "judo." These *crackpot ideas* may yet have their day, though. 381 And I want to be on record.

– Provide basic *firearms safety training* in schools, *in return for comprehensive sex education.* Think about it! Isn't this one of those positive-sum, win-win scenarios? It lets us judo past the NRA's trenches by offering the one thing they *want* that might actually help reduce gun violence!382 While forcing them into a deal that would help reduce teen pregnancy, STD and abortion rates by empowering girls and women. (And help divide them from their fundie allies.)383 A head scratcher? Well, just let it sit there, among less busy neurons at a corner of the mind.

– As of mid 2019, Bernie Sanders came aboard supporting this proposal that long predates even my own interest384… a *small tax on financial transactions.* As low as 0.01%, it would not be noticed by average human investors. But it could stymie the AI programs at major Wall Street firms that make up to a billion trades a day. Advantages include a way to limit volatility, plus helping to control a "churn-hungry" financial caste. But I have a bigger reason: it could diminish the likelihood of those cryptic, unscrupulous Wall-Street firms unleashing artificial intelligences that are *by design* voracious, parasitical, predatory, amoral and utterly insatiable potential "skynets."385

---

[381] A blog on crackpot notions! http://www.davidbrin.com/nonfiction/crackpotsuggestions.html

[382] Envision every elementary school kid encouraged to tattle on Uncle Bob's unsafe and unsecure shed fulla bazookas, while praising dad for the responsible rifle safe. Oh, the NRA would split over this! Then imagine red skulls imploding as liberal and minority kids learn weapon basics.

[383] Abortion rates decline more in blue than in restrictive red states, why? All studies attribute it to sex education. https://www.npr.org/2019/09/18/761753866/u-s-abortion-rate-continues-long-term-decline

[384] Transaction taxes might save us all. http://www.davidbrin.com/nonfiction/transactionfee.html

[385] The amount of money in the top three investment funds alone is now equal to the GDP of China.https://www.bloomberg.com/graphics/2019-asset-management-in-decline/
http://statisticstimes.com/economy/projected-world-gdp-ranking.php
https://www.pionline.com/article/20190221/ONLINE/190229952/fidelity-sees-record-revenue-operating-income-despite-dip-in-aum

– Ban interlocking corporate directorates among a narrow CEO clan of golf buddies voting each other vast compensation packages. The Greatest Generation wisely forbade this conniving incest. They also banned massive stock buybacks. (See Chapters 10 and 11.)

– Give capital gains tax breaks only to long held and voted stock or (more radical, but justifiable) *only* to *new issues* that actually raise new money for companies.

– Revise "corporate democracy" to reward involved, long-term stockholders and purchasers of new issues, while limiting the power of passive proxies and shell companies, especially those shells who don't devolve to real human owners.

– More mind-blowing still, even though techno-liberals like Stewart Brand have pushed it for years, and it might help reduce carbon emissions significantly… consider making new allies and crucial support for environmental action in exchange for accelerated development of two or three of the truly impressive new types of ultra fail-safe nuclear power plants?

– Establish an *Institute for Verification and Re-test.* One problem with modern science – it emphasizes *new* discoveries over the *verification* process upon which the whole thing relies. Postdocs and professors don't find it sexy to merely check out or replicate a recent finding, nor does that lead to prizes and fame. Necessary for the peer review process to work, we need some way to encourage tests to reproduce results. A possible role – if properly set up – for burgeoning networks of amateur scientists?

Even more crackpotty!

Okay, you were warned… several grains of salt…

– *Revive rural ghost towns* as subsidized havens of all kinds. Seriously, does anyone look for win-win solutions, anymore? There are rural villages dying all across America. Some show leadership and verve, adapting, experimenting and thriving with new models… and we must help those, generously! Yay that. Incentives might encourage folks in three out of four small, dying towns to ingather with the one that has real prospects.

Then what to do with those abandoned three, where local farmers workers and merchants just couldn't quite make a profit? Once we've helped those folks *get* profitable on their own feet in a vibrant town, are there *modern problems that might be helped* by offering the bought-out or abandoned ones to certain groups across America? Offering those groups a completely voluntary, subsidized life in fresh air, gardening or farming or running businesses that need merely to break even, *not* make a profit?

You can guess I am talking about groups who are already receiving aid (or expensive caretaking or else restricted movement) far more expensively in cities or shelters or minimum security facilities. In a village, taxpayers need only under-write a *marginal bit,* for the garden farm or restaurant or fix-it shop to crest at viability. If you can't imagine half a dozen potential uses and constituencies in just a minute or two – from purely voluntary homeless redoubts to safe places for refugees to do their paperwork, to... well... just try again. There are dozens.

– *Revive air travel the simplest way.* One sign of our spiral toward levels of class war last seen in 1789 France is how the rich are abandoning us to our fates in deteriorating airports and airlines, fleeing from First Class into charters and corporate jets, thus avoiding all the frisking and hassles. History is clear. When elites abandon a mode of transportation (e.g., railroads in the 1950s, and ocean liners) that utility starts to die! Moreover, the gulf between the mighty and little people widens to unsupportable levels. (See David Rothkopf's book *Superclass: The Global Power Elite and the World They Are Making.*) This can be solved with some decent agitation, followed by the right taxes and fees. Metaphorically speaking – and *so far* I am still talking in metaphors – we must lift torches and pitchforks, break into the elite lounges and chase those moguls *back into First Class,* where they belong! Enjoy the champagne. But fly with us.

– *Ban the undergraduate business major.* Let them go for an MBA after four years spent creating or delivering goods and services. You think I'm joking? Ten years later, you'll think we entered a Golden Age. (The Chinese leadership consists almost entirely of managers who were promoted from their start as engineers. See Chapter 9.)

– *Stop letting taxpayer-subsidized companies "shout" into space.* All right, this one sounds *super*-crackpot. But as we speak, private companies using dishes that were paid for by the U.S. taxpayer are beaming commercial stunt messages – for everything from snack food companies to Craig's List – into outer space – supposedly to sell music videos and garage sale items to aliens! Sure, it sounds harmless, and it might be. But that's the problem, we just don't know. And at minimum it violates laws against amateur interference in diplomacy with foreign powers.386

Okay, there are lots of these items that may seem marginal or crackpot today... like votes for women, back 120 years ago. We'll get to more of them way late in the book, as treats for those who hang around.

Meanwhile... well... there's my proposed *priority list from Chapter 12.* The things that desperately must happen, to save America and the Enlightenment Experiment from the restoration of 6000 years of oligarchic feudalism.

I hope one thing above all. That sane American voters – and in other nations allied for the future – will give us the power to wrangle over these things, and enact a lot of them.

---

[386] See my evaluation of the cult phenomenon called METI or "Message to Extraterrestrial Intelligence." http://www.davidbrin.com/meti.html

Acknowledgements & Thanks

This volume, unlike anything I've done before and almost as complex as *The Transparent Society*, benefitted greatly from pre-read suggestions and other help from numerous wise-heads, starting with Cheryl Brin, Stephen Potts, Alfred Differ, Pat Scannell, Jonathan Armstrong, David Bray, David Ivory, Mike Nelson, Stefan Jones, Dr. Allen Bryan, Scott Foster and Barbara and Chris Fransden. And special thanks to Larry Yudelson for reformatting the Kindle edition for print-on-demand.

About the Author

David Brin is a scientist, tech-speaker/consultant, and author. Brin's novels include NY Times bestsellers and Hugo award winners, and have been translated into more than twenty languages. His 1989 novel, *Earth*, foreshadowed global warming, cyberwarfare, and the worldwide web. A film by Kevin Costner was based on Brin's novel, *The Postman*. His latest – about humanity's potential survival in the near future, is *Existence*.

Brin serves on the external advisory council of NASA's Innovative and Advanced Concepts program (NIAC). He has appeared on shows such as Nova, The Universe, and Life After People. He has keynoted major events for the likes of IBM, GE, Google, Boeing and the Institute for Ethics in Emerging Technologies.

Brin's nonfiction book, *The Transparent Society: Will Technology Make Us Choose Between Freedom and Privacy?* won the Freedom of Speech Award of the American Library Association.

Brin Website: http://www.davidbrin.com/
Contrary Brin Blog: http://davidbrin.blogspot.com/
Twitter: http://twitter.com/DavidBrin @davidbrin

Made in the USA
Monee, IL
16 November 2019